Navigating Comprehensive School Change

A Guide for the Perplexed

Thomas G. Chenoweth

Robert B. Everhart

EYE ON EDUCATION

6 DEPOT WAY WEST, SUITE 106

LARCHMONT, NY 10538

(914) 833–0551

(914) 833–0761 fax

www.eyeoneducation.com

Library of Congress Cataloging-in-Publication Data

Chenoweth, Thomas G., 1945–
    Navigating comprehensive school change : a guide for the perplexed / Thomas G. Chenoweth and Robert B. Everhart
    p.   cm.
    Includes bibliographical references and index.
    ISBN 1-930556-31-4
    1. School improvement programs—Handbooks, manuals, etc. 2. Educational leadership—Handbooks, manuals, etc. 3. Educational change—Handbooks, manuals, etc. I. Everhart, Robert B. II. Title.

    LB2822.8 .C55 2002
    371.2—dc21

                                                                2001055603

10 9 8 7 6 5 4 3 2

Editorial and production services provided by
Richard H. Adin Freelance Editorial Services
52 Oakwood Blvd., Poughkeepsie, NY 12603-4112
(845-471-3566)

About the Authors

Thomas G. Chenoweth, Ph.D., received his doctorate from Stanford University in 1984, and is currently an associate professor at Portland State University. A former public school principal and teacher, his primary interest is in helping school leadership teams find meaning and work through comprehensive school change initiatives. He recently served as a Satellite Center Director and as a National Policy Advisory Board Member for the Accelerated Schools Project. Currently, he is the Program Coordinator for the K–12 Administrative Licensure Program at Portland State University. His recent publications, *Redefining Faculty Teaching Roles for the 21st Century—Educational Leadership and Administration* (2000) and *Building Initial Commitment to Accelerate—Accelerated Schools in Action* (1996), focus on principal preparation and leadership in school reform environments. Together with coauthor Robert Everhart, he provides technical assistance and training to schools and school districts involved in comprehensive school change. He can be reached at chenoweth@pdx.edu.

Robert B. Everhart, Ph.D., received his doctorate at the University of Oregon and is currently a professor at Portland State University. Prior to his current position, he was dean of the Graduate School of Education at Portland State University for 12 years. He began his career in education as a middle school teacher and has also worked in school districts in the area of program evaluation. His current interests are in the areas of educational policy, school change, and education for early adolescents. His most recent publications include *Flirting on the Margins: An Educational Novel* (1998) and a book chapter, *Toward a Critical Social Narrative of Education* [forthcoming in George Noblit (ed.), *Playgrounds of Postcritical Ethnography* (2002)]. He can be contacted at everhartr@pdx.edu.

Table of Contents

Figures and Tools

With Appreciation

Tool 2.1, p. 27: Used with permission of the Northwest Regional Education Laboratory (NWREL), Portland, OR.

Tool 2.2, p. 29: Reprinted by permission of the publisher from *Best Practice: New Standards for Teaching and Learning in America's Schools* by Steven Zemelman, Harvey Daniels, and Arthur Hyde. Copyright © 1998. Published by Heinemann, a division of Reed Elsevier, Inc., Portsmouth, NH.

Skill- and Content-Based Reform Models, pp. 40–41: Used with permission of the Northwest Regional Education Laboratory (NWREL), Portland, OR.

Tool 2.4, p. 44: Adapted from a training module, *Teaming with Excellence,* and used with permission of Brenda Le Tendre, Pittsburg (Kansas) State University.

Figure 2.3, p. 45: Adapted from a training module, *Teaming with Excellence,* and used with permission of Brenda Le Tendre, Pittsburg (Kansas) State University.

Tool 2.5, p. 48: Adapted from Brenda Le Tendre, *Teaming with Excellence,* and M. Doyle and D. Strauss (1976), *How to Make Meetings Work,* New York, Jove Books.

Figure 2.4, p. 52: Adapted and used with permission of the National Center for the Accelerated Schools Project, University of Connecticut, Storrs, CT.

Figure 2.5, p. 53: Adapted from *Practical Action Research for Change* by R.A. Schmuck, copyright © 1997. Used by permission of Skylight Professional Development, www.sky lightedu.com.

Too 4.1, p. 94: Used with permission, *Teachers in Charge.* Ontario Teacher's Federation/Fedèration des enseignantes et des enseignants de l'Ontario.

Tool 4.2, pp. 99–100: Ruth S. Johnson (1996). *Setting Our Sights: Measuring Equity in school Change.* Los Angeles: The Achievement Council. Used with permission.

Tool 4.3, p. 106: Adapted from *Creating New Visions for Schools: Activites for Educators, Parents, and Community Members* (p. 23). Learning Innovations at WestEd (formerly the Regional Laboratory for Educational Improvement of the Northeast Islands). © 1991. In *Work in Progress: Restructuring in Ten Maine Schools.* Cox, P.L. and deFrees, J. The Regional Laboratory for Educational Improvement of the Northeast Islands and the Maine Department of Education.

Tool 4.4, p. 109: Reprinted with permission from Pankake, A. M. *Implementation: Making things happen.* Larchmont, NY: Eye On Education, 1998, p. 26.

Figure 4.2, p. 115: From C. Finnan, et al. (Eds.). (1996). *Accelerated Schools in Action: Lessons from the Field.* Thousand Oaks, CA: Corwin Press, p. 189. Used with permission.

Tool 6.1, pp. 177–178: Copyright 1999 by Alfie Kohn. Reprinted with the author's permission from *The Schools Our Children Deserve.* Boston: Houghton-Mifflin, 1999. For more information, visit www.alfiekohn.org.

Figure 6.1, p. 180: Adapted from P. Senge, et al. (2000). *Schools that Work.* New York: Doubleday.

Foreword

by Michael Fullan
University of Toronto

How can you resist a book with the title *Navigating Comprehensive School Change*? This book is brilliantly conceived. It takes an enormously complex topic, and guides the reader through the key aspects of dealing with fundamental educational reform. It never underestimates the complexity of school change while providing practical insights and advice.

First, we are provided with a short course on navigation. This primer on change is the on land dry run establishing the basics—focus on student learning, be comprehensive, leadership as key, build a democratic environment, reculture and understand the key factors in the change process.

We are then treated to five chapters that help us through the journey of change. In turn, critical ideas and steps are formulated involving: getting started (Chapter 2); building commitment (Chapter 3); achieving implementation (Chapter 4); sustaining change (Chapter 5); and evaluation and assessment (Chapter 6).

In the final two chapters, Chenoweth and Everhart put the voyage of change in perspective by suggesting New Beginnings for remembering the keys to future and ongoing change (Chapter 7), and by consolidating the Lessons Learned about change (Chapter 8).

Navigating Comprehensive School Change is at once deep and practical—a rare accomplishment in the literature on educational reform.

The ideas and lessons identified are consistent with my own recent reviews of the field, and engagement in multiyear change initiatives in several countries as reported in my two books *The New Meaning of Educational Change,* 3rd edition (New York: Teachers College Press, 2001), and *Leading in a Culture of Change* (San Francisco: Jossey-Bass, 2001).

Chenoweth and Everhart, however, take the big concepts of change and work them through operationally at the level of day-to-day practice. We learn how to form leadership teams, the importance of focusing on capacity-building and reculturing, how to build commitment while dealing with dissatisfaction, problem-solving during implementation, how to keep going, and how to go beyond standardized testing in developing a range of alternative assessment strategies.

Navigating Comprehensive School Change is a unique and relentlessly helpful book designed to take us through the worst storms as we search for and consolidate successful school reform.

Acknowledgments

We are grateful for the many suggestions and steadfast support we received throughout our navigation of the seas of change. First we thank our families, Shelley Everhart, Lenore Fines, and Marilyn Chenoweth for their patience, valuable feedback and editing help at the most critical times. We also want to acknowledge the contributions of Tom Ruhl of Lewis and Clark College and Dan Johnson, Gayle Thieman, and Amy Petti at Portland State University, who carefully read earlier drafts. We also appreciate the encouraging feedback received from our students, future leaders in the Beaverton School District (OR) administrative cohort program. Moreover, we wish to thank Henry Levin, Gene Chasin and our many colleagues from the Accelerated Schools Project for their encouragement and the many opportunities to truly learn about school reform. We'd also like to thank the reviewers who critiqued early versions of the manuscript: Lew Allen, Debbie Constable, Donald Curtis, Elaine Hassemer, Bruce Patt, and Brenda Tanner. Finally, our deepest gratitude goes to Bob Sickles, whose enthusiasm for the project never wavered and who directed us to safe harbors at times when we were in danger of going adrift.

Preface

Purpose of this Book

The purpose of this book is to provide for busy practitioners and students of change an accessible and useful resource on the usually difficult, always complex, and critically important process of change in our nation's schools. We strive to help schools navigate school change in part through the story of a new school principal (Mary) and her staff at South Central Middle School. South Central is experiencing rapid changes in the composition of its community and student body, one result being an increasing number of poor and minority students at the school. In the face of these changes, South Central has been a school with a historical reluctance to change despite clear evidence that current practices have not been effective for the majority of its student body.

As the authors of this book, we are part of the story because we served as technical assistants to South Central for the first three years of its involvement in a fictitious national comprehensive change model which we call Project Improve. Although Project Improve does not exist in reality, both of us have been involved in change initiatives very similar to Project Improve. One of us (Chenoweth) has been part of the Accelerated Schools Program and is currently on the Project's national advisory board. Both of us have a history of working with schools on a number of school improvement projects similar to Project Improve. Thus, our roles in this book as facilitators of the process of change as it emerged at South Central Middle School are based on actual experiences. We've shared with numerous schools the rewards of seeing progress made, as well as the disappointment of efforts that weren't so successful.

As Mary once reflected, being part of a change effort in a school is akin to trying to change a tire on a car while it speeds down the road at sixty miles an hour. Yet, schooling goes on as long as the students are there, and schools will keep speeding down the educational highway at the same time that new change initiatives are introduced and mandated. How can educators become better prepared to successfully cope in such a rapidly moving environment? Indeed, how might educators become more proactive in *leading* change efforts rather than mostly *following* them? And how would school leadership need to evolve in order to better meet these goals? We have written this book to help school practitioners respond to these and other serious questions about better meeting the demands of inevitable educational change.

Change in schools is like trying to change a tire while the car is moving.

As we begin the twenty-first century, the imperative for changes in public education is greater than ever. Indeed, the American public ranks education as one of its top priorities. At the same time, the leadership that is needed to spark and sustain these change efforts is often ill-defined and unprepared. Turnover at the district and building level is high, with superintendents of urban school districts averaging three years in office. In addition, the number of qualified individuals who are interested in leadership positions in districts is dwindling. Leadership succession in the principalship frequently stalls school reform in its tracks. Central office functions are depleted as the result of a resource-scarce environment. Teachers experience numerous and often conflicting new role demands that cause them to feel overloaded and powerless. And although there are calls for family and community involvement in school change, too often community members are only marginally involved in the re-creation of their schools.

Despite these challenges, the pressure for higher school achievement and the accountability of educators to enable such performance will only increase in the future. All of which raises our key question: who will provide the leadership for school change that is needed in such difficult times? It is our belief that leadership for school change must be shared amongst *All* members of the school community. All members—administrators as well as teachers, staff, parents, and community members must thus become more knowledgeable about the change process and more proficient at working through it. Such is the purpose of this book.

Navigating Comprehensive School Change: A Guide for the Perplexed is primarily intended for *Leadership Teams*, comprised of educators and community members, which must become the vanguard for school change in the twenty-first century. Such teams will need to play an important role in bringing out the leadership capacities of many people, both within and outside of schools, whose roles are critical to effective change. Because of its focus, this book should also be useful in university leadership preparation programs that train teachers and administrators for new roles. The book is research-based, yet written in a style that we hope is more appealing and accessible to school practitioners. It is intended to provide the necessary information about the change process as well as to guide you to some of the best practices for change. It is designed to stand somewhere between the sometimes obtuse and abstract change literature written for academics, and the many normative (and non–research-based) books and guides, which can lead to numerous checklists and simplistic formulas for change.

Leadership for change must be shared amongst all members of the school community.

At times, we've characterized the book as a cross between two genres. First, we view it as "tourist guide"(e.g., how to think about the journey, how to prepare for it, what to pay atten-

---

* Indeed, as we finish this book, the new Superintendent of Memphis, Tennessee (a district previously at the forefront of comprehensive school change) announced that the district would terminate its five-year school reform effort because there was a lack of significant gains in achievement scores and return to "the basics." See Viadero, D. (2001). Memphis scraps redesign models in all schools. *Education Week, 20*(42), 1, 19.

tion to upon arrival, dealing with the unexpected, etc.). But we also hope that the book will serve as a "consumer report" (e.g., identifying some of the best tools and sources about change, accessing useful information about the change process, providing information about the strengths and challenges of various strategies). We believe you'll find these two objectives are met in the pages that follow.

We view this book as a cross between a tourist guide and a consumer's report.

The information presented is a distillation, synthesis, and a recasting of the best literature about school change/improvement. Yet the book does not actually review the literature *per se*. Rather, we use selected literature in two ways. First, we guide readers to the best comprehensive reviews of the school change literature, e.g., the *International Handbook of Educational Change*.[1] We feel that this is particularly helpful for those readers who want to access the change literature in more depth. Second, we refer to the literature that is particularly helpful in addressing our thesis that successful school change occurs when the entire school community assumes leadership for developing and implementing a process of continuous improvement.

Because both of us have been involved in the Accelerated Schools program (Chenoweth in particular), you'll see frequent references to lessons and experiences gained over the 15-plus years of the Accelerated Schools Program (ASP). We don't mean by this to infer that the ASP is necessarily better than many of the other comprehensive school change models. However, much of what has been experienced in this long-term project has clear connections to school change in general, and so we borrow liberally from these lessons learned. The fact that educators have learned so much from the ASP confirms what Levin said a few years ago about the prospects of success for the project:

> In fact, our greatest success will be if this approach becomes so highly accepted in U.S. education that it does not need a label, but is the standard approach to educating children.[2]

There are many books that are excellent sources of information and perspectives on school change (Fullan,[3] Elmore[4], Wilson,[5] Sarason,[6] etc.). Yet, we believe that most of them connect to scholars of the change process rather than doers of change. In fact, we've used some of these books in our own university courses and the response of many of our practitioner-oriented students to those sources has stimulated us to write this book. Our students tell us that they want a book that links common dilemmas and problems in the change process to possible solutions and /or resources about those dilemmas. They want a book that they can keep on their desk or in a briefcase, and they envision a book that becomes dog-eared and a bit rumpled from regular use. We've tried to write the book with these uses in mind. Indeed, the book is grounded in the critical review of drafts by teachers and administrators who read early drafts of the book. Their commentary served us well and many of their suggestions are reflected throughout the text.

Organization of the Book

This book is intended for two broad audiences, although these audiences certainly are not mutually exclusive. The first audience consists of leadership teams in schools or individuals interested in forming such teams. Leadership teams are charged with the tricky job of providing direction for change while at the same time empowering others to do the same. Thus, they must lead but also involve others in leadership. This is no easy task. The second audience consists of students/practitioners of the change process, which could include educators involved in building/district staff development activities as well as those who are part of a university-based class or seminar on the general topic of educational change. Whether you are part of one or both of these audiences, we've tried to anticipate your needs as you engage in the important process of school reform. We believe that a book designed for these audiences should be based on sound knowledge about the change process, provide ready access to some of the best practices of school change, and serve as a guidebook that can alert the book's users to important issues about change.

The audiences for this book are school leadership teams and students/ practitioners of change.

The content of the book is based upon some of the most recent empirical literature on school change, especially the best practices in school change. School leadership teams will need to become connoisseurs and critical consumers of literally hundreds of change possibilities. The best hope for understanding these possibilities is to become as mindful and thoughtful about the change process as possible. There are numerous processes that connect the "usually messy, unpredictable, and quite often convoluted dynamics of changing—(and) there are no hard and fast rules but rather a set of suggestions and implications given the contingencies specific to a local situation."[7] So, we have to learn to use the knowledge about school change thoughtfully and selectively, moving between perspectives and strategies all the while utilizing our knowledge to match these strategies to different contexts and challenges.

It's important to be thoughtful and selective when examining the research about change.

You've already been introduced to Mary. You'll hear more about her and her colleagues because we've developed a *story* about school change that runs through the book. The story is a composite of smaller tales about change that we've seen or participated in during our own professional lives. We think that the story will help you to understand that the process of change is an everyday occurrence in the life of schools, and thus you will be better able to identify with discussions about change contained in the book.

The book is organized around a series of questions that practitioners usually ask about the change process. We've adopted a metaphor about sailing because we believe that being successful at change is much like the competent navigation of a seagoing vessel.

- Chapter 1, *How About a Short Course in Navigation?,* provides an outline of the assumptions we used in compiling this book. It's important you are aware of these assumptions because they guide what we cover as well as what we don't cover throughout the book. Next in this chapter, we summarize seven key points about change distilled from the hundreds of studies on school change (reviewed more extensively in Chapter 8). We provide an early overview of these key points in order to provide quick entry into the chapters that follow. These key points are intended to give you a quick, short course on navigating school change.

  Success at change is like the successful navigation of a ship.

- Chapter 2, *"Launching the Ship: How Do We Prepare This Thing to Float?"* discusses the process of leadership team formation and identification of a high stakes problem, the buy-in process, and capacity building. Here, the focus is on pre-initiation and initiation issues. Here we introduce the Project Improve Design model, used by South Central in its change process. The Project Improve model also serves as an organizer for this book.

- *"Is Everybody on Board?"* is the key question in Chapter 3. This question focuses on the important process of building commitment through creating dissatisfaction with the status quo, creating a school-wide vision, taking stock in curricular areas, and establishing school-wide goals.

- Chapter 4, *"Did You Say Turn Port or Starboard?"* discusses the often messy but critical process of implementation—that is, attempting to put into practice what is intended. Matters discussed include: clarifying assumptions, handling setbacks, how to honor past practices, maintaining the vision, and following a systematic problem-solving approach.

- Chapter 5, *"Was this Rock Really on the Map?"* discusses the process of sustaining change. This chapter focuses on bringing in new members to the change effort, a continuing attention to improved student learning, and maintaining a process of continuous improvement.

- In Chapter 6, we address the question of *"How Do We Know When We've Arrived?"* by addressing issues of evaluation (the extent to which an intended change is being implemented) and assessment (whether the change has an impact on student learning). Assessment is a key factor in change, especially in this era of standards-based school reform. In this chapter, we examine how you'll evaluate the implementation of change as well as the impact of that change on student learning.

- Chapter 7, *Conclusions and (New) Beginnings* pulls together the major themes and perspectives that run throughout the book.

♦ In Chapter 8, *Doesn't Somebody Out There Have a Chart?,* we return to the literature on school change summarized in Chapter 1. Here we go into detail as to the literature on school change and what it tells us. The chapter organization corresponds to the other major chapters of this book, providing for ready access to the corresponding discussions in Chapters 2 through 6.

Schools involved in change efforts have available to them a considerable inventory of resources that can be utilized. Indeed, there are so many resources available that it is difficult for the busy educator to know where to turn in order to access these resources. We've tried to provide easy access to some of the most useful resources in the *"Ports of Call"* section at the back of the book. This section helps you gain access to sources provide key information and link you to other useful sources. We've classified resources into seven broad categories, and then listed the resource and its address. You'll note of course that, in this electronic age, Web pages are commonplace.

Be sure to consult the "Ports of Call" section at the end of this book.

Finally, because school change is so complex and the path to successful results so fraught with hazards, we've developed *charts* to help navigate through some of these hazards. A chart is presented at the beginning of each chapter (*Chapter Highlights*) and provides an overview of the topics included in the chapter. We've also included navigational markers along the way in the form of a series of *icons* that alert the user to directions, choices, and possibilities. Icons that you will encounter are: key point (key icon), useful tool (wrench icon), resources (book, video/film, TV, computer icons), organizations (atom icon), and things to think about (thinker icon). At the end of each chapter, we also provide a *reculturing map* that outlines the changes in the values and activities that will be needed in order to successfully enact the change process. We hope that by paying attention to these guideposts, users will be able to better handle change rather than feeling that change is handling them.

We move now to Chapter 1 and a discussion of the assumptions of the book and a short primer on navigating school change.

References

1. Hargreaves, A., Lieberman, A., Fullan, M., & Hopkins, D. (Eds.). (1998). *The international handbook of educational change*. London: Kluwer Academic Publishers.
2. Levin, H. M. (1996). Accelerated schools: The background. In Finnan, C., St. John, E., McCarthy, J., and Slovacek, S. (Eds.), *Accelerated schools in action: lessons from the field*. Thousand Oaks, CA: Corwin Press, p. 22.
3. Fullan, M. (1993). *Change forces*. London: Falmer Press.
4. Elmore, R. (1990). *Restructuring schools: The next generation of educational reform*. San Francisco: Jossey-Bass.
5. Wilson, K. G., & Daviss, B. (1994). *Redesigning education*. New York: Henry Holt.
6. Sarason, S. B. (1971). *The culture of the school and the problem of change*. Boston: Allyn and Bacon.
7. Fullan, op. cit., p. vii.

HOW ABOUT A SHORT COURSE ON NAVIGATION? Assumptions and Key Lessons About Change

---

Chapter Highlights

♦ *Clarify assumptions.* It is important for all participants to know, understand, and support the essential premises on which a comprehensive school change proposal is based.

♦ *Explore the research on change.* There are many valuable lessons found in the research on school change. Using these lessons can significantly improve the change process.

The Story of South Central Middle School and Educational Change

Mary was a dedicated and conscientious teacher. Indeed, her positive reputation was amply supported by the numerous awards that she'd received within her district and the recognition accorded her by the state chapter of the Association for Supervision & Curriculum Development (ASCD). What's more, Mary always attracted many parent volunteers who were willing to assist in the classroom as well as to participate in the variety of field trips and after-school events for which Meadowlark school was well known. Though Mary had received her administrative licensure a few years ago, and had been an elementary vice-principal for two years as well as principal in the summer school program for one summer, she wasn't seriously considering school administration at the age of 49. Mary would be eligible to retire from teaching in another eight years and she loved working directly with students—a passion that she was afraid she'd no longer experience if she entered the pressure-cooker environment of building administration.

In October of 1998 however, Bruce Tolliver, the principal of Meadowlark, invited Mary into his office, closed the door and, after the usual small talk about children, family, and district politics, said to her in very direct terms: "Mary, there's a middle school principal position open next fall and the superintendent wants you to consider it. While I dread losing you, I agree with her."

Teaching has room for very few promotions, and the administrative route is one of the few. Although Mary was honored by Bruce's comments, she knew that administration was an honor she could easily decline. Besides, why would she want to leave Meadowlark for South Central Middle School? Everyone in the district knew that South Central ate up administrators and spat them out with regularity. Indeed, no principal had lasted more than three years in the past decade, and no wonder. Student performance was low on virtually every scale, and student mobility was at 40 percent per year. Parental involvement at South Central was negligible—except when an outraged parent's complaint got the attention of a local civil rights organization, which in turn then broadcast their complaints before the school board and the media.

"Thanks Bruce, for considering me, but my answer is no," Mary replied. As much as Bruce tried to talk her into keeping an open mind, he couldn't get her to reconsider. He had expected as much.

Superintendent Jennifer Craig, however, had yet to use her charm on Mary. Jennifer was in her third year as superintendent and had already made her mark in the community on the theme of improved student learning. Jennifer was of the opinion that when students failed to meet educational standards, it wasn't because they lacked the capacity. Rather, the fundamental problem was that the schools had not found the best strategy to teach those students. Given that student learning was at the heart of schooling (and most especially in poor and minority neighborhoods like that served by South Central), Jennifer believed that schools had to become invested in the improvement of student learning.

-- To meet this challenge, Jennifer didn't issue edicts from the central office or promulgate strategic plans. Her approach was much more incremental, more long-range. She believed that the schools themselves had to take charge of their own destiny—to struggle with facing what wasn't working, why it wasn't working, and to develop their own plans to meet the challenges. She subscribed to the philosophy that her principals should be empowered to find ways to effectively involve the entire staff in the process of comprehensive school change, and indeed should form leadership "teams" within the school in order to maximize that involvement. In this envi-

ronment, Jennifer viewed the role of the school board as one of establishing broad policies to facilitate school-based change efforts. The responsibility of the superintendent's office was to create the environment to support those policies and to hold the schools accountable. Finally, the individual school buildings were to be charged with devising the most effective means to meet these goals.

Jennifer also tried to put her money where her rhetoric was through her actions of reducing the budget of the central administration by some 10 percent and transferring most of those funds to the schools themselves.

As charismatic as she was, however, Jennifer had her weaknesses. Oftentimes, she was too impatient to change and some felt that she was so far ahead of her staff that she lost many of them in her wake. Additionally, while Jennifer was great at long-term visioning, she was less adept at crafting the details of how to reach those long-term visions. These characteristics left some staff thinking that Jennifer's activity was designed more to enhance her career mobility than it was to serve the schools and children of the Bridgeport School District.

After Jennifer called Mary into her office to discuss her philosophy and strategy, Mary had to admit that she was impressed by Jennifer's enthusiasm and vision. When she listened to Jennifer review her aspirations for all schools, and especially troubled ones like South Central, Mary realized how similar her own philosophy was with that espoused by Jennifer. She liked the notion of shared leadership and a democratic environment within which to make decisions about teaching. Her perspective clearly recognized the strengths of the professional educators and provided the space to effectively utilize those strengths. A focus on student learning had always been at the heart of what Mary did in her classroom, and she believed that was one reason why she had consistently been successful at raising student achievement. Finally, Jennifer had a way of advocating for change without making it appear that everything from the past was bad and the people who did it were incompetent. Rather, change was a natural process, and advocating for change was really a strategy for continuous renewal within the school. A few days after talking to Jennifer, Mary called us to ask what we thought. Because we had been the university faculty members who led the administrative cohort preparation program in which Mary had been enrolled five years ago, she thought we might be able to help her think about the plusses and minuses of Jennifer's offer. Mary had been one our best students in the cohort, and we encouraged her to accept the position.

So, it was with anticipation (as well as a bit of nervousness) that Mary attended the school board meeting in January of 1999 where it was announced that she had been appointed the new principal of South Central Middle School, effective July of that year. Certainly the task before her would be challenging, but with a supportive superintendent, Mary felt confident that she could play an important role in changing the expectations for students at South Central School.

Not surprisingly to us however, within a few days of the announcement of Mary's appointment, we received a message on our voice mail. "Help," said the voice on the recording. "You know who this is; you helped get me this job, now you have to help me prepare to meet the faculty of South Central in a week. What do I say? I need a crash course in school change. Call me back—today!"

We did return Mary's call and reminded her that the challenges of school change were formidable and couldn't be overcome with a cookbook. We knew, however, that she needed some "talking points" to help prepare her comments for the meeting with the faculty. So the next day we met Mary after school and reminded her that much of what she needed to say to the faculty were points that had been raised during her administrative licensure program that we directed a few years ago. We also reminded her of the key issues critical in any change effort. Slowly, Mary became more confident and realized that she knew more than she thought she did. She was ready to meet with her new faculty to begin navigating school change at South Central.

After reading this chapter, you'll understand what Mary and other future school leaders learned in the administrative program that we taught. More specifically, we introduce you to the assumptions about school change that we discussed with the group over the year and why we think they are so important. These assumptions, which underlie the organization and content of this book, represent fundamental values that we hold about the change process.

You'll also be exposed to a snapshot of key critical factors about change that we believe are prerequisites for successful change. When Mary asked us for a "crash course" on school change, these factors were the ones we thought might be included in a syllabus for such a course. Indeed, these factors are integral to this book and are derived from key findings from the research on change(discussed in depth in Chapter 8) as well as our own experiences in assisting schools with comprehensive change efforts.

Our Assumptions

Change in schools, as in any formal organization, is a highly complex process bounded by many conditions. We believe, however, that there are some basic assumptions that must be introduced, debated, and ultimately adopted if change is to be successful in your school. This book is guided by these assumptions and it is important for us to spell them out.

Major Assumptions of this Book

◆ Change must focus on improved student learning

◆ School change must be comprehensive, not piecemeal

◆ Effective school change demands shared leadership

◆ All relevant stakeholders must be involved in the change process

◆ Effective change means changing school cultures

Focus on Student Learning

First, when we discuss educational change, we're operating under the assumption that all such change is directly targeted toward the improved learning of all students. It might seem unnecessary to state this as an obvious assumption of this book; however, we believe otherwise.

A strong focus on student learning is necessary.

Many educational changes can be characterized as focusing on factors that are only indirectly related to student learning. For example (and we know that some will disagree with us on this) factors such as site-based decision making, enhanced school climate, and some staff development activities do not necessarily influence increased student learning of academic concepts, skills, or processes. We argue that school change must focus on primary change factors—those that are most directly related to the improvement of student learning. Changes that directly influence the student's capacity for what Darling-Hammond calls "meaningful learning" are fundamental to the rationale for change.[1] By this she means the use of higher-order thinking skills, application of these skills to meaningful situations, and the utility of prior learning in complex problem solving.

Comprehensive Change

2)

Change must focus on the totality of conditions affecting student learning.

One of the problems with so many change efforts has been their piecemeal approach. Many of you have experienced this—the adoption of new reading materials one year, tweaking classroom management procedures the next, the introduction of technology comes after, and so on. Then it's back to redoing the things that were changed a few years back. No wonder that so many teachers become cynical about the change process.

When changes are adopted one at a time, they are unlikely to have much of a cumulative effect. It's analogous to trying to keep an older car's electrical system operative by replacing only the battery, or the starter, or the coil. The reality is that the electrical system is interactive, and replacing one part at a time, although it may be necessary, may not be sufficient to create a reliable electrical system. So it is with schools. In order to address the improved learning of students, we need to attend to the totality of what affects children's learning. Certainly, some of these factors are external to the school and often we do not have control over how much television children watch or how frequently their parents assist them with homework. Yet we DO have control over many in-school factors, and need to examine them in the composite. We know that student learning is affected by the quality of teaching, the availability of instructional resources, the organization of learning environments, and, yes, even something as hard to define as "school climate." As Firestone and Corbett note, "the most productive schools have a distinctive normative structure that supports quality instruction."[2] Simply said, that means that comprehensive change is something in which participants feel ownership, and is a process reinforced throughout the entire school day. We believe this approach is a necessary ingredient of effective school change.

School Leadership

The third assumption of this book centers on the nature of leadership in schools. In order for schools to dedicate themselves to student learning, they must develop a leadership configuration dedicated to that good. When the term "leadership" is used, it normally conjures up the image of a strong administrator—one who is charismatic and able to mobilize people and resources for a common purpose. Although we don't wish to necessarily negate the value of such an individual, we believe that school change is hindered when educators rely too much on such a view of leadership.

What's wrong with the notion of a strong and influential administrator? Much depends on how we view that person's role. If by strong and influential we mean an individual to whom we look to set the vision and direct the implementation of effective strategies, then we have to question the consequences of such centralized authority. Is this the only person on whom we rely for guidance? Is this the person who will define and translate the change process for the staff? If the vision of the leadership is not easily grasped or understood by the staff, how are those differences reconciled? If there is a change in leadership, is there sufficient investment in the change process to continue the agenda?

These questions signal our discomfort with the traditional perspective on school leadership. We've simply seen too many attempts at change fall flat due to overreliance on one or two individuals to direct the agenda. We ourselves have worked on comprehensive change efforts, only to see these efforts die on the vine as a result of the transfer of a principal or the departure of a superintendent. Lee Bolman and Terry Deal state that it is

> misleading and elitist to imagine that leadership is provided only by people in high positions. Such a view causes us to ask too much of too few. Popular images of John Wayne, Bruce Lee, and Sylvester Stallone provide a distorted and romanticized view of how leaders function. We need more leaders as well as better leadership.[3]

Sergiovanni refers to "leadership density" as a prerequisite for long lasting school change and improvement. According to him "leadership density is the extent leadership roles are shared and the extent to which leadership is broadly exercised."[4] These perspectives reflect our views on leadership for change.

③

Leadership must be broadly shared and exercised.

In summary, we believe that any change effort worth its salt is one that will involve change in the multiple areas of the curriculum, teaching, and leadership as mentioned earlier by Darling-Hammond. We believe also that such changes are developmental and will take considerable time to evolve. With the complexity of issues that are bound to emerge, school leadership needs to provide consistent support and direction. This goal is difficult to achieve if there is over reliance on gladiators on white stallions. Our assumption in this book, then, is that leadership is participative and broadly shared. Many people within a school, district, or community possess the needed skills to help provide direction to the change effort. The secret (if there is one) is identifying those skill sets, locating the individuals who can best provide them, and involving them as equal partners in the change initiative. Thus, an effective school or district leader is one who is willing to put his or her need to always be the center of attention on a shelf and to facilitate the conditions that helps others to assume leadership roles. As Lao-Tzu once said, the effective leader is "one of whom it is said: we did it ourselves."

Democratic Environment

Our fourth assumption follows from our discussion of shared leadership. We believe that effective school change occurs best within a democratic environment—one wherein decisions about vision, direction, and practice are made openly and shared by all relevant stakeholders. Only when all parties understand the issues that are being ad-

④

All participants must agree to the practices that are to be changed.

dressed and the practices being proposed will they be willing to share the responsibilities for making change happen.

You are probably thinking, of course! How could it be any other way? Well, we invite you to reflect about your role in education. How many times have you felt that a new program was being adopted with sketchy knowledge on your part or without solicitation of your input? Indeed, in our own state of Oregon, an entire statewide effort at standards-based education was approved by the state legislature some ten years ago with only two open legislative hearings (both with little advance notice). The legislative leadership justified such quick action on the assumption that the professional teachers association would resist the change. It's been uphill ever since!

Despite the rhetoric about shared decision making and the like, it's far too common that decisions about change do not involve those who will have to make the change. Undoubtedly, a democratic environment for change may seem to be slower and messier than a change handed down from the top. Yet, in the long term, attempting to ensure the involvement of the many rather than just the few may be the more expeditious route. In the case of Oregon's ten-year career of implementing a standards-based curriculum, we find that many of the proposals that were part of the original legislation have never seen the light of day(and most of these are ones that required additional funds). We wonder how much good was accomplished by developing a reform with so little involvement by the very people who would be asked to implement the legislation.

Seymour Sarason, a long-term student of the change process in schools, developed a theme in a 1971 book that was to become an enduring regularity in the many books he has authored since: "the more things change, the more they stay the same."[5] That is a recurring theme in our book as well. His basic point was that so much of school change turns out to be rhetoric about change rather than valid programmatic changes in behavior and outcomes. There are, of course, many reasons why the rhetoric is so strong, fundamental among them the fact that so many school change efforts are politically inspired rather than being educationally based. Yet Sarason speaks eloquently about how the absence of dialog and understanding about change so often sinks the implementation of change. He says that "one of the central reasons for this self-defeating process is the tendency for change proposals to emanate on high without taking into consideration the feelings and opinions of those who must implement the changes, i.e., the teachers."[6] It is for this reason that a major tenet of this book is that change must occur within a broad-based democratic context.

Reculturing

Our last assumption in planning this book is based on the currently popular concept of organizational culture. As is common with many such terms, culture has been used in a variety of ways and for a variety of purposes, making it difficult to say with precision what organizational culture means. The educational anthropologist Harry Wolcott defines the nature of culture as "the various ways different groups go about their lives and the belief systems associated with that behavior."[7] In this sense, culture has to do with the taken-for-granted nature of everyday life within groups, communities, and societies. Because we live so much of our lives in organizations, it is logical to assume that organizations also are settings within which cultures arise. Edward Schein discusses this in terms of "the accumulated shared learning of a given group" and goes on to note that the distinctiveness of organizational cultures is that they produce patterns and integration, creating meaningful wholes that "make sense" of a group's experience.[8]

All schools, then, are in the process of creating and modifying their collective history. In the vast majority of cases, this culture is constructed and re-constructed at an *ad hoc* subconscious level where teachers and administrators are scarcely aware of the cultural nature of what it is they take for granted. Thus, learning is defined in a particular way (e.g., teacher presents materials and students demonstrate that they have learned it), and student abilities are characterized likewise (the good students do well on tests because their parents care about education; poor students don't test well because their parents don't care). Once these views of everyday life are set into place, it is difficult to interrupt the atmosphere of "common-sense" that the culture creates.

We believe that effective school change requires that common-sense patterns be broken down, examined and, where appropriate, changed. The fundamental nature of our assumption lies in the very essence of what culture is—a deep pattern of shared perspectives and behavior as well as the rootedness of culture within organizations. As Sarason has consistently noted, one of the reasons why in educational circles, "the more things change, the more they remain the same" is that the regularities of schooling (i.e., its culture) are rarely examined or changed. In this book we assume that schools interested in significant changes in teaching and learning must "reculture" in ways that are bound to challenge past practices. Such reculturing will create stresses and strains, but these are necessary and hopefully positive stresses. If reculturing is done within a democratic environment (as we defined it earlier), and all parties openly share the process, then reculturing need not be viewed with fear. Because this book is directed toward leadership teams in schools, Schein's challenge to school leadership is direct and to the point: "that we must examine the assumptions of our practice at every level, knowing full well that in so doing we are creating anxiety that can result in a countertrend to do as little as possible."[9]

Common-sense patterns should be broken down, examined, and where necessary, changed.

Reculturing necessarily means challenging current practices.

Key Factors in the Change Process

Now that you've been introduced to the values we believe are important in any change effort, what does the research literature tell us about what is important for school change? Although Chapter 8 explores this research literature in detail, we present below a summary of seven factors identified in the research that we believe are crucial (with a notation of the chapters that focus on these factors). These are also the points that Mary emphasized to her faculty during her introductory "short course on school change" session:

Elements of a Short Course on School Change

- **Use a design model to guide the change effort**. Once defined, the purpose of change should be carried out through a well-developed design model, informed by previous work, best practice, and research. Such a model provides a template for decision making and helps connect the pieces of change into a coherent whole, thereby minimizing the tendency to tinker anew each time a change is proposed. (Chap. 2).

- **Build staff capacity for change**. It is critical to build the capacity of your staff in the content of school change (what needs to be done and why) as well as the process of change (how to do it). Change can be sustained only through the shared leadership that grows out of enhanced staff capacity. Failure to invest in this capacity-building process almost always guarantees subsequent failure (Chap. 2).

- **Create meaning and purpose**. The purpose of any change effort should be to enhance teaching and learning. This purpose must be clearly defined through a visioning process involving all relevant stakeholders. Change happens best when a problem is well defined, owned, and personalized by those who will carry out the change (Chap. 3).

- **Work towards changing the culture of the school.** Understanding the present culture of a school (how people think and act) is fundamental to successful change. Even more important is to understand the elements of that culture in need of change. Making these changes is called the reculturing process, and is the critical link between the words of change and the actions of change (Chap. 4).

- **Create a culture supportive of continuous improvement**. Change must be viewed as integral to everyday life in schools rather than as an "add-on" with a finite life cycle. This continuous improvement must become a focus of the reculturing effort in schools (Chap. 5).

- **Focus school change on improved student learning**. Change must facilitate all students to meet high standards. However, it's important to understand the role of state/national standards to benefit all students while also going beyond these standards to create a more powerful learning environment (Chap. 6).

- **Develop a means by which to measure progress**. Schools must evaluate their fidelity to the change process and assess its impact on student learning. The evaluation and assessment of change is key to continuous improvement, and must be built into your design model from the earliest stages (Chap. 6).

The key principles above appear throughout the subsequent chapters. Keep them in mind as you turn next to Chapter 2 and a discussion of how to launch comprehensive change in your school.

References

1.   Darling-Hammond, L. (1997). *The right to learn*. San Francisco: Jossey Bass, p. 105.
2.   Firestone, W.A., & Corbett, H.D. (1988). Planned organizational change. In N. J. Boyan (Ed.), *The handbook of research on educational administration*. New York: Longman, p. 336.
3.   Bolman, L.G., & Deal, T. (1997). *Reframing organizations*. SanFrancisco: Jossey Bass, p. 295.
4.   Sergiovanni, T. (1995). *The principalship: A reflective practice perspective*. Boston: Allyn and Bacon, p. 136.
5.   Sarason, S. (1971). *The culture of the school and the problem of change*. Boston: Allyn and Bacon, p. 2.
6.   Ibid., p. 221.
7.   Wolcott, H. F. (1999). *Ethnography: A way of seeing*. Walnut Creek, CA: Alta Mira, p. 25.
8.   Schein, E. H. (1997). *Organizational culture and leadership*. San Francisco: Jossey Bass, p. 10.
9.   Ibid., p. 27.

LAUNCHING THE SHIP: HOW DO WE PREPARE THIS THING TO FLOAT?
Pre-Initiation & Initiation

Chapter Highlights

- ◆ *Form your leadership team.* Careful thought will need to inform leadership team selection and delineation of its responsibilities. Make sure that there is a high stakes problem that can serve as the leadership team's catalyst and rallying point for school change.

  ☐ Select your leadership team.

  ☐ Clarify roles and expectations.

  ☐ Rally around a high stakes problem.

- ◆ *Orchestrate a buy-in period.* The leadership team will need to facilitate discussion, create meaning, build understanding, and encourage reflection leading to a staff decision to initiate comprehensive school change.

  ☐ Visit other schools.

  ☐ Attend state showcases.

  ☐ Form study groups.

- ◆ *Build staff capacity to better understand the content (the what) of school change.* The leadership team and staff will need to become active learners of the content of school change.

  ☐ Become familiar with conceptual frameworks for thinking about both organizational and individual change.

  ☐ Know key lessons learned from research.

  ☐ Explore comprehensive school reform models.

- ◆ *Build staff capacity to better understand the process (the how) of school change.* The leadership team and staff will need to become active learners of the process of school change.

  ☐ Develop group process skills for dealing with difficult people, reaching consensus, and creating ground rules or group agreements.

  ☐ Hone your meeting management skills by developing clear agendas, assigning and clarifying roles, and meeting regularly.

  ☐ Utilize systematic problem-solving processes like inquiry and action research.

After reading this chapter, you will be ready to form a dynamic and representative leadership team. The team will be able to delineate its responsibilities and will understand its need to rally around an agreed upon high stakes problem. The team will be capable of facilitating a "buy-in" period in which staff explore and reflect upon the many change possibilities before them. Your team will also be prepared to build its own knowledge base about both the content of change (change frameworks, lessons learned from the research, and comprehensive change models) and the process of change (group process, meeting management, and systematic problem solving skills). The team will then be equipped to lead other staff members through a similar course of action in which the school as a whole will be set to make an informed and willing decision to initiate comprehensive school change.

Initiation at South Central School

Mary felt excited to be named the incoming principal of South Central Middle School. Her picture and accompanying story appeared on the front page of the community newspaper. Parents even hosted a potluck dinner for her and the school community. Everyone's expectations seemed so high.

Yet all the interest, friendly phone calls, and welcoming notes had overwhelmed her and Mary began to feel somewhat unprepared for all of the attention. She knew that she would have to work very hard to maintain her strong reputation in the district. She had been a superb teacher and someone to whom her colleagues gravitated. Suddenly, reality set in. Mary wondered what would she do to get her new school moving? Should she take a slow concerted approach and really get to know everyone or should she actively initiate change?

That very spring her question was answered. The state had forced her hand by issuing report cards for all of its schools. Although it was common knowledge that South Central had many low-achieving students, it became vividly clear that South Central was one of the state's most challenging schools. Data revealed that many students were not meeting state standards in reading and math.

At her very first faculty meeting in August, Mary held up the school's report card and said to her staff, "Change is in the air. We do not have a choice about whether or not to change. We can't remain the same. But we do have a choice about how we will change." She then invited her school community to "take stock" of its strengths as well as its challenges and from there to create a vision for where the school should be in the coming years. She added, "We will need to explore all of the change possibilities before us and make a commitment to significantly increase student engagement, promote powerful learning, raise student achievement and meet state standards." She went on to tell her staff that she wanted and expected everyone's active involvement. And, to guide their school into and through a change process, she decided to truly empower the site council as the school's leadership team. Members were nominated by the school community at large and then democratically elected to serve two-year terms. The membership consisted of five teachers, two instructional assistants, two parents, and one community member, as well as Mary.

Knowing that there would be new openings on the site council, Mary worked to ensure that its composition truly represented the school's diverse student population. Within two months, the team attended a state showcase of national school redesign models, visited lighthouse schools, and invited the two of us to help them make sense of their many and complex school change options. The leadership team discussed their case for school change at a faculty meeting and began to explore change options that seemed to best fit their particular needs and context. Already the school was beginning to be more involved in an active discussion of how to better meet the needs of its students

After five months of inquiry and vision development, the school community narrowed its options down to three comprehensive school redesign models. Mary and her team then facilitated a session in which the school staff listed the perceived advantages and disadvantages of each model. Finally, after some heated deliberation, the vast majority of the school community, swayed by the site council's strong endorsement, decided to propose the adoption of Project Improve because it seemed to be the best fit for their existing school culture (see Figure 2.1, pp. 18–19).

Project Improve required that the school community, through a secret vote, demonstrate support for, and a willingness to commit to, the project. Mary and the leadership team knew that there were still some resisters in the staff, so they set a high standard of at least 90 percent staff commitment to begin the change project. After the first vote, there was an 83 percent majority in favor of adopting the project. Mary then polled her staff, asking them what it would take to get the required 90 percent. Two staff members wanted a guarantee of budgetary support and long-term commitment from the district. Mary arranged for the superintendent, two board members, and the business manager to visit the school, talk to the staff, and make a commitment to support the school for at least three years. Mary also personally talked to one very reluctant 8th grade teacher and gave him the option to transfer to another district school. With his subsequent transfer and the potential of hiring of two new enthusiastic and idealistic young teachers, Mary felt the school was again ready to vote a second time. This time there was a 93 percent vote from the staff to begin the Project Improve change process.

Project Improve is a nationally recognized comprehensive school redesign project affiliated with the New American Schools (NAS). Staff chose Project Improve not only because of its "Good Housekeeping Seal of Approval" from NAS, but also primarily because of its rigorous standards assuring "design-based assistance" throughout the course of the project. In their investigations, staff found many models attractive, but ultimately lacking in technical support and assistance required for the duration of long-term school change. One of us, in fact, had served as a Project Improve facilitator and trainer during the past four years. Project Improve came with a well-designed school change process geared toward building the capacity of the school community to better address its own particular school challenges. It also offered content-based instructional materials in reading and mathematics for schools that needed them. Regular staff trainings and laboratories, geared toward infusing constructivist learning principles and best teaching practice into classrooms, were also to be offered throughout the course of the change process.

Figure 2.1 (pp. 18–19) offers a map of the *Project Improve Design Model*. This model offers a systematic process for continuous school improvement. It is adapted and based upon lessons learned in our review of the educational change literature. It also represents a synthesis of best practice and lessons from our own experience with the Accelerated Schools Project (ASP) and the experiences of numerous practitioners with whom we have worked over the years.

Forming Your Leadership Team

In our story, Mary had decided to use the school's existing site council as the school's leadership team. She knew that in the past the site council had not been active and that it wasn't truly representative of the school community. We encouraged her to be mindful and systematic in establishing the new site council, especially given the recent low scores on the state report card and the imperative for school improvement. Members would need to be committed and ready to initiate the change process.

In these pre-initiation stages, we believe it is necessary to create what Sergiovanni[1] describes as "*leadership density*—the extent to which leadership roles are shared and the extent to which leadership is broadly exercised." We feel that leadership density is a key ingredient to strengthening, sustaining, and widely investing participants in the renewal of their schools. With it we can help ensure that school improvement takes hold and persists in spite of unpredictable personnel changes and numerous environmental challenges.

"A community is like a ship; everyone ought to be prepared to take the helm."—Henry Ibsen

Leadership Team Selection

Based upon a broadened notion of leadership, we proposed some important criteria for screening members of the leadership team:

School Leadership Team—Qualifications

♦ Commitment to school-wide change

♦ Colleague respect

♦ Leadership potential based upon past experience and the perception of others

♦ Good interpersonal relationship skills

♦ Ability to initiate projects and gets things done

Figure 2.1. Map of Project Improve Design Model

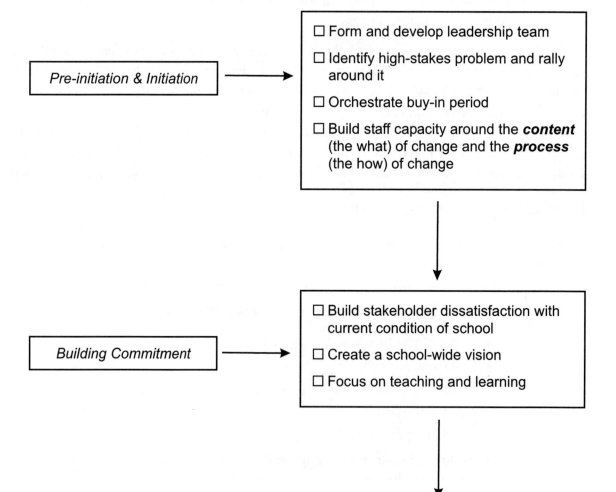

Figure 2.1. Map of Project Improve Design Model (continued)

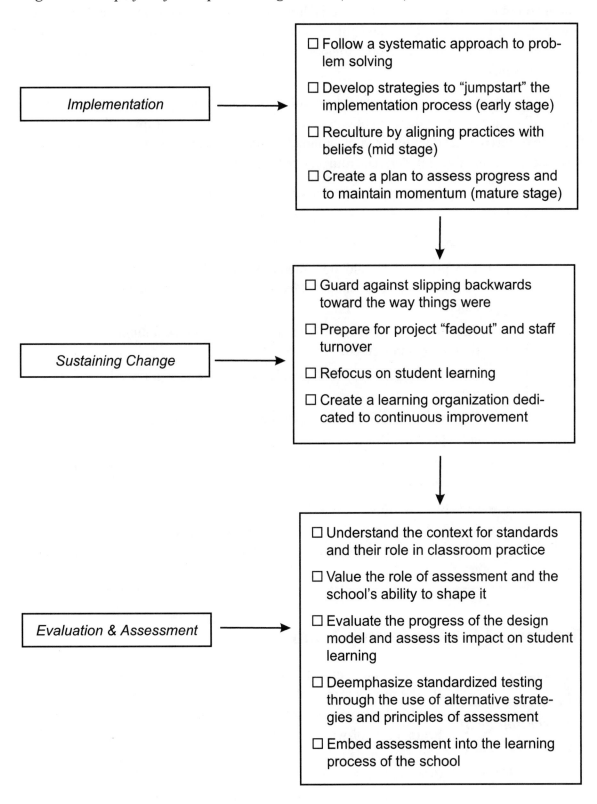

We also recommended that the leadership team be large enough to be representative of the school community, but not so large that it is difficult to work with and manage. Maeroff recommends four to eight members and points out that in industry leadership teams are typically composed of six to twelve members.[2] Elementary schools may have smaller sized teams than secondary schools.

There are a variety of ways to select team members and no one way is right or wrong. You will need to check state or district policies and, if you have them, your own school's by-laws. Possible means of selection, for example, might include voluntary sign-up, election, principal designation, or membership derived from an existing group.

Finally, we offered Mary some general selection guidelines:

School Leadership Team—Selection Guidelines

♦ The principal should not impose choice. If the principal names the team, she should at least do so in consultation with others.

♦ The diversity of the staff, student body, and community should be represented.

♦ Be aware of cliques and people who do not work well together.

♦ Be sure that grade levels, departments, and/or special areas are represented.

♦ Include instructional assistants and those who actually live in the community.

♦ Consider a central office advocate.

♦ Secure the advice and technical support of outside friendly critics like university professors and school reform providers.

The Role of the Leadership Team

Many schools tend to focus on issues external to the core technology of teaching, learning, and assessment.

Now that your team has been selected, it will be important to clarify the team's responsibilities. First and foremost, they will need to mindfully manage the school change process to seize the moment to begin a school-wide improvement process focused on student learning. This focus is key, because many schools tend to focus on issues external to the core technology of teaching, curriculum, and assessment. Issues like resources, school climate, and governance structures become the ends of school reform rather than the means. Schools that follow this path often end up feeling like they are spinning their wheels rather than making improvements in student learning.

Your leadership team will certainly have questions about its responsibilities. What are we committing ourselves to? Will we receive a stipend? Is there sufficient release time? How will we mange the process and content of the change project? Will my colleagues treat me differently when I am formally recognized as a school leader? Is the principal truly receptive to change and sharing power? Do we have the support of central office? Maeroff offers a helpful set of responsibilities for school leadership teams.[3]

Leadership Team Responsibilities

◆ Modeling the kinds of behavior that the team would like to elicit from colleagues

◆ Anticipating objections so that answers are provided before some of the negative reactions are registered

◆ Remembering that each member is only part of the team and does not speak for the team as a whole unless delegated to do so

◆ Taking every opportunity to share ownership with the school community

◆ Providing enough time for others to interact with the team

◆ Striving to get ample opportunity in the school's schedule for time to work on the change process with the rest of the school

◆ Keeping the school community informed about progress

◆ Being positive whenever possible

◆ Maintaining a sense of humor about what the team is trying to accomplish

---

Identifying a High-Stakes Problem

As previously mentioned, your leadership team will need to seize the moment to begin a school-wide process of improvement. Different critical incidents can serve as catalysts for school change. In the case of South Central Middle School, the critical incident was the sudden and dramatic release of the State Report Card. In other schools it can be the creation of a School-Wide Title I Plan, the development a School Improvement Plan, a School Accreditation Visit, School Reconstitution, the announcement of new national and/or

Different critical incidents can serve as catalysts for school change.

state reports, or the newspaper posting of student achievement data. Whatever the case, the leadership team will guide the change process as it unfolds and develops at the school site.

At South Central, the recent release of the school's state report card (Figure 2.2, pp. 23–23) served as a rallying point and catalyst for school change. Data revealed that 8th grade student achievement was low across the board in reading, writing, and math. At least 70 percent of students were not meeting state standards across all of the tested areas. Student attendance was at an all time high and even surpassed state averages. Yet, classrooms were still fairly traditional and uninspiring to most of the school's students. And even though the staff was experienced, it seemed stuck in its ways.

Given these realities, Mary had skillfully held up the school's report card and said, "We do not have a choice about whether or not to change. We can't remain the same, but we do have a choice about how we will change." The school had a significant student achievement problem, yet Mary's style was indirect and invitational. She made staff feel as though they had some control over their future school change initiatives, yet also indicated that they must begin the improvement process now.

Buy-In Period: Deciding to Initiate Comprehensive School Change

An essential responsibility of your leadership team is to engage the school community in a discussion of the need for change, best instructional practices, and possible models for change. The goal of this phase is to achieve a critical mass of support so that a comprehensive effort to improve your school can begin. Your work here is important in that you will begin to lay a foundation of meaning and understanding about what needs to be done. You will need to lead school-wide discussions about the challenges you face, become better educated yourselves, and then educate your community about what you have learned. Together you will need to visit successful schools, participate in statewide showcases, attend conferences, and dialogue about what you have seen and learned, all the while thinking about what will work most effectively and fit your own school culture.

The goal of the "buy-in" phase is to achieve a critical mass of support so that a comprehensive effort to improve your school can begin.

Figure 2.2. State Report Card, South Central Middle School

STUDENT PERFORMANCE

Rating: Low

The student performance rating is based on annual state test results. Improvement over time and percent of students meeting the standards in 1999 are combined to calculate this rating.

IMPROVEMENT OVER TIME

The table below shows your school's improvement on reading and mathematics multiple choice test results over four years—1996 through 1999.

YOUR SCHOOL'S STUDENT PERFORMANCE	
	Improved over time
X	Stayed about the same over time
	Declined over time
	Unable to determine improvement over time *

PERCENT OF STUDENTS MEETING STANDARDS

The graph below shows the percent of students at your school who met state standards on 1999 reading, writing, mathematics multiple choice and mathematics problem solving tests. Results for the same grade level of students in Oregon schools with similar demographics (comparison schools) and the state also are shown.

GRADE 8

Reading: School 23%, Comparison Schools 37%, State 56%
Writing: School 30%, Comparison Schools 50%, State 68%
Math Multiple Choice: School 24%, Comparison Schools 32%, State 52%
Math Problem Solving: School 21%, Comparison Schools 38%, State 55%

■ School ▨ Comparison Schools □ State

STUDENT BEHAVIOR

Rating: Exceptional

The student behavior rating is based on student attendance.

ATTENDANCE

The table below shows the percent of students attending your school and the statewide average for grades 6 through 8.

	SCHOOL	STATE
1995-96	82.1%	92.6%
1996-97	80.4%	92.6%
1997-98	83.9%	92.7%
1998-99	96.5%	92.8%

SCHOOL CHARACTERISTICS

Rating: Satisfactory

The school characteristics rating is based on the percent of students taking state tests.

PERCENT OF STUDENTS TAKING STATE TESTS

The table below shows the percent of students who took 1999 state tests in your school and the state.

	SCHOOL	STATE
Students taking state tests	90%	98%

OTHER INFORMATION

Here is additional information from the state about your school that may be of interest to you.

INSTRUCTIONAL STAFF

The table below shows the education and experience of your school's instructional staff and the average for all instructional staff in Oregon in the 1998-99 school year.

	SCHOOL	STATE
Master's degree (or higher)	44%	46%
Average years of experience	15 years	14 years
Average years of experience in district	13 years	10 years

As we gather more data, we hope in the future to report how education dollars are spent statewide, class sizes, student participation in extracurricular activities, school safety and student discipline.

Specific data and calculations contributing to your school's rating and report cards for all schools and districts in the state are posted on the Oregon Department of Education web site at www.ode.state.or.us/reportcard.

* Improvement over time cannot be determined because:
☐ Too few students
☐ Incomplete data
☐ New school (less than 3 years)
☐ Missing data or under appeal
☐ No students in grades 3, 5, 8 and 10

Visiting Other Schools

We recommend that you build motivation and readiness to change by visiting schools that are actively involved in a school change process that is similar to what you eventually hope to do at your school. Nothing is more persuasive to staff than hearing and seeing school-change stories from the perspectives of other practitioners.

Yet, although such visits can be insightful, they also can be analogous to the somewhat superficial understanding of Mexico obtained from a three-day visit to Cancun or Acapulco.[4] Impressions gleaned from a brief visit abroad to any culture usually provide an insufficient basis upon which to draw complete conclusions about culture. To assist you in the school visit, we have prepared a "tour guide" that offers some *must see* and *don't miss* areas. We organize our tour guide around the *meaning, organization*, and *effects* of change. Meaning has to do with staff feelings, perceptions, and understanding of the changes they are trying to make. Organization focuses on supportive structures such as governance systems and assessment processes. The effects of change focuses directly on the classroom and the student experience. We offer a set of questions noted below to help you learn about the school during a relatively short and quick school tour.

> *Our tour guide is organized around the meaning, organization, and effects of change.*

Meaning of Change

- **Readiness for Change**. Is a high percentage (80 to 90 percent) of the staff supportive of the change initiative?

- **School Vision**. Is there a shared sense of purpose? Are staff members able to articulate the school's vision and priorities?

- **Understanding**. Does the leadership team understand the complexity and delicate nature of the change process? Does the staff have a model of change in mind? Does the staff have access to specific skills and knowledge necessary for a successful implementation?

- **Success**. Are there notable examples of success?

Organization or Structure of Change

- **Organization and Governance**. How are decisions made and who makes them? Are there procedures for problem solving and school-based inquiry?

♦ Culture. Is collegiality evident through mutual sharing, assistance, and collaborative work? Does staff have adequate meeting management and group process skills? Are staff members able to work with diverse views?

♦ **Instruction and Curriculum**. Are instructional practices teacher-centered or do they include opportunities for cooperative learning, peer and cross-age tutoring, and increased student responsibility? Does the curriculum present concepts in the abstract or are concepts applied to real, personal, and concrete experiences?

♦ **Feedback and Assessment**. Does the school openly solicit diagnostic information from multiple sources? Does the school reflect upon its practices?

♦ **Support**. Are adequate financial and time resources available? Is there support from key administrators in the district? Is the required technical knowledge available and accessible?

Effects of Change

♦ **Active Learning**. Do students take an active role in learning or do they largely "consume" what teachers have planned for them to do?

♦ **Authentic Learning**. Is instruction based upon application to real life situations or issues?

♦ **Interactive Learning**. Do students collaborate with each other in pairs and small groups sharing knowledge and expertise, completing projects, and critiquing each other?

♦ **Inclusive Learning**. Are all students (including children who are LEP or have special needs) actively involved by exploring, reading, collaborating, listening, touching, and moving?

♦ **Continuous Learning**. Are connections made in lessons to previous learning? Are prior knowledge and student strengths accessed and built upon?

State Showcases

A relatively new phenomenon in the last few years has been the development and evolution of state and regional showcases of promising school improvement projects and practices.

As occurs in automobile design shows, the latest educational change models are presented to prospective consumers or school leadership teams. "Providers" from various reform initiatives throughout the country like Accelerated Schools, the School Development Program, Expeditionary Learning, Reading Recovery, etc., present their comprehensive or subject-based school reform models or packages (see *Ports of Call* section at the end of the book). Each has a specific focus, claims about its effectiveness, information about how it supports teachers, what technical support or curriculum it offers, how much it costs, and materials as well as information about whom to contact for further information.

In this environment it is very easy to be "seduced" and eventually make choices and decisions that may not be in the best interest of your school. It is very important that your leadership team seriously reviews your student performance data and is well aware of your school's strengths and challenges. Finding the best fit for your school is crucial. You also need to consider your school's particular context and history before committing to a particular path of school reform. Some models are more open-ended and might fit a staff independent and proud of its professionalism; others are more directive and may be better for a relatively inexperienced staff. Each model has specific strengths and areas of focus. The true test of a model's ability to improve student learning, though, is the degree to which your teachers can benefit from the model's approach to improve teaching and student learning within your particular school context. Remember, any educational change design model cannot be simply dropped into any school setting. Rather, you must pay particular attention to your own unique school context and history. Some schools will have already adopted a literacy and math series, but still need a process for creating staff unity and democratic participation. Others may have good interpersonal chemistry and be in need of specific curricular packages. What's most critical is that your leadership team asks a series of pertinent questions about the proposed change. The Northwest Regional Education Laboratory offers a set of guiding questions that your leadership should consider[5] (see Tool 2.1).

Some design models are more open ended and might fit a staff independent and proud of its professionalism; others are more directive and may be better for a relatively needy or inexperienced staff.

Remember, any educational change design model cannot simply be dropped into any school setting.

Tool 2.1. School Reform Showcase: Finding the Best Fit

Guiding Questions

1. What is an example of how a particular reading or math skill is taught?

2. Is specific content taught at specific grade levels?

3. What materials are necessary? Are new books, technology, and other materials required in order to implement this model? Are they provided under the cost of the program?

4. How will the materials we already have work with the model?

5. Will we need to change staffing in our building? What additional staff (or roles) will be required with this model? (e.g. facilitator, parent outreach coordinator)

6. How much additional staff development time will be required for the whole staff? For a smaller group of teachers?

7. How closely will this model link with assessments required by our district/state?

8. Will we need to change how our school works, i.e., who makes decisions and how they are made?

9. With what type of student population has this program worked effectively?

10. How long does it take a school to successfully implement all aspects of this model?

11. What types of implementation interventions are stressed by this model?

    - On-site visits?

    - On-site facilitators?

    - Whole school training?

    - Facilitator training?

Synthesis/Reflection: How will this change model affect what I do in my classroom?

Study Groups

One good role for your leadership team is that of a study group. You will want to begin your study with existing school data, especially as it pertains to student learning. Based upon your assessment of student strengths and challenges you will want to identify some tentative but specific student needs. Next consider examining what the research and key professional organizations say is best practice as it relates to comprehensive school reform and major curricular areas.

We particularly like the recommendations assembled by Zemelman, Daniels, and Hyde in their well crafted book, *Best Practice: New Standards for Teaching and Learning in America's Schools:*[6] These are described below in a simple "less of/more of" framework (see Tool 2.2).

Murphy and Lick define the primary goal of study groups as:

> To center the entire school faculty on implementing, integrating, and managing effective teaching and learning practices that will result in an increase in student learning and a decrease in negative behaviors of students.[7]

Thus, we recommended that Mary and her leadership team become a study group as they began to initiate a change process at South Central. The study group would serve as a catalyst and model for the school as a whole. Once a design model had been chosen, it was expected that other study groups would arise and be formed around the key content areas assessed by the state, i.e., reading, writing, mathematics, and science.

Capacity Building: Managing the *Content (the What)* of School Change

It is essential for your leadership team to become as mindful and thoughtful about the content of change as possible. By content or the basic conceptual ideas about the "what" of school change, we mean: (a) frameworks for thinking about organizational and individual change, (b) lessons learned from research, and (c) guidelines for selecting comprehensive school design models.

Tool 2.2. Common Recommendations
of National Curriculum Reports

- ♦ **LESS** whole-class, teacher-directed instruction, e.g., lecturing
- ♦ **LESS** student passivity: sitting, listening, receiving, and absorbing information
- ♦ **LESS** prizing and rewarding of silence in the classroom
- ♦ **LESS** classroom time devoted to fill-in-the-blank worksheets, dittos, workbooks, and other "seatwork"
- ♦ **LESS** student time spent reading textbooks and basal readers
- ♦ **LESS** attempt by teachers to thinly "cover" large amounts of material in every subject area
- ♦ **LESS** rote memorization of facts and details
- ♦ **LESS** stress on the competition and grades in school
- ♦ **LESS** tracking or leveling students into "ability groups"
- ♦ **LESS** use of pull-out special programs
- ♦ **LESS** use of, and reliance on, standardized test
- ♦ **MORE** experiential, inductive, hands-on learning
- ♦ **MORE** active learning in the classroom, with all the attendant noise and movement of students doing, talking, and collaborating
- ♦ **MORE** emphasis on higher-order thinking; learning a field's key concepts and principles
- ♦ **MORE** deep study of a smaller number of topics, so that students internalize the field's way of inquiry
- ♦ **MORE** time devoted to reading whole, original, real books and nonfiction materials
- ♦ **MORE** responsibility transferred to students for their work: goal setting, record keeping, monitoring, evaluation
- ♦ **MORE** choice for students; e.g., picking their own books, writing topics, team partners, research projects
- ♦ **MORE** enacting and modeling of the principles of democracy in school
- ♦ **MORE** attention to affective needs and the varying cognitive styles of individual students
- ♦ **MORE** cooperative, collaborative activity; developing the classroom as an interdependent community
- ♦ **MORE** heterogeneously grouped classrooms where individual needs are met through inherently individualized activities, not segregation of bodies
- ♦ **MORE** delivery of special help to students in regular classrooms
- ♦ **MORE** varied and cooperative roles for teachers, parents, and administrators
- ♦ **MORE** reliance upon teachers' descriptive evaluation of student growth, including qualitative/anecdotal observations

We wanted Mary and her leadership team to realize that there are numerous well-developed change frameworks, a considerable number of research studies, and hundreds of school reform models. Some of these are better than others and the best of these sources we felt could provide South Central with direction and a map for charting and following their own particular school reform journey. Furthermore, information from these multiple sources can be used selectively and thoughtfully and matched to South Central's particular context and challenges. They can help South Central's leadership team become aware of predictable stages and pitfalls in their journey. In the end, we felt that this knowledge about the content or "what" of school change would help South Central become more of a purposeful traveler with an itinerary rather than just a random hitchhiker looking for a ride.

There are numerous well-developed change frameworks, a considerable number of research studies, and hundreds of school reform models.

Frameworks for Thinking About School Change

A useful way to think about school change is with the organizational framework of Project Improve that we presented at the beginning of this chapter. Since this book is actually organized around this framework, our discussion here will be brief.

Project Improve Model of School Change

♦ Pre-initiation and Initiation

♦ Building Commitment

♦ Implementation

♦ Sustaining Change

♦ Evaluation and Assessment

In the *pre-initiation* phase, leaders of school change (in this case the school leadership team and us as university facilitators) engage the school staff in a discussion of the need for change and a model for change, and in the end garner the initial commitment and support needed to embark upon a major school transformation. The goal of this phase is to begin building a shared meaning and commitment around a particular reform model and to achieve a critical mass of staff support so that efforts to change the school can begin.

During the *initiation* phase school staff members build their knowledge base and receive training in the skills, knowledge, and attitudes that are required for the model to succeed. Requisite skills and knowledge include working in teacher teams, developing group process and meeting management skills, using inquiry or action research to identify and solve school problems, and improving their the knowledge of instructional and curricular practices designed to create powerful learning experiences for all children.

The pre-initiation and initiation phases includes the formation of a leadership team, identification of a high stakes problem, a "buy-in" process, and staff capacity building around both the content and process of change. We recommend that the pre-initiation period be no longer than three to five months and the initiation period be no longer than a year; otherwise, initial enthusiasm for change will diminish.

It's one thing to initiate change and another thing to really get behind the change effort. Accordingly, we have developed a phase in which staff work on building commitment to school change that is both passionate and long-term. Killing the myth that the school is doing the best it can or that the students and their families are defective is a fundamental step in significant school change. We also find that developing a school-wide vision to be very motivating and uplifting. We ask the members of the school community to think of their dream school or the one to which they would ideally like to send their own child. Then we ask that staff specifically assess their school's strengths and weakness around the major curricular areas. We purposefully focus on issues related to student learning and achievement rather than spinning our wheels on peripheral issues like resources or working conditions. We take note of Lortie's research, which points to teachers' ability to connect with, and teach, students, as being their most rewarding activity.[8]

Killing the myth that the school is doing the best it can or that the students and their families are defective is a fundamental step in significant school change.

During the *implementation* phase, we concentrate on basic issues like following a systematic problem-solving process and finding adequate resources. We also think of implementation as having distinctive stages. Early implementation focuses on helping staff make transitions from time-honored practices and encourages networking with other educators and community members. Mid-course implementation centers around school reculturing, a process in which school beliefs are aligned with changes in practice. Finally, the late stages of implementation focus on the maturation of the change process. Returning to the school vision for direction is important, as is beginning to use evaluation and assessment tools for determining how well your plan is working.

Once change is implemented we must work on *sustaining* it. We find that this is the point when most school change efforts begin to drift or break down. In view of that we focus on socializing new staff members and dealing with inevitable changes in leadership. This phase is also a time of recommitting to the school's vision and increased student learning. It is a time in which an ethic of continuous improvement must become embedded in the culture of the school.

Evaluate implementation and assess student learning.

The final *evaluation and assessment* phase should actually be an ongoing activity. Here we want to evaluate whether the design model has actually been implemented and assess whether or not it has led to increased student learning and more students meeting state standards. We feel that evaluation and assessment must not be an afterthought but something developed from day one.

Our process corresponds roughly to what Rosenblum and Louis have called the rational model of school change, whereby change is viewed as a logical, sequential process of readiness, initiation, implementation, and continuation[9] (a framework originally developed by Berman and McLaughlin, 1976[10]). We propose our five-phase model mainly as a heuristic device for understanding some of the essential steps in successfully implementing school change.

We realize that the actual change process is hardly as linear and sequential as this framework suggests. For example, capacity building is an ongoing activity, and cultural change can begin when new ideas are introduced, discussed, and assimilated among staff members. Furthermore, changes in teaching practice should be considered from the beginning as new ideas are experimented with and introduced to the school staff. We also believe that change is best viewed within a systems framework, recognizing that planned change is embedded within an existing school structure, culture, and environment that can either support or impede the school's transformation.[11] Nonrational processes as well as rational planning are part of the change process, most notably the political forces and personalities within and outside of the school that define the context for change. Still, thinking about change as we develop in Project Improve helps to identify issues that seem to arise at different phases of the change process.

In addition to the Project Improve design model, there are numerous other resources and frameworks that we like and feel can help us to better understand the elements of change. For example, Miles' "Triple I" model described in a video on managing change focuses on Initiation, Implementation, and Institutionalization of change with special attention given to the *implementation dip*.[12] Here, staff are typically excited about school improvement until as a rule they become stuck when the realty sets in that change takes time and lots of effort.

Our own work has centered on discovering "What's Happening" in schools with a focus on the "Meaning, Organization and Structure," and "Effects of Change on Students"[13] (see "Buy-In" section in this chapter on Visiting Other Schools). Conley's "Comprehensive View of Restructuring" framework points out that Curriculum, Instruction, and Assessment must be the central, or end, variables in school reform.[14] We strongly recommend Hall and Hord's "Concern's Based Adoption Model" (CBAM) and its application to participant feelings, perceptions, or concerns about the change process.[15] Stages of concern range from becoming aware of the change and then managing it to refocusing and actually making an impact. The CBAM framework helps us to assess and read individuals' levels of understanding, buy-in, and commitment and take a developmental approach in managing their participation in the change process. Finally we would like to point the reader to the work of Robert Evans.[16] This work distinctively focuses on the individual or human side of change in school settings. His discussion of teacher resistance and the failure of school reformers to help teachers come to grips with perceived loss and finding continuity in their work is very illuminating.

We particularly value William Bridges' Three-Phase Model, which focuses on how individuals can manage personal transitions so that larger organizational change can happen.[17]

> ### Three-Phase Model of *Individual* Transitions
> ♦ Ending
> ♦ Neutral Zone
> ♦ Beginning

Bridges points out that change is situational: the new school, the new principal, the new leadership team, the new policy, or in our case the new school change effort, Project Improve. Transition, on the other hand, is the psychological process staff will need to go through to come to terms with Project Improve. Transition is an individual or internal psychological process whereas change is more of an external or organizational event. Bridges importantly points out that unless transition occurs, change will not work out. His model is unusual in that it begins with an ending. Transition starts with an ending or personal loss and it is virtually impossible to get change without getting into personal challenges. Managing transitions at South Central is about helping staff through the predictable stages of loss and disorientation. Staff and community members at South Central will need help in letting go of their past and coming to grips with their school's future, both in terms of their own personal work and beliefs about how children learn best.

Transition is an internal process whereas change is more of an external event.

Following Bridges' framework, perceived losses must be recognized and compensated for during the ending phase. Holding public rituals helps participants to let go of the past and begin to accept the proposed change. For example, we recommended to Mary that the school hold a community celebration with the completion of its visioning process.

Bridges' neutral phase is the time when meaning and sense making are critical. It is important to help participants understand how the proposal change fits with the school's vision and needs. Goals and benchmarks must be set and risk taking is to be encouraged. Accordingly, we recommended to Mary that decision making be consistent with and supportive of the school's vision and the values of the Project Improve process.

During the "last" or beginning phase, participants must be provided with a clear picture and sense of purpose. There should be a game plan and all stakeholders should actively participate in the proposed change. We recommended that Mary carefully follow the Project Improve design model process to guide her school's change efforts. Thus, her staff members would have a clear picture of where they were headed. Greater clarity and purpose for staff also emerged as the leadership team began to model appropriate behaviors consistent with Project Improves' philosophy of practicing shared leadership and creating a democratic environment. Accomplishments, like developing a school vision and receiving a Comprehensive School Reform Demonstration (CSRD) grant, were celebrated.

There are predictable stages and road blocks to consider in the change process.

These frameworks and others like them can give us direction for charting and following our own particular courses. They point out that there are predictable stages and destinations to consider in our journey. They help us to be mindful and thoughtful tourists rather than random hitchhikers.

Finally, although various frameworks and resources for change must be considered and used when applicable, the critical departure point for school change is when staff members as individuals commit to changing themselves. We utilize the following statement with school practitioners when they become bogged down or stuck in their school reform work. It creates a certain tension or dissonance that helps them renew their commitment to school change:

The starting point for improvement is not system change, not change in others around us, but change in ourselves. Waiting for others to act differently, results in inaction and no change.

Lessons Learned About Change from Research

There are a few key issues about successful change that are constants across the research. They were first discussed in Chapter 1 and will be reintroduced in greater detail in the following chapters. Here we summarize what is basic and essential for your leadership team to know about school change. First and foremost there must be a buy-in period in which meaning and purpose are created and developed by all of the participants. A foundation of understanding, meaning, and commitment must be laid during this initiation process. Collaborative work groups in which leadership is shared have the best chance of being successful throughout the change process. These groups must focus on both the content and process of change. Participants will need to become well-informed and critical consumers of the numerous educational change possibilities before them. The changes on which they work must be comprehensive and cultural rather than piecemeal. To this end, successful schools develop learner-centered visions that focus on improving student learning.

There must be a buy-in period in which meaning and purpose are created and developed by all of the participants.

You will need to become well informed and critical consumers.

Secondly, implementation is really a process of local adaptation. Any effort at change will run into, and be affected by, an already existing pattern of thinking or acting within the school. Thus, change efforts conceived outside of the culture of the school invariably are changed by the already existing patterns of behavior within the school. Change is very context-dependent. Schools don't so much implement change as much as they adapt to change. Once schools adapt the change to meet the conditions of their environment, the context in which educators work is the overall driving force affecting the implementation process. Low success rates of implementation are attributable to program developers who often fail to consider the specific cultural elements of the schools in which the changes are to be imbedded.

Any effort at change will run into, and be affected by, an already exisiting pattern of thinking or acting within the school.

Third, the key to sustaining change centers on the attempt to maintain and build upon those cultural regularities that are in place and interact to support the change efforts, i.e., collaborative work groups and an ethic of continuous improvement. The school leadership team must work at sustaining genuine participation by facilitating the school community to continually define and redefine its values and beliefs, which in turn ultimately drives the change process. By so doing, deep understanding, involvement, and commitment are sustained through the deliberate creation of a culture of reflection and change. A specific focus on student learning mobilizes the school community to examine how its students learn in school and the role of the adult community to improve that process.

Build upon those cultural regularities that are in place.

Finally, change must be viewed as integral to everyday life in schools rather than as an add-on with a finite life cycle. Most of us see change as something that has a clear beginning and usually, a definable end—and we can't wait for its end. In a healthy school however, change is seen as the constant, not the exception.

Guidelines for Selecting Comprehensive School Design Models

One of your first responsibilities as a leadership team is to explore and survey the vast land of comprehensive school reform possibilities before you. Wilson and Davis note that until recently, making changes in schools has been a "cottage industry of lone tinkerers" with little prior knowledge being shared or effectively used.[18] Comprehensive school reform is akin to what they refer to as a "redesign process." Such a process involves the integration of research and development efforts along with the testing of these ideas in actual school sites, which leads to model refinement. It's what Wilson and Davis believe to be the "missing link" in educational reform.

Comprehensive school reform is akin to a "redesign process."

The Southwest Educational Development Laboratory in Austin, Texas reports that currently there are *289* school change models receiving government funding through the Comprehensive School Reform Demonstration Program (CSRD). According to the Northwest Regional Education Laboratory (NWREL):

> Comprehensive school reform is a means to improve student achievement through reorganizing and revitalizing entire schools, rather than implementing isolated programs. It uses well-researched and well-documented models for school-wide change that are supported by expert trainers and facilitators. Challenging academic standards, strong professional development, and meaningful parent and community support are all part of a comprehensive school reform program (http://www.nwrel.org/CSRD/).

The Mid-continent Regional Education Lab defines comprehensive school reform as follows:

> Comprehensive school reform is a congressional initiative focusing on reorganizing and revitalizing entire schools, rather than on isolated piecemeal reforms. The purpose of this initiative is to provide financial incentives for schools to develop comprehensive school reforms based on reliable research and effective practices and including an emphasis on basic academies and parental involvement, so that all children can meet challenging state content and performance goals (http://www.mcrel.org/CSRD/).

These models, catalogued in the above sources, are being implemented in districts throughout the nation. We warned Mary and her leadership team that they would need to become well-informed of the many change possibilities before them. Becoming assertive consumers, they would need to find the right fit for their school or even design their own change project from the ground up. Congress initially named 17 comprehensive school change models in its CSRD Program legislation. Since this initial list was offered by Congress, other comprehensive reform models have been funded, along with numerous curricula-based programs that fit into locally developed comprehensive school plans.

Some comprehensive reform models (e.g., Success for All and Core Knowledge) espouse that school reform needs to be structured and explicit, even prescriptive, to achieve results.

Prescriptive reforms are keyed to "quickly implemented changes to core elements." Principle based reforms are keyed to "longer-term change and building staff capacity."

These *prescriptive* reform models are keyed to specific task and instructional practices. They have well-defined learning objectives, and teachers utilize specific instructional practices and curricular materials in order to meet these objectives. On the other end of the continuum (e.g., Accelerated Schools and Coalition for Essential Schools) are *principle-based* reform models, which call for guiding principles that become a lens for school decision-making. Principle-based reform models call for the professional development of teachers, permitting practitioners more discretion to define learning objectives, and the processes to direct them. Bodily describes prescriptive reforms as those keyed to "quickly implemented, task level change to core elements." In contrast, Bodilly explains principle-based reforms as those keyed to "longer-term change and building school-level capacity to promote self-improvement.[19]

The Northwest Regional Education Laboratory in Portland, Oregon, and the Laboratory for Student Success at Temple University have prepared a catalog and interactive handbook, respectively, of school reform models that identify skill and content-based or curricular reform models. These are available at: http://www.nwrel.org/csrdp and http://www.reformhand book-lss.org. The Northwest Regional Educational Laboratory offers a guide for evaluating whole school reform efforts, as does the Mid-Continent Region Education and Learning, available at http://www.mcrel.org/CSRD/. These last two guides are based upon the assumption that the school has already decided to implement a comprehensive school reform model. They could be particularly helpful when your leadership team visits innovative school sites or participates in state and regional showcases.

What criteria might you use to determine if these models fit your needs? CSRD has developed nine criteria to help schools in their selection process. We find these guidelines to be very helpful in assessing the strengths of particular comprehensive school reform models (see Tool 2.3, p. 38). You will also find a reference to "School CSR Self-Assessment Tool" at the NWREL Web site previously mentioned.

Tool 2.3. Nine Components of Comprehensive School Reform Programs

1. **Effective, research-based methods and strategies**: A comprehensive school reform program employs innovative strategies and proven methods for student learning, teaching and school management that are based on reliable research and effective practices, and have been replicated successfully in schools with diverse characteristics.

2. **Comprehensive design with aligned components**: The program has a comprehensive design for effective school functioning, including instruction, assessment, classroom management, professional development, parental involvement, and school management that aligns the school's curriculum, technology, and professional development into a school wide reform plan designed to enable all students—including children from low-income families, children with limited English proficiency, and children with disabilities—to meet challenging State content and performance standards and address the needs identified through a school needs assessment.

3. **Professional development**: The program provides high-quality and continuous teacher and staff development and training.

4. **Measurable goals and benchmarks**: A comprehensive school reform program has measurable goals for student performance tied to the State's challenging content and student performance standards as those standards are implemented, and benchmarks for meeting the goals.

5. **Support within the school**: The program is supported by school faculty, administrators, and staff.

6. **Parental and community involvement**: The program provides for the meaningful involvement of parents and the local community in planning and implementing school improvement activities.

7. **External technical support and assistance**: A comprehensive reform program utilizes high-quality external support and assistance from a comprehensive school reform entity (which may be a university) with experience or expertise in school-wide reform and improvement.

8. **Evaluation strategies**: The program includes a plan for the evaluation of the implementation of school reforms and the student results achieved.

9. **Coordination of resources**: The program identifies how other resources (federal, state, local, and private) available to the school will be utilized to coordinate services to support and sustain the school reform.

The following list from the Northwest Regional Educational Laboratory is a sample of what's possible in both principle and prescriptive-based reform options. Your leadership team's job is to research some models that would be good fits with your school culture, teaching and learning needs, and school district politics. These design models demonstrate the array of possibilities from which you can draw as you consider the direction of your change effort. You will want to become a well-informed and assertive consumer of these change possibilities that range from entire school reform models to skill and content-based reform models. The *Ports of Call* section found at the end of the book will guide you to multiple resources that will help as you decide what to do and how to do it.

Entire-School Reform Models

- ◆ Accelerated Schools Project (K–8)
- ◆ America's Choice School Design (K–12)
- ◆ ATLAS Communities (PreK–12)
- ◆ Center for Effective Schools (K–12)
- ◆ Child Development Project (K–6)
- ◆ Coalition of Essential Schools (formerly 9–12, now K–12)
- ◆ Community for Learning (K–12)
- ◆ Community Learning Centers (PreK–Adult)
- ◆ Co-NECT Schools (K–12)
- ◆ Core Knowledge (K–8)
- ◆ Different Ways of Knowing (K–7)
- ◆ Direct Instruction (K–6)
- ◆ Edison Project (K–12)
- ◆ Expeditionary Learning/Outward Bound (K–12)
- ◆ Foxfire Fund (K–12)
- ◆ High Schools That Work (9–12)
- ◆ Audrey Cohen College: Purpose Centered Education (K–12)
- ◆ High/Scope Primary Grades Approach to Education (K–3)
- ◆ Integrated Thematic Instruction (K–12)
- ◆ League of Professional Schools (K–12)
- ◆ MicroSociety® (K–8)
- ◆ Modern Red Schoolhouse (K–12)
- ◆ Montessori (PreK–8)

- ◆ Onward to Excellence (K–12)
- ◆ Paideia (K–12)
- ◆ QuESt (K–12)
- ◆ Roots & Wings (PreK–6)
- ◆ School Development Program (K–12)
- ◆ Success for All (PreK–6)
- ◆ Talent Development High School with Career Academies (9–12)
- ◆ The Learning Network (K–8)
- ◆ Urban Learning Centers (PreK–12)
- ◆ Ventures Initiative and Focus® System (K–12)
- ◆ Matrix of Components

Skill- and Content-Based Reform Models

Reading/Language Arts

- ◆ Breakthrough to Literacy (K–2)
- ◆ Carbo Reading Styles Program (K–8)
- ◆ Cooperative Integrated Reading and Composition (2–8)
- ◆ Early Intervention in Reading (K–4)
- ◆ Exemplary Center for Reading Instruction K–12
- ◆ First Steps (K–10)
- ◆ Junior Great Books (K–12)
- ◆ National Writing Project (K–16)
- ◆ Reading Recovery (1)
- ◆ Strategic Teaching and Reading Project (K–12)

Mathematics

- Comprehensive School Mathematics Program (K–6)
- Connected Mathematics Project (6–8)
- Core Plus Mathematics Project/Contemporary Mathematics in Context (9–12)
- Growing with Mathematics (K–5)
- Interactive Mathematics Program (9–12)
- MATH Connections (9–12)
- University of Chicago School Mathematics Project (K–12)

Science

- Developmental Approaches in Science, Health and Technology (K–6)
- Foundational Approaches in Science Teaching (Middle School)
- GALAXY Classroom Science (K–5)
- Iowa Chautauqua Program (K–12)

Other

- ACCESS (PreK–1)
- Basic Skill Builders (K–6)
- COMP: Creating Conditions for Learning (K–12)
- Feuerstein's Instrumental Enrichment (4–12)
- HOSTS: (Help One Student To Succeed) (K–12)
- HOTS: (Higher Order Thinking Skills) (4–8)
- Lightspan Achieve Now(K–6)
- Positive Action (K–12)
- Responsive Classroom® (K–8)
- Success–in–the–Making (K–9)

Capacity Building: Managing the *Process (the How)* of Change

This section focuses on the process of change. By process we mean group process, meeting management, and problem-solving skills. These are all elements that contribute to the manner in which change actually occurs. Today, the challenges faced by school communities are more complex than ever, ranging from dealing with increasing student diversity, new state standards, and preparing students for unforeseen jobs in the twenty-first century. These challenges are too complex to work on in isolation or alone. Thoughtful solutions to our challenges will come from the synergy of school communities working together.

The challenges faced by today's schools are too complex to work on in isolation or alone.

You will want to select members who have good interpersonal skills themselves. School change is filled with ambiguity, uncertainty, and its ups and downs. It is crucial that the leadership team is good at working with people and models behaviors that will be expected of the staff as a whole. You may be asking teachers and instructional assistants, who have spent most of their time working alone in classrooms, to suddenly begin working collaboratively in problem solving groups. Furthermore, teachers often feel as though they have insufficient time for their own classrooms let alone school-wide change issues. Therefore running meetings that are well organized, efficient, and participatory will be of utmost importance. Developing meeting agendas, assigning and practicing roles of facilitator, recorder, and timekeeper, learning inquiry and/or action research skills for group problem solving, and writing thoughtful action plans will all need to be addressed and considered as well. Three critical skills are needed for productive group work: *(a) group process, (b) meeting management,* and *(c) problem-solving skills.*

Group Process Skills

Dealing with Difficult People

When your school decides to initiate comprehensive school change, it will become necessary to ask teachers, staff, and parents to work more collaboratively. Yet, in many schools, training is rarely provided to develop the interpersonal skills needed for staff and community members to work harmoniously in groups. With significant school change comes the need for work in varied problem-solving groups ranging from the site council and school as a whole to various task and study groups.

Training is rarely provided to develop the interpersonal skills needed to work harmoniously in groups.

For one reason or another, most of us view groups and meetings as pretty dysfunctional and unproductive. Too often when a group of reasonable and intelligent people get together, something happens with the group chemistry—people don't seem to get along, they can't seem to reconcile different points of view, and not much gets accomplished. Consequently, people leave feeling frustrated and as though they have wasted their time. To head off such problems and to develop strong interpersonal skills, groups need to be aware of what can go wrong in groups and how to help things go right. We recommend the activity "Agnes and Her Friends," in Tool 2.4 (pp. 43–44), as one way of raising awareness about these issues.

"Agnes and Her Friends" is an activity that allows groups to explore ways in which unproductive behaviors can impede the group in accomplishing its work and meeting its goals. After eliciting typical dysfunctional behaviors from group participants and assigning these behaviors to one of the character types described in "Agnes and Her Friends," the group then hypothesizes what caused each of the characters to behave as he/she does. Following a brainstorm of "why," participants then turn to generating ways in which the group can structure meetings and support the person so that the unproductive behaviors become unnecessary. This activity becomes a mirror for the group to analyze its own unproductive behaviors because we can all be "Agnes and Her Friends." Furthermore, a lot of these unproductive behaviors are unconscious behaviors that we all engage in from time to time. We can all learn skills for prevention and correction of these unproductive interpersonal behaviors.

Reaching Consensus

Democratic school change requires that participants become aware of the various parameters of decision making. In our own work with schools, we discuss three types of decision making: first, *command* decisions made by one person or group of persons without input from others; second, *advisory* decisions made by one person or group of persons after gathering input from others; and finally, *shared* decisions made by the whole group or representative group. In comprehensive school change, we would expect to see increased shared decision making, especially around significant issues requiring the support and buy-in of everyone.

Expect to see more shared decision making.

Shared decisions must be reached through the consensus process. The collective wisdom of the group creates a certain type of synergy that typically leads to very thoughtful decisions. Staff are more likely to support decisions reached through consensus because of their involvement in the decision making process. Figure 2.3 (p. 45) demonstrates how decision making shifts when a school moves from a traditional top-down orientation to a democratic site-based decision-making pathway. An increase in shared decision making necessitates an expanded need for making decisions by consensus.

Tool 2.4. Guidelines for "Agnes and Her Friends"

Introduction: Each of you has no doubt attended meetings where the group's business was impeded because of unproductive behaviors by some group members. These meetings could have occurred in a community group, PTA, church group or at your school. Would you take a minute to reflect on a meeting that you've attended where the behavior of one or more members has hindered the group in getting its work completed. List some of the behaviors that you've observed.

Reflection: Group takes 1 to 2 minutes to jot down some of the behaviors they've seen occur.

Group Share: The facilitator then asks for observations that have been made by participants. The facilitator assigns the behaviors to one of the following characters: Agnes (Aggressor), Beatrice (Blocker), Clarence (Clown), Dora (Dropout), and Simon (Saboteur).

Five sheets are posted where recorders can list the behaviors as reported by participants. Each sheet is headed with the name of one of the characters. The reflection and group brainstorm of unproductive behaviors usually takes about 15 minutes.

Hypothesize Why: The facilitator then asks the group to hypothesize why Agnes behaves as she does in a group setting. The hypotheses are listed on the left side of a piece of chart pack or butcher paper.

How Can the Group Structure Meetings and Support the Person?: The facilitator then asks the group to generate ways to deal with Agnes based on their hypotheses about what causes Agnes to behave as she does. Participants should think about what can be done before, during and after the meeting.

Small Group Activity: After the facilitator models with the large group the process of examining Agnes' behavior, she then assigns a character to each small group to repeat the process. The same character can be assigned to more than one group if groups outnumber characters. The following agenda can guide the small group session:

	Task	*Time*
1.	Select a facilitator, recorder, timekeeper, and reporter.	2 min.
2.	Hypothesize WHY your person uses unproductive behaviors in the group.	5 min.
3.	Generate ways to deal with the person in positive ways and eliminate or limit their negative behaviors. Think about before, during, and after the meeting.	8 min.
4.	Post, share, and receive additional group input.	15 min.

The data generated by the group should be typed and shared with group members.
Materials needed for activity:

♦ Sheets of paper labeled *Agnes, Beatrice, Clarence, Dora* and *Simon*

♦ Sheets of paper labeled *Why?* on the left side and *How to Deal With* on the right side

♦ Felt pens, tape

Figure 2.3. Types of Decision Making in Traditional and Collaborative Schools

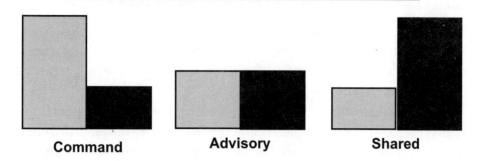

Command   **Advisory**   **Shared**

Command: Made by one person or group of persons without input from others.

Advisory: Made by one person or group of persons after gathering input from others.

Shared: Made by whole group or representative group.

Traditional School ▢   Collaborative School ◼

We define group consensus as substantial agreement, not necessarily 100 percent agreement. It is a process that embodies the following tenets:

- ◆ I believe you understand my position.
- ◆ I believe that I understand your position.
- ◆ I will go along with the decision because it was reached in and open and fair way.

Group consensus means substantial agreement, not necessarily 100 percent agreement.

A concrete application of these tenets is illustrated by Ben Franklin's last speech to the Constitutional Convention in 1787:

> I confess that there are several parts of this Constitution which I do not at present approve, but I am not sure I shall never approve them; for having lived long, I have experienced many instances of being obliged, by better information or fuller consideration, to change opinions even on important subjects which I once though right, but found to be otherwise.

> …For when you assemble a number of men to have the advantage of their joint wisdom, you inevitably assemble with those men all their prejudices, their passions, their errors of opinion, their local interest, and their selfish views.

> …The opinions I have had of its (The Constitution) errors I sacrifice to the public good.

...On the whole, Sir, I cannot help expressing a wish that every member of the convention who may still have objection to it would with me on this occasion doubt a little of his own infallibility, and, to make manifest our unanimity, put his name to this instrument.

After much research and dialogue there comes a point when a decision must be made so that you can proceed with school change. We share a strategy for reaching consensus that has worked extremely well in our own work with whole school communities. We ask the entire group to indicate to us their current level of support for the proposed change. By raising their fingers we can quickly see the groups current level of support for the proposed change. Participants who raise one or two fingers are asked to share their concerns. Once they have expressed their concerns, we ask them what it would take for them to live with the proposed change? Then with the permission of the entire group we try and make modifications or tweak the proposal enough to gain the support of those with concerns. It's a give and take process, but ensures a public hearing of concerns and in the long run heads off resistance and even potential sabotage.

Consensus Strategy

Coming to Conclusion

Straw Vote: (Five Fingers)

Use to test for consensus. Members of the group hold up their fingers simultaneously to indicate their support for the group's decision.

     5 Fingers = I'm all for it. Best Decision.

     4 Fingers = I support it. Good Decision.

     3 Fingers = I'm willing to support it.

     2 Fingers = I have concerns.

     1 Finger   = I can't support it. I'll work toward an alternative.

Group hears objections of 1s and 2s and modifies decision as needed.

Developing Ground Rules and/or Group Agreements

After initial group discussion and efforts in dealing with difficult people and in consensus building, a group should develop its own ground rules for ensuring group harmony and productivity. Begin by asking the group for suggestions about behaviors that might keep the group productive and list them on chart paper. Conclude by studying the proposed ideas making sure that there are no omissions or duplications and that everyone can live with the list. Ground Rules serve as a powerful means of preventing and even correcting conflict and group disharmony. When a problem arises the group will confront its ground rules rather than one another. For example, if participants are beginning to arrive late for meetings, the facilitator or any group member can simply review the ground rules and ask the question "how are we doing at being on time?" The following list provides a thoughtful example developed at one of our schools:

A group should develop its own ground rules for ensuring group harmony and productivity.

Ground Rules

- ◆ Start and end on time
- ◆ Stay on task
- ◆ Allow no put downs
- ◆ Allow no side-talking
- ◆ Be focused: no grading papers or "knitting"
- ◆ Be a good listener: one person talks at a time
- ◆ Come prepared: reading, research, snacks, etc.
- ◆ Be collaborative rather than competitive
- ◆ Be nonjudgmental: reserve judgment and look at the whole picture; it's okay to disagree
- ◆ Use "I" messages and offer constructive feedback with permission

---

Meeting Management Skills

Agenda Development

First and foremost, it is crucial that you have a clear agenda to guide the proceedings for each meeting. There is a tendency in busy schools to "wing it" and have meetings on the run. We have developed an agenda format that works well for us (see Tool 2.5, p. 48). A unique feature of this agenda is that it includes places for identifying a group process skill on which to work and for debriefing the meeting as a whole. For example, to discourage meeting domination by one or two participants you might simply list the group process skill of "equal participation" or "active listening." We also recommend that you end your meeting by debriefing your group process by simply asking the question, "how did we do as a group today?" As Doyle and Straus advise, in a successful meeting there must be an equal emphasis on process and content.[20]

Tool 2.5. Agenda Format

Meeting Facilitator:

Group Members:
(check if present)

Recorder:

Timekeeper:

Meeting Purpose/Type:

Materials/Preparation Needed:

Date:

Time:

Place:

Bring to the Meeting:

EXPECTED RESULTS:

GROUP PROCESS SKILL:

What/Who	*How*	*Time*

Debrief Group Process

Next Meeting:

Time: _____   Place: _____

Facilitator: _____

Recorder: _____

At the conclusion of each meeting, a time and place for your next meeting should be set. We also strongly encourage you to develop a tentative agenda as the last thing you do before dis-

Develop a tentative agenda as the last thing you do before adjourning.

banding. By doing so, you can really "hit the ground running" at your next meeting and not waste time trying to reconstruct what the purpose of the meeting is. During the time between the meetings the facilitator can fine-tune the agenda and then at the beginning of the next meeting, take a short period of time to review and renegotiate the agenda as well as make any last minute revisions regarding the timeallocated to each agenda item. It goes without saying that a meeting should follow the agenda. When participants introduce topics that are not on the agenda, the meeting facilitator can acknowledge the concern, but place the item on a post-it note in what we call the "parking lot." That way the concern is acknowledged and recorded for future agendas, discussion, and attention.

Assigning Roles

There are four basic roles for most meetings: facilitator, recorder, timekeeper, and group member. We recommend that you switch meeting roles periodically, especially those of timekeeper and recorder. The facilitator is critical and should be filled by a person who has excellent group process skills (see Tool 2.6).

Tool 2.6. Meeting Management Roles			
Facilitator:	*Recorder:*	*Timekeeper:*	*Group Member:*
◆ Substantially neutral	◆ Maintains group memory	◆ Uses agenda to monitor time and keep group moving along	◆ Concentrates on the content
◆ Focuses group on common task	◆ Accurately records group ideas	◆ Reminds group when time is running out for the agenda item	◆ Participates fully
◆ Suggests alternative procedures and methods	◆ Checks with group on accuracy	◆ Assists group in renegotiating the agenda when necessary	◆ Keeps the group productive
◆ Protects individuals from personal attack	◆ Uses variety of techniques to highlight and separate ideas	◆ Assists group in staying on task by reminding them of remaining time	◆ Actively listens
◆ Encourages participation		◆ Brings "bird walkers" back to the group's work	◆ Keeps an eye on the recorder's minutes for accuracy
◆ Helps find win/win solutions			

Frequency of Meetings

Significant school improvement often means an increase in meeting time. We have found that there is typically a need for more small task group meetings and fewer traditional whole group faculty meetings. Task groups will typically need additional time to work on improving student learning in key curricular areas, which are assessed by the state. How often and for how long you will meet depends on a variety issues raging from contract guidelines, finding more release time for planning, and how you decide to structure the workday.

Calhoun and Joyce, in reviewing characteristics of successful school change efforts, found that in the most successful sites school reform work took up approximately 10 percent of the workweek and occurred on a weekly schedule.[21] This seems like a worthy goal, although it is a bit higher than what we have found in the schools with whom we have worked. Regardless, you will need to meet regularly, more frequently, and be opportunistic about finding ways to find release time for deeper levels of understanding and implementation. Schools have developed numerous ways of capturing time, ranging from groups of teachers meeting during enrichment assemblies or common planning times to "banking" time where the school day is extended four days a week and shortened one day so that teachers can meet during the shortened day for an extended period of uninterrupted time.

Find time to meet regularly and more frequently.

Problem-Solving Approach

Your school will need to develop a means of problem solving and addressing the challenges it faces—what Glickman terms a "critical study process."[22] We recommend two possibilities. One, the Inquiry Process based on John Dewey's Scientific Process and used in the Accelerated Schools Project and the other, Action Research, a problem solving process used widely by schools across the United States.

Your school will need to develop a means of problem solving and addressing the challenges it faces.

Both of these approaches run counter to the existing cultural regularities found in most schools. Teacher work for the most part has been defined as contact time with students. Many teachers report that they lack the discretionary time to even leave their classrooms for a restroom break! In such an environment, teachers are not as reflective as they could be, and, when faced with a problem, they tend to leap to solutions.

This situation in schools is analogous to the story of an Oregon logger who was frantically trying to saw some wood. An observer pointed out, "You would be able to cut more wood if your saw was sharper," and the logger responded, " Yes but, I haven't enough time to sharpen my saw." Through approaches like inquiry and action research, we are asking teachers to slow down and take more time away from their traditional classroom responsibilities to find deeper solutions to the challenges they face. The point is that as a leadership team, you will need to find the time for your task groups to "sharpen their saws" and practice routines such as inquiry and action research to find thoughtful and long-lasting rather than band-aid solutions to the challenges they face.

The *Inquiry Process* is a means or path for working together to critically examine and address a school's major problems or challenge areas. There are five stages in the Inquiry Process (see Figure 2.4):

1. **Focus on the Challenge Area**

   Explore the problem informally and hypothesize why the challenge area exits. Test the hypotheses. Interpret the results of testing and develop a clear understanding of the challenge area.

2. **Brainstorm Solutions**

   Look inside and outside the school for ideas and expertise. Determine which existing resources can be reasonably applied to assist in solving the problem.

3. **Synthesize Solutions and Develop an Action Plan**

   Make sure that the solution(s) move you toward your vision. Anticipate possible obstacles and determine if the solution(s) is reasonable and doable. Determine goals as well as the necessary actions, who will complete them, and timelines for each solution.

4. **Pilot Test and /or Implement the Plan**

   Seek school-wide approval and designate specific staff members to coordinate the implementation and assessment of the pilot program.

5. **Evaluate and Reassess**

   Did the action plan bring the school closer to the school vision? Did it meet the cadres (task groups) preestablished goals and objectives? Were the various components of the plan successfully implemented as planned?[23]

Figure 2.4. The Inquiry Process

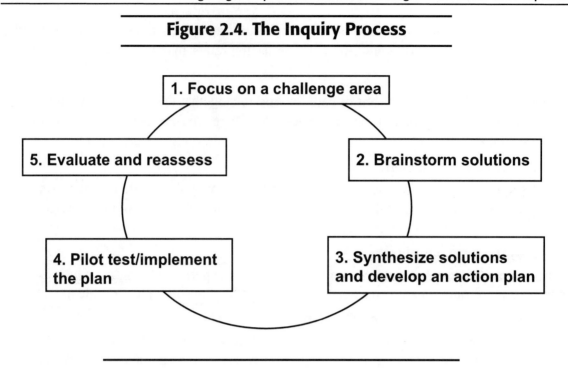

The *Action Research* model proposed by Richard Schmuck is another systematic process for problem solving and creating a culture of continuous improvement (see Figure 2.5) Schmuck describes action research as

> Planned inquiry—a deliberate search for truth, information, or knowledge. It consists of both self-reflective inquiry, which is internal and subjective, and inquiry-oriented practice, which is external and data based....Action research consists of planned, continuous, and systematic procedures for reflecting on professional practice and for trying out alternative practices to improve outcomes.[24]

The model has much in common with the Inquiry Process. Specifically, there are six steps:

1. **Try a new practice**

   Initiate a teaching practice that is new to your repertoire and is research-based.

2. **Incorporate hopes and concerns**

   Situate them within the classroom and school context and compare the current situation to a preferred state in the future.

3. **Collect data**

   Use a variety of research techniques such as questionnaires, interviews, observations, or documents.

4. **Check what the data mean**

   Did the new practice work? What merit did it have? Share the data with colleagues, students, and parents.

Figure 2.5. Action Research Process

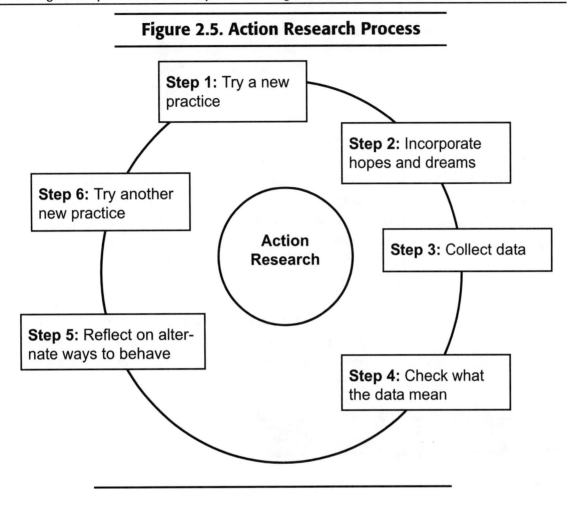

5. **Reflect on alternative ways to behave**

   Your own interpretations and others' understandings of the data help determine a future course. What will you do differently?.

6. **Try another new practice**

   One cycle of proactive action research has been completed. Begin a new cycle of continuous improvement.

Inquiry and Action Research appear deceptively simple, but in reality we have found that faithfully and thoughtfully following these approaches is one of the most challenging aspects of school change. Inquiry is the process we recommended for South Central's curriculum task groups to follow. It was especially useful for *a priori* complex problem solving when the problem is not well defined and the scope is large. Here, using the Inquiry Process for significant school-wide challenges such as developing an enrichment approach to student learning and aligning it with state standards makes the most sense. Action Research, on the other hand, is particularly useful in classroom applications where challenges are more clearly defined and less ambitious in scope. For example, individual teachers can use Action Research as they attempt to implement new and enriching learning experiences in their classrooms. Following the Action Research process will give teachers specific feedback that they will need in order to know whether or not the changes made have been successful.

Inquiry and Action Research appear deceptively simple, but in reality faithfully and thoughtfully following these approaches is one of the most challenging aspects of school reform.

Inquiry and Action Research can be slow moving, but have the potential to craft changes that will endure and make a difference. Both approaches to problem solving will require support and the creation of new expectations and rewards for teacher work in schools. Without substantive support for collaborative, problem-solving work, successful change won't happen. School leaders will need to model, as well as facilitate and encourage it. There will be many obstacles to overcome, ranging from finding the time and meeting regularly to having a consistent focus on student learning and providing coaching at the school level. Even schools with the best intentions tend to become complacent and backslide. Once the initial excitement and novelty wears off, there is a tendency to take short cuts and regress back to the way things were. Inquiry and action research take constant vigilance and a commitment to problem solving as part of an ongoing process of continuous improvement.

Chapter Summary

In this chapter, we have stressed the importance of the pre-initiation and initiation phases of the school change process. Quite often, these phases are underplayed or even overlooked by school reformers. William Bridges describes the "marathon effect" where front-runners often finish the race before recreational runners have even begun. So, too, your leadership team will want to help all participants begin the "race," become vested, and grow to be excited about school change.

To truly optimize your chances of long-lasting school change, your leadership team will need to be assembled and developed in a mindful fashion. Leadership team qualification criteria, selection processes, and specific responsibilities must be clarified up front. Also, building an early foundation of meaning and purpose for all stakeholders must not be overlooked. The process must be invitational and ultimately constructivist in nature as participants learn, share, and come to understand by constructing their own meaning and knowledge. You will also want to be thoughtful and creative in how you help to build the capacity of participants to better understand and use the knowledge base and tools pertinent to both the content and process of change. Finally, you will need to develop a systematic approach to problem solving and stick with it for the long haul. Inquiry and Action Research approaches are recommended.

In the next chapter, we discuss ways for your leadership team to build long lasting staff commitment to school change. It's one thing to initiate a school change project like Project Improve, but another to lay the groundwork for foundational and long-term staff commitment to making Project Improve actually happen. Strategies like building dissatisfaction with the current situation, creating a school-wide vision, and focusing on the improvement of teaching and learning will be discussed.

Reculturing Map

What behavioral changes should you look for during the pre-initiation and initiation phases of the change process?

Increase:	*Decrease:*
☐ Collaboration	☐ Working Alone
☐ Shared Leadership	☐ Reliance on the Principal
☐ Involvement	☐ Selective Participation
☐ Discussion and Dialogue	☐ Direct Presentation of Information
☐ Knowledge Base and Reflection	☐ Leaping to Solutions
☐ Meaning and Purpose	☐ Drifting
☐ Focus on Teaching and Learning	☐ Peripheral Issues
☐ Buy-In Period	☐ Top Down Mandates
☐ Recognition of Past History and Existing Culture	☐ Blind Implementation
☐ Crisp and Purposeful Meetings	☐ Deadly and Time-Wasting Meetings
☐ Consensus	☐ Majority Rule
☐ Problem Solving	☐ Superficial or Band-Aid Solutions

References

1. Sergiovanni, T. (1995). *The principalship: A reflective practice perspective*. Boston: Allyn and Bacon.

2. Maeroff, G. I. (1993). *Team building for school change: Equipping teachers for new roles*. New York: Teachers College Press, p. 32.

3. Ibid., p. 111.

4. Chenoweth, T., & Everhart, R. (1991, Fall/Winter). The restructured school: How do you know if something is happening? *The Journal of Planning and Changing, 22*(3-4), 178–190.

5. Northwest Regional Education Laboratory. (1998). School reform showcase: Finding the best fit (guiding questions). Available: http://www.nwrel.org.

6. Zemelman, S., Daniels, H., & Hyde, A. (1998). *Best practice: New standards for teaching and learning in America's schools*, (2nd ed.). Portsmouth, NH: Heinemann, pp. 4–6.

7. Murphy, C. U., & Lick, D. W. (1998). *Whole-faculty study groups: A powerful way to change schools and enhance learning*. San Francisco: Jossey-Bass.

8. Lortie, D. C. (1975). *Schoolteacher: A sociological study*. Chicago: University of Chicago Press.

9. Rosenblum, S., & Louis, K. S. (1981). *Stability and change*. New York: Plenum.

10. Berman, P., & McLaughlin, M. (1976). Implementation of educational innovation. *Educational Forum, 40*(3), 345–370.

11. Rosenblum, S., & Louis, K. S. *Stability and change,* op. cit.

12. Miles, M. (1993). The triple i model. *Video Journal of Education, 2*(4).

13. Chenoweth, T., & Everhart, R. The restructured school: How do you know if something is happening? *The Journal of Planning and Changing,* op. cit.

14. Conley, D. T. (1993). *Roadmap to restructuring: Policies, practices, and the emerging visions of schooling*. University of Oregon: ERIC Clearinghouse on Educational Management.

15. Hall, G. E., & Hord, S. M. (2001). *Implementing change: Patterns, principles, and potholes*. Boston: Allyn & Bacon.

16. Evans, R. (1996). *The human side of school change: reform, resistance, and the real-life problems of innovation*. San Francisco: Jossey-Bass.

17. Bridges, W. (1991). *Managing transitions: Making the most of change*. New York: Addison-Wesley.

18. Wilson, K. G., & Daviss, B. (1994). *Redesigning education*. New York: Teachers College Press, p. 135.

19. Bodilly, S. (1998). *Lessons from new American schools' scale-up phase: Prospects for bringing designs to multiple schools.* Santa Monica, CA: Rand Corp., p. 113.

20. Doyle, M., & Straus, D. (1976). *How to make meetings work.* New York: Jove Books.

21. Joyce, B., & Calhoun, E. (1998). Inside-out and outside-in: Learning from past and present school improvement paradigms. In Hargreaves, A., Lieberman, A., Fullan, M., & Hopkins, D. (Eds.). *International handbook of educational change.* London: Kluwer Academic Publishers, pp. 1286–1298.

22. Glickman, C. D. (1998). *Renewing America's schools: A guide for school based action.* San Francisco: Jossey-Bass.

23. Hopfenberg, W. S., & Levin, H. M. (1993). *Accelerated schools: Resource guide.* San Francisco: Jossey-Bass.

24. Schmuck, R. A. (1997). *Practical action research for change.* Arlington Heights, IL: Skylight, pp. 28–29.

IS EVERYBODY
ON BOARD?
Building
Commitment

Chapter Highlights

- **Build dissatisfaction.** Your leadership team can build staff commitment to school change by building dissatisfaction with the current condition of your school and the life chances for success of your students.
  - ☐ Know who's coming to school.
  - ☐ Redefine the meaning of "at-risk."
  - ☐ Use a high-stakes problem as a rallying point and leverage for school change.
  - ☐ Motivate participants through portraits of successful schools.
- **Create a vision.** Creating a vision of your dream school will be uplifting. It will give your school a compass that will inspire and guide it through the rough times ahead.
  - ☐ Develop an image of your dream school, the kind of school you would send your own child to.
  - ☐ Follow a systematic process to create a shared vision and set of belief statements.
  - ☐ Celebrate and publicize your vision
- **Focus on Teaching and Learning.** Change focused on teaching and learning will enable you to get to the heart of the matter, improving student learning.
  - ☐ Concentrate on state-assessed curricular areas.
  - ☐ Develop short- and long-term learning goals.
  - ☐ Move towards an enrichment model of teaching and learning that builds on student strengths and interests.

After reading this chapter, your leadership team will be better able to lay the groundwork for foundational and long-term commitment to school change. You will learn some new strategies for creating staff "dissatisfaction" through the use of multiple data sources that demonstrate those current practices that are not working well. You will also be able to identify the practices that influence poor performance and contribute to challenging life outcomes for many students. Your team will also discover how to redefine the "at-risk" problem and how teachers think about the students with whom they work. You will uncover the importance of believing that it is the school, rather than students, that is at-risk. By so doing, you will be able to create a new sense of hope and teacher efficacy about the challenges they face. You will also become skilled at developing a vision statement and accompanying belief statements that can serve as a school compass to inspire and guide you through the challenging times ahead. After that, you will learn some specific procedures for assessing student strengths and challenges around key curricular areas like reading, writing, and math. Finally, you will find out how to create specific student learning goals so that your staff can achieve some early successes or quick-wins.

Building Commitment at South Central

South Central School had come a long way in the past several months. A strong and effective leadership team had been established, and the school community had become more thoughtful and mindful about the need for school change. The school community's knowledge base about the content and process of change had grown exponentially. After much research and dialogue, a majority of the school staff and parent leaders had decided that they wanted to implement the Project Improve Design Model of change. The final school site visit to another Project Improve school downstate served as a catalyst for making a decision to sign on with Project Improve. Although the staff liked what the leadership team had to say about Project Improve and its apparent good fit with South Central's culture, hearing it from teachers in another school was most convincing.

Mary knew that she and the leadership team were ahead of the staff in terms of their knowledge about school change. They were, as Everett Rogers points out, early adopters.[1] Mary decided to do some more foundational work to build a deeper and long-lasting commitment to the work that was before them. Mary knew that change is typically short-lived because participants can make superficial commitments and then often bail out when the going becomes challenging. John-

son points out that schools can actually strengthen commitment to school change by building dissatisfaction among the school community about low educational outcomes for so many students.[2] Strong dissatisfaction becomes the impetus for creating a culture of achievement for all students. Compelling data must be used and shared to persuade the school community that many current practices are not working and that there is a real need for change.

Accordingly, the school community began to look very closely at its recently released school report card and pertinent school-wide data. They also looked at national education and economic trends dealing with the relationships between education and earning potential and patterns of student tracking. Portraits of successful and unsuccessful schools were also examined. The staff spent a great deal of time discussing a recent *Education Week* report titled "Children of Change,"[3] that describes in detail the changing demographics that are affecting schools across the country. They also tackled traditional definitions of what it means to be "at-risk" and began to look at schooling from an enrichment, rather than a remedial, perspective.

The enrichment perspective argues that students should receive an education based on the premises of gifted and talented education rather than remedial education stressing memorization and drill. Student strengths were to be recognized and built upon. There would be less telling or direct instruction and more opportunities for exploring and problem solving in multiple learning situations like projects, field trips, and community-based experiences. Staff began to understand that cultivating beliefs and attitudes supportive of enrichment could be determinants of their students' future success and satisfaction with school.

Next, the school began a visioning process. Participants were in agreement about learning experiences they wanted for their own children, but no initial consensus could be reached regarding the students they were entrusted to teach at South Central. About 20 percent of the staff continued to believe that students still needed a heavy dose of basic learning skills before moving into enrichment activities. Mary and the leadership team, however, pointed out that years of teaching basic skills and focusing on mastery learning hadn't worked very well at South Central and that now was the time for the school to try changing its basic orientation to curriculum and instruction. After considerable discussion, these teachers agreed to at

least not offer their students a steady diet of direct instruction and agreed to begin to explore more of an enrichment approach. The leadership team members knew that they had their work cut out for them.

In spite of some haggling over its wording and an extended period of wordsmithing, an inspirational and memorable vision statement was crafted through the consensus process. The entire school community had a touching vision celebration. Students sang songs, released pigeons, and buried a time capsule. The local newspaper and television station covered the event.

At the end of all this, we reminded the staff not to confuse the means of school reform (team building, capacity building, visioning, etc.) with the ends of school reform (improved teaching practice and increased student achievement). The staff began an assessment process around the major curricular areas. They identified student strengths as well as challenges in relationship to state standards. Clear student learning priorities were set for each of the curricular areas.

Building Dissatisfaction

Paradoxically, school-wide commitment to change can best be developed by creating deep dissatisfaction among the school community about low educational outcomes for many students. Strong dissatisfaction can then become the impetus for creating a culture of achievement for all students. However, compelling data must be used to persuade the school community that many current practices are not working and that there is indeed a real need for change.

In the following discussion, we provide illustrations of how you can build dissatisfaction with your school's current condition and begin to build a deep commitment to doing something about it. We begin our discussion by examining who's coming to school. How do we respond to issues such as increasing student diversity and poverty? Are we sensitive to the present lives of our students? Then, we focus on how we think about our students. Are they at-risk or is the school at-risk? We discuss these issues by utilizing the recent release of the state report card for South Central Middle School and how staff discussions of it led to the identification of a high-stakes problem. Finally, we will discuss the usefulness of looking at portraits of successful schools and teachers. What do successful schools and teachers look like and how did they become so effective?

Who's Coming to School?

We believe that a major problem in school reform is that many teachers continue to teach with outdated images of their students. In our work with schools, we find it helpful to take a closer look at who's really coming to school. We start with the actual lives of the teachers themselves and ask them a series of questions to help get them in touch with their own childhoods. We call this activity "Remember When:"[4]

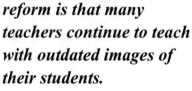

A major problem in school reform is that many teachers continue to teach with outdated images of their students.

- ♦ What games did you play as a child?
- ♦ What did you do after school?
- ♦ What skills were needed for those games?

The rich discussions initiated by these questions more often than not paint a picture of middle-class America and the world of *Leave It to Beaver.* When many teachers were children, they arrived home where an adult, typically their mother, was in the house. Usually, there was a prepared snack and a period for getting started on homework assignments. There was also conversation about the school day and what went well or didn't. Before the family dinner, most kids played outside for a while in a safe neighborhood or in a nearby park. And if they stayed inside the house, they played board games like *Clue* or *Monopoly.* Not only were these games fun, but they also reinforced the development of good social skills and critical thinking.

When we shift the focus to today's children, these same teachers generate dramatically different images of children. Many of today's children are "latchkey," who let themselves into empty homes or apartments after returning from school. Mom (or Dad) is typically unavailable to supervise children after school and is often working in a low-skilled, low-paying job (South Central's poverty rate based upon free and reduced-rate lunch counts was 65 percent). Single parents who move in and out of poverty head many families. Many of the homes are what some critics call "total television environments" where the TV is on virtually all day and evening. There

Above all, there is a significant lack of adult presence in the lives of children.

are no board games to be found in the home. Moreover, many young people in these homes have never even played a board game unless it was during a rainy day at school. Above all, there is a significant lack of adult presence in the lives of these children. They are left to their own ways, and the absence of meaningful activity is often filled with inappropriate and misdirected behaviors like sexual activity, drug use, and gang membership.

The point of all of this is that many students in our classrooms today are vastly and significantly different than the typical student of past generations. One in five children lives in poverty, and a disproportionate number of these children are ethnically, culturally, and linguistically diverse. By the year 2020, one in every three citizens will be what we now call a "minority."[5] And by 2056, "the average U.S. resident will trace his or her descent to Africa, Asia, the Hispanic world, the Pacific Islands, or Arabia—almost anywhere but white Europe."[6] Instead of blaming students for these changes, we must ask ourselves, "Who's coming to school and how do we change our schools to better meet the needs of this new group of students?" We will need to know our students better and honor their life experiences rather than turn back the clock to the way we view our own past.

Redefining the At-Risk Problem

Bridges points out that one of the first steps in change is to clarify and communicate the purpose of the proposed change.[7] Another way of saying the same the same thing is "what is the problem?" Bridges also points out that "you need to sell problems before you try to sell solutions."[8] Frequently, problems are not clear or agreed upon, and they have not been explained in ways that are meaningful to those who will be responsible to implement the solutions. The problem must be real, understood, shared, and internalized before the change process can begin.

"You need to sell problems before you try to sell solutions."
—William Bridges

In our story, South Central has just received its first state report card. Staff knew that they were working with a diverse inner-city student population, but for years they had largely externalized the problem. They had viewed the "problem" as related to family and community, not as the school's problem. When Mary held up the report card at a faculty meeting and said, "we must do something," many of the staff really thought that there really wasn't much that they could do either individually or as a school. The problem was viewed as beyond them.

We've learned that that a helpful way to begin is to ask one's colleagues, "When you hear the words 'at-risk' what do you think of?" Inevitably, participants will mention characteristics such as dysfunctional families, drug addiction, rampant crime, lack of motivation, discipline problems, poverty, etc. All of these conditions are external to the school and are life circumstances over which the school has no direct control. Teachers often feel resigned or fatalistic about them. It's too easy, then, for teachers to throw up their hands and say, "there's really not much that we can do." In these situations, teacher efficacy is low and teachers come to feel powerless to make a difference.

We propose an alternative definition of "at-risk." It is one that we borrow from our work with Accelerated Schools and it states: "children are not at-risk, rather they find themselves in at-risk situations." Schools are viewed as at-risk when they are not organized in a way to build on student strengths and personal interests. This notion of at-risk is based on the premise that all young people are curious and want to learn about their world. They also bring rich personal life experiences, expressive and receptive language skills (albeit often not the ones used by the school), and diverse and interesting cultural identities. The challenge to the school is to redesign itself to meet these conditions.

"Children are not at-risk, rather they find themselves in at risk- situations."
—Henry Levin

Promising research from Barbara Means and Michael Knapp points out how we must re-organize our schools for students who have traditionally not been successful

> Instead of taking a deficit view of the educationally disadvantaged learner, the researchers developing the alternative models described here focus on the knowledge, skills, and abilities that the child brings. Early accomplishments, attained before coming to school, demonstrate that disadvantaged children can do serious intellectual work. What we need to do is design curricula and instructional methods that will build on that prior learning and complement, rather than contradict, the child's experiences outside of school.[9]

To further clarify this alternative way of thinking about "at-risk," we find it helpful to look at emerging research that supports the idea that all kids can learn and be successful. Lisbeth Schorr in her enlightening book *Within Our Reach*[10] explains that damaging outcomes for kids are caused by a multiplicity of risk factors that interact and multiply exponentially as these factors increase. She points out that numerous research studies on human behavior lead to the conclusion that:

"The question is not how smart you are, but how you are smart."
—Howard Gardner

> These studies provide powerful evidence that it takes more than a single risk factor to produce damaging outcomes.…Lasting damage occurs when the elements of a child's environment—at home, at school, in the neighborhood—multiply each other's destructive effects.…The implication is clear: The prevention of rotten outcomes is not a matter of all or nothing.[11]

We all have risk factors that range from health problems and learning disabilities to economic challenges and marital problems. But because most of us educators are well educated and economically (relatively) secure, we are usually able to cope and live relatively successful and productive lives. The point here is that if a school can ensure that it, too, is not a risk factor, one major ingredient of risk will have been removed from the lives of many students and thus will increase their chances of success in life. Risk factors are not an all or nothing game. Success can come to those who live under trying conditions. With poor and minority students, it is doubly important that their school not

Risk factors are not an all or nothing game. Success can come to those who live under trying conditions.

become another risk factor in their lives. The schools that they attend must become alive and engaging, a place where students are cared for, supported, and helped to succeed academically.

We like John Dewey's advice that "a problem well defined is a problem half solved." How we think about the students we work with strongly influences their chances for success and happiness in life. Defining who is at risk is a major first step to this problem-solving process. It's not an all-or-nothing game. We must ensure that the schools we work in are not just another risk factor in the lives of its students.

"A problem well defined is a problem half solved."
—John Dewey

High-Stakes Problem

For many years, South Central's staff had been averse to regularly using data for decision making. They knew that student achievement rates were low, but generally believed that, given their diverse inner-city student body, the teachers were doing the best that they could. However, the pressure of their state report card (discussed in Chapter 2) had a sobering effect on the school community. The progress of students at the school had become very public and required a response. With a new and change-minded principal and an emerging leadership team, South Central needed to be proactive; otherwise, the school could face reconstitution or even closure.

Mary and the Leadership Team used the report card adroitly as a lever for school change. Staff began to examine the report card data because it was simple and it focused on the school as a whole. Mary tried to ensure that no individual teachers were singled out or felt threatened. Although the South Central staff had always collected data on individual students, they had never aggregated data and discussed it publicly.

State report card data revealed that approximately 70 percent of 8th grade students at South Central were not meeting state standards in reading, writing, and math. Furthermore, the school was performing significantly worse than schools with similar socioeconomic indicators. At the same time, student attendance was at an all time high and even surpassed state averages, an indicator that last year's campaign to encourage attendance had worked. District data also projected that 35 percent of South Central students would eventually drop out of high school, a figure significantly above the state average. Mary and the leadership team knew that many classrooms at South Central were fairly traditional and uninspiring to most of the school's students. Although the staff was experienced and appeared as committed as those from schools across the district, they were stuck in their ways. The leadership team asked the staff to look at some census data on potential income and levels of education (see Figures 3.1 and 3.2).

Figure 3.1. Education Level and Yearly Income

Education Level	Male	Female	Both Sexes
Advanced degree	$74,406	$42,625	$61,317
Bachelor's degree	$46,702	$28,701	$38,112
Associate's degree*	$31,426	18,933	$25,181
High school grad	$27,642	16,161	$22,154
Not high school grad	$17,826	10,421	$15,011

* Or some college

Source: *Time Almanac 1999.*

Figure 3.2. Child Poverty by Race and Ethnicity

In 1998, 18.9 percent of children (13.5 million) were living in poverty. Minority children under age 18 were far more likely to live in poverty than non-Hispanic white children.

Percent of Children Under Age 18 Living in Poverty
(Percent poor; number poor in thousands)

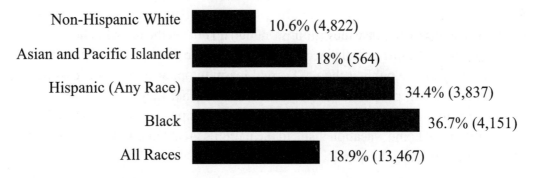

Non-Hispanic White — 10.6% (4,822)
Asian and Pacific Islander — 18% (564)
Hispanic (Any Race) — 34.4% (3,837)
Black — 36.7% (4,151)
All Races — 18.9% (13,467)

NOTE: Living in poverty is defined as households with incomes below the federal poverty line ($16,600 for a family of four in 1998).

SOURCE: U.S. Census Bureau, data from March 1998 Current Population Survey.

These census data suggested that too many South Central students could be headed for low-paying, low-skilled jobs. This was especially troubling for many South Central community members because the county had just celebrated the year 2000 by proclaiming that it was moving into a new world in need of high-skilled information-age workers. Because many South Central students were nonwhite, first- or second-generation immigrants, or poor, they were most likely to be left behind in this occupational transformation. Nationwide, nearly 19 percent of U.S. children—about 13.3 million—live in poverty. Although child poverty rates have decreased 4 percent since 1993, extreme poverty is becoming more concentrated in central cities. Furthermore, the number of children living in "working poor" families has grown dramatically. Poverty rates at South Central had actually tripled over the last thirteen years, with 65 percent of the students qualifying for the free and reduced-price lunch program.

Students who are nonwhite, first- or second-generation immigrants and refugees, or poor are most likely to be left behind in 21st century occupational transformations.

Census data also revealed that by 2015, Black and Latino students will make up 60 percent of the children living in poverty and that one-third of these children will have immigrant parents. Moreover, concentrated poverty in schools like South Central is associated with lower student achievement for poor and nonpoor alike.[12] Given these conditions, it was also important for the South Central school community to become more sensitive and develop a better understanding of issues associated with poverty.

Mary used provocative and insightful quotes to further help her staff explore and understand this challenge. Hill, for example describes the impact of school experiences for poor children:

> It is precisely because they (poor students) do not get the out-of-school experiences middle and upper-middle income children receive that low-income students rely so heavily on the public schools. Formal learning opportunities for low-income minority young people are largely restricted to what they have the opportunity to learn in school, unsupplemented by museum trips, access to computers and the Internet at home, vacation visits to the nation's great landmarks and national parks, or opportunities to spend a few weeks traveling abroad."[13]

Thus, the importance of the experience students receive and participate in during the school day gains even more significance. As mentors, we continuously pointed out to Mary and the leadership team that it is the hours that poor students spend in public schools that may very well determine their future. Haberman concurs, and Mary used his passionate statement to further make her case:

> For the children and youth in poverty from diverse cultural backgrounds who attend urban schools, having effective teachers is a matter of life and death. These children have no life options for achieving decent lives other than by experiencing success in school. For them, the stakes involved in schooling are extremely high.[14]

Finally, Mary used Ruby Payne's insightful book, *A Framework for Understanding Poverty*, to present some additional and very pertinent information about poverty.[15] Mary took a very courageous stand about what the staff should know and do to help South Central students become successful.

- ◆ For many South Central students, she explained, "the circumstances that cause poverty are situational. We have many recent immigrants from Mexico and South East Asia and refugees from Bosnia and Somalia. Culture shock and language challenges are significant factors contributing to our families' poverty."

- ◆ "Our school operates from middle-class American norms and uses the hidden rules of the middle class. We do not directly teach these rules to our students."

- ◆ "For our students to be successful, we must understand these hidden rules and teach our students the strategies that will make them successful at school and eventually at work."

- ◆ "We can neither excuse our students nor blame them for not learning. As educators we must teach them well and raise our expectations."

Most schools operate from middle-class American norms and use the hidden rules of the middle class.

All of these considerations have serious implications for our society in general and South Central in particular. If we do not educate all students well and ensure the success of the students who will make up the bulk of our labor force in the twenty-first century, then we all pay the price. Not only must we teach these students an enriched and challenging curriculum, we must also, as Payne implies, become mentors and advocates for our students and teach them the "hidden rules"—or as Delpit states, the "codes of power"[16]—that will permit these students to be the leaders of tomorrow.

Finally, Mary shared with her staff the need to be especially mindful of these challenges because African American, Latino, and low-income students at South Central have historically been tracked into remedial and vocational education with an emphasis on low-level work and attainment of the "right" attitudinal skills, rather than on higher order and critical thinking skills. Moreover, Mary pointed out that the typical occupations that utilize these low-level work skills are becoming less relevant in the labor market. Unfortunately, schools like South Central have tended to have lower expectations for low-income and minority students, who in turn rarely gain access to college gatekeeper courses such as algebra. This, in turn, has influenced the aspiration levels of students, and, as a result, their teachers and counselors have come to define them as incapable of attaining higher-order and critical thinking skills.

As a school community, you'll need to become outraged and morally committed to addressing and solving the challenges that lie before you.

In conclusion, it is essential that school communities like South Central develop an informed and clear picture of their students and begin teaching in ways that build on student strengths and interests. Your leadership team will need to vividly demonstrate, through the use of compelling data, that indeed there are complex and interrelated problems. As a school community, you'll even need to become outraged and morally committed to addressing and solving the challenges that lie before you. Developing meaning and purpose in your work and recommitting to making a difference in the lives of your students will help carry you through the tough times ahead.

Portraits of Successful Schools and Teachers

There are many stories where myths about minority students who live in poverty and have little success in school are dispelled. In the movie *Stand and Deliver*, we see how Hymie Escalante was capable of successfully teaching advanced placement calculus to large numbers of inner-city students.[17] Deborah Meier's school, Central Park East, is another success story worthy of examination. Central Park East (founded after the original K–8 school) is a small public high school in New York City's East Harlem, affiliated with the Coalition of Essential Schools. Its curriculum is organized around questions that foster what Meier calls "habits of mind," and students are assessed on exhibitions and portfolios of their work. About 90 percent of its students go on to college.[18] The Holibrook Elementary School in Houston is another success story. It's part of the Accelerated School's Project and its story is one of how ordinary teachers and administrators achieved extraordinary results. By working together, teachers transformed their school from one of the district's most dismal schools to one of its most exciting and successful schools.[19]

Mary and her leadership team made copies of these and other successful school stories and placed them in faculty mailboxes. The leadership team even showed a clip from *Stand and Deliver* at the beginning of a faculty meeting. The leadership team also arranged for groups of teachers to visit regional Coalition of Essential Schools and Accelerated Schools that had reduced their achievement gap. Finally, when one of the teachers was at a conference in Boston, she visited with Deborah Meier. All of these visits and stories were explicitly shared as part of an attempt to create a culture of what's possible and to develop a sense of discomfort with maintaining the status quo at South Central.

Gordon Calwelti's monograph "Portraits of Six Benchmark Schools: Diverse Approaches to Improving Student Achievement" describes how six exemplary American schools turned low achievement patterns around.[20] Common characteristics of these schools include:

- The school-wide focus is on clear standards and on efforts to improve results that can be measured. The main goal is to improve results on state assessments or other standardized tests.

- Teamwork is a way of life and helps ensure accountability. The staff meets regularly to examine assessment results and plan instruction based upon these results. Teachers are empowered to improve academic achievement.

- The principal is a strong instructional leader. It is difficult to initiate or sustain any meaningful change without a supportive principal. Different leadership styles are right for schools at different times in their development.

♦ Staff members are committed to helping all students achieve. They believe in their students and want to teach at their school. They spend extra time working with their students and planning to make the school better. Without truly committed teachers, you are unlikely to raise student achievement significantly.

♦ Multiple changes are made to improve the instructional life of students, and these changes are sustained over a period of at least three to five years. District professional development activities for principals (leadership teams) emphasize these elements.

There are many such success stories, and, as Ron Edmonds once pointed out, we only have to see one effective to school to know that it can be done.[21] These stories and practices are very

consistent with the recommendations found in this book and they provide practitioners with specific examples of what successful schools look like. Certainly, there are others and we encourage you to look for them as you begin to build staff commitment to change and write your own success story. Your leadership team can use numerous data sources (as noted below) in its mission to create a sense of dissatisfaction with the status quo at your school.

"We only need to see one effective school to know that it can be done."
—Ron Edmonds

**Possible Data Sources for Creating
School-Wide Dissatisfaction**

♦ State Report Card

♦ Student Achievement Data

♦ Annual Income and Levels of Education

♦ High School Graduation Rates

♦ Ethnicity/Race of Entrants Into the Labor Market

♦ Evidence of Tracking and Ability Grouping

♦ Access to Gatekeeper Courses

♦ Portraits of Successful Schools

Creating a School-Wide Vision

Everyone these days seems to stress the importance of having a vision, but few of us have either the knowledge or skills to create a shared vision and the ability to maintain it. Senge describes shared vision as a "force in peoples hearts" and at its simplest level as the answer to the question, *"What do we want to create?"*

A vision is truly shared when you and I have a similar picture and are committed to one another having it, not just to each of us, individually, having it. When people truly share a vision they are connected, bound together by a common aspiration.[22]

Senge further points out that most visions are one person's or one group's vision that is then imposed on the school. Such visions force compliance rather than true commitment. In order to build commitment to the shared vision, your leadership team will need to be genuinely committed, be honest and open about potential benefits and problems, and let others freely choose to become involved.

Participants will never feel committed to a shared vision if they don't see their own personal visions reflected in the larger shared vision.

Hopfenberg and Levin define a school vision as the "there" in contrast to the "here and now," or an ideal picture of where you would like your school to be. Vision is "both your inspiration and your destiny."[23] Senge's, and Hopfenberg and Levin's, perspectives on vision also stress the importance of the development of personal visions and of forging them into a shared vision. Participants will never feel committed to a shared vision if they don't also see their own personal visions reflected in the larger shared vision.

One way of forging personal visions into a shared vision is to ask participants to think about the school that they would design for their own child or a child that is very dear to them.

"The schools that we would want for our own children are the ones we should want for all children."—John Dewey

John Dewey's notion about the kind of school you would want for your own child is a helpful stimulus. Many public school teachers who teach poor and minority students enroll their own children in private or suburban schools. Moreover, many of these same teachers believe that the schools in which they teach are doing a pretty good job, all things considered. Yet, these schools are not good enough for teachers to enroll their own children. This can be a bottom-line outcome or realty check to spark a discussion of whether or not your school is a good school. Would your teachers enroll their own children in the school? Why or why not? Once issues like this have been publicly discussed and shared, it becomes apparent to participants that the aspirations they have for their own children should influence their aspirations for the school in which they teach. Such is the beginning of a shared school vision.

Creating a vision can be done if you have some guidelines with which to work. Let us share with you a specific process for developing a school wide vision statement and set of accompanying belief statements (see Tool 3.1). Although most schools realize the value of creating a positive and shared vision of their future, few have a tool or specific process to do so.

Tool 3.1. Creating a School Vision

Step I: Dream School Activity

Purpose: To begin the visioning process and enhance buy-in and commitment from all stakeholders.

Materials: Puzzle pieces from precut large (wall-size) red schoolhouse, felt tip pens, masking tape, and table space for small group work.

Directions:

♦ In small groups (5 to 8) brainstorm what your "dream school" would look like. What actions, behaviors, instructional practices, etc. would you see?

♦ Come to consensus and write down these ingredients on your puzzle piece.

♦ At the end of this activity fit your puzzle piece in the appropriate place on the wall.

♦ Report your group's dreams from your "puzzle piece" to the larger group.

♦ Discuss patterns and commonalities with the large group.

Notes: This activity can be done with a variety of stakeholder groups: staff, students, parents, community members, etc. Be sure and ask the group, "Whose voice is not heard here?"

Step II: Brainstorm Power Words

Purpose: To brainstorm strong and meaningful words related to the dream school that will become the foundation for a vision and set of belief statements.

Materials: Chart paper, felt-tip pens, and masking tape.

Directions:

♦ Give the group permission not to be perfect. Remember that consensus means substantial agreement, not 100 percent agreement.

♦ Discuss why we need a vision. View the JFK video in which he enlists NASA "to have a man on the moon by the end of the decade." Share other examples of powerful visions.

♦ Review Dream School. Look for key words, ideas, and concepts.

♦ Divide the group into small groups of 5 to 8.

Tool 3.1. Creating a School Vision (continued)

♦ Assign the following activities to three groups:

• Group 1: This group works on developing a list of nouns (person, place, or thing…students, parents, community, etc.).

• Group 2: This group works on developing a list of verbs (action words…support, encourage, facilitate, etc.).

• Group 3: This group works on developing a list of adjectives and adverbs (how it will look, frequency, quality…active, hands-on, engaging, etc.).

♦ Each of the groups works for around 10 minutes to develop these lists. If the number of participants is high, multiple groups can work on the same assignment. When they finish their assignment, have them meet with like groups and pare down their lists to one final version.

♦ The final lists of nouns, verbs, and adjectives/adverbs are then placed in front of the room. Each person is given five sticky dots for use in voting and told to place no more than two dots in any one category.

♦ After everyone has voted on the words, the group stands back and looks for key concepts and words that jump out to the group.

Notes: You can actually tally the votes for each of the words. Leave enough space between words for placement of sticky dots.

Step III: Write Vision Statement

Purpose: To write a vision statement using the most important power words.

Materials: Half sheets of chart paper, felt tip pens, masking tape, and lists of power words generated during last activity.

Directions:

♦ Review last activity. Point out the most salient power words. Share some sample visions.

♦ Review consensus and give the group permission not to write "perfect" vision statements.

♦ In small groups of 5 to 8, craft a vision statement of 14 words or less using key power words. Use the words that received the most votes. Add articles and prepositions as needed. Don't worry if a particular word does not appear in your vision statement, because it can appear in the belief statements, which will be developed following this activity.

Tool 3.1. Creating a School Vision (continued)

♦ Small groups combine and consolidate their vision statements. For example, consolidate 6 vision statements into 3 vision statements. Discuss and compare the vision statements. Does any one clearly speak for the entire group?

Notes: The final three vision statements can be placed in the staff lounge for further review and discussion. The leadership team can do some word-smithing and develop a single vision statement. Visions must be memorable and inspirational. We recommend 14 words or less and that the vision be grounded in the kind of school you would want for your own child.

Step IV: Write Belief Statements

Purpose: To write an accompanying set of belief statements, which gives the vision precise meaning and makes it come alive.

Materials: Sentence strips, felt tip pens, and masking tape.

Directions:

♦ Review three vision statements and the editing work of the leadership team. Come to agreement on one vision statement using the consensus process.

♦ Define and give examples of belief statements.

♦ In small groups of 5 to 8, develop four belief statements. Write each belief statement on a sentence strip. Use high-saliency words not reflected in the vision.

♦ Post sentence strips on chart paper attached to a wall in the front of the room. When the first group is done, have the group members post their sentence strips according to perceived categories. For example, all sentence strips having to do with teaching should be clustered together.

♦ The next group should do the same thing, again looking for perceived categories or creating new ones as needed.

♦ When all of the sentence strips are posted, have the large group review them and check to see if they are all clustered or categorized properly. Rearrange or create new categories as needed. Also look for redundancies and eliminate them with the permission of the group who created them in the first place.

♦ Assign names to each category—e.g., beliefs, teaching, community, etc.

♦ Give each group one or two sheets of chart paper with the attached sentence strips and have them pare them down to one or two belief statements. Eventually, you should have anywhere from six to twelve belief statements.

Notes: This is a fun activity and models best teaching practice. It's really a concept attainment lesson.

After developing your vision and belief statements, there should be a celebration and public display of your school's future dreams. Be aware, however, that many visions never take hold and die prematurely. As we discuss throughout this book, you need to be open to revisiting your vision, especially as new staff and families become part of your community. It is also important to keep your vision out in front of your community, especially when community members feel burdened as they manage their current reality.

After developing your vision and beliefs statements, there should be a celebration and public display of your school's future dreams.

In summary, a school-wide vision is an idealized picture or dream of what your school would look if it were functioning perfectly well. Its gives participants a preview of what they must strive for in the future. Belief statements help to operationalize and further clarify the vision. Together, a school-wide vision and belief statements should inspire a school community and serve as a reference point for future decision making (see example of vision and beliefs statements of the Bridgeport School, below). Participants will need to ask themselves if what they are considering doing is consistent with their vision and beliefs. If it is, then its probably a good decision, and, if its not, then it needs to be reconsidered. Above all, the vision and belief statements need to be learner-focused. In the next section, we discuss how to ensure that your efforts to improve the school are directly related to teaching and learning.

Particpants will need to ask themselves if what they are considering doing is consistent with their vison and beliefs.

Bridgeport School Vision

The Bridgeport community honors its diversity and builds partnerships that encourage & celebrate powerful learning.

We Believe:

♦ Diversity enriches our community by increasing our understandings beyond personal experiences.

♦ Collaboration strengthens our community of learners.

♦ Each member of the Bridgeport Community is a learner.

♦ All learners have the right to build self-esteem and a sense of belonging through academic, social, and emotional success.

♦ Every learner can reach his or her potential.

♦ All learners have the right to learn in a nurturing environment that is safe, accepting, and positive.

♦ Powerful learning is learning that is relevant and valued by the learner.

Focus on Teaching and Learning

Concentrate on State-Assessed Curricular Areas

The best way to build commitment to school change is to get right to the heart of the matter, that of improving teaching and learning. Many reform efforts literally "spin their wheels" on peripheral issues like governance, resources, or school climate, and never make changes that directly impact the classroom. For this reason we believe it is crucial to begin with the major curricular areas that are assessed by your state. In our own state of Oregon, this means reading, writing, math, science, and social studies. Teams of staff members and representative parents should be encouraged to self-select an area of interest and/or expertise for further inquiry and problem solving. For example, reading may be a problem area in your school, and, therefore, one group could collect data on reading performance at your school in relationship to comparable schools. We recommend that leadership team members serve as facilitators for each of these tasks groups.

Many reform efforts literally "spin their wheels" on peripheral issues like governance, resources, or school climate, and never make changes that directly impact the classroom.

The Carousel Simulation, Tool 3.2 described below, is a step-by-step process for beginning a school community dialogue about school change that is focused on key curricular content areas. It provides a picture of the here and now that you can compare to your vision (the there), beliefs statements, and the specific learning needs of "who's coming to school." The discrepancies between where you are and where you want to be as a school will become the basis for setting specific student learning goals in each of the key curricular areas. Focus on what you will need to know about this curricular area to:

♦ Improve student achievement

♦ Increase student engagement

♦ Promote active learning

♦ Meet state standards

Tool 3.2. Assessment Around Key
Curricular Areas: A Carousel Simulation

Step I: Select an area to study. The entire school community is divided into balanced groups (e.g., consider assigned grade levels, subject matter expertise, specialty areas, new and veteran teachers, male and female balance, racial/ethnic diversity, personality conflicts, etc.) Groups can self-select or be assigned by the leadership team. We recommend self-selection with some judicious reassignments as needed.

Step II: For each assigned content area (e.g., reading, math, writing, etc.) generate a list of questions on chart pack paper you think will be important to answer in order to create an accurate picture of your school as it is today in this particular curricular content area. Aim for a list of at least 10 questions. Follow rules of brainstorming. Post the best questions in different areas around the room. Time allotted: _____

Step III: At the signal, move to the next list of questions. Reflect on the content area this group is researching. Review that group's list of questions. Make a notation of any that you do not understand. After reviewing their list, add at least one additional question they could ask to fully understand the selected curricular area. Time allotted: _____

Step IV: Continue rotating, following directions in Step III, until time is called and you have reflected on each group's chart. Time allotted: _____

Step V: Return to your original chart. Review what has been added to it or questions noted. Begin at the top of the list, and identify and record one way (preferably more) that this information or data can be obtained. Are there any questions on the list that leave you unable to think of where to find the information? Circle these questions. Time allotted: _____

Step VI: Take one of the questions and describe how you would involve students and community/families in collecting the information and interpreting the results. Write this briefly on your chart. Time allotted: _____

The *Carousel Simulation* process is the beginning step in an Action Research or Inquiry Process model for your school. With input from the entire school, community teams can begin to research and answer their site-developed questions and then to craft action plans with both short- and long-term goals. We recommend that these teams work weekly on developing their plans and that they get needed feedback and support from the leadership team on a regular basis.

Establishing Short- and Long-Term Student Learning Goals

Schmoker points out that many school reform projects demonstrate plenty in terms of process, but little in terms of results. It is not uncommon to find considerable testimonial and positive quotes from individual teachers and students, but little in terms of measurable student progress. He also finds a marked difference between vague, well-intentioned school improvement efforts and carefully targeted, goal-oriented, short-term efforts, which characterize business organizations and are aimed explicitly at getting measurable, substantive results quickly. A results-driven emphasis, however, can look to short-term gains, often to the detriment of a long-term commitment to change.

"Many school reform projects demonstrate plenty in terms of process, but little in terms of results."—Mike Schmoker

In the education literature we are advised to avoid an impatient quick-fix orientation. Yet, Schmoker points out that we are beginning to see the utility of sustained rapid improvements as long as they are balanced with a vision that values a long-term perspective for change:

> When no results came time after time, we began to examine whether change could or should be expected to come quickly. We concluded that since we took a long time to get into a mess, we would need a long time to get out. We decided it was foolish to expect a quick fix; real change is deep, systematic, and cultural. And so we gave up on short-term expectations of change….But short-term planning and measurement promote the successes that add hope to the apparent futility of large-scale reform attempts.[24]

We view the Carousel Simulation within the context of enrichment and powerful learning as a way to jump-start school change around the core technology of schooling, that is around state-assessed curricular areas. One way to focus on the heart of the matter is to plan for, and achieve, "quick wins" related to student achievement. Joyce, Wolf, and Calhoun report that in their review of research on effective school improvement efforts "where significant improvement has happened, it has happened rapidly." They also report that "innovation can be implemented and gains can be seen in student achievement within a year by paying attention to already existing approaches that work and work fast."[25] Moreover, Schmoker points out that we can get "rapid results" using the "breakthrough strategy," that is, by focusing on small but immediate improvements.[26] Scaffer originally defined this breakthrough strategy as:

One way to focus on the heart of the matter is to plan for and achieve "quick wins" related to student achievement.

> Locating and starting at once with the gains that can be achieved quickly, and then using those first successes as stepping-stones for increasingly ambitious gains.[27]

We also recommend that each of the content area task groups deliberately read some of the latest and best research on curriculum, teaching effectiveness, and student achievement noted below.

Resources for Raising Student Achievement Rapidly

♦ Cawelti, S. (Ed.). (1999). *Handbook of research on improving student achievement* (2nd ed.). Arlington, VA: Educational Research Service.

♦ Cotton, K. (1995). *Effective schooling practices: A research synthesis*. Portland, OR: Northwest Regional Education Laboratory.

♦ Cotton, K. (1999). *The schooling practices that matter most*. Portland, OR: Northwest Regional Education Laboratory.

♦ Wang, M. C., Haertel, G. D., & Walberg, H. J. (December 1993/January 1994). What helps students learn? *Educational Leadership*, 74–79.

♦ Zemelman, S., Daniels, H., & Hyde, A. (1998). *Best practice: new standards for teaching and learning in america's schools* (2nd ed.). Portsmouth, NH: Heinemann.

From this reading and subsequent discussions, the curricular task groups should identify a number of short- and long-term goals around their chosen curricular areas. The short-term goals are "quick-wins" that pay attention to already existing research based approaches that work, and work fast. Long-term goals relate more to the school's particular context and address more ambitious and complex teaching and learning challenges. Both short and long-term goals need to be developed simultaneously, but task groups should work on their short-term goals immediately. As an example, the South Central math task group created a table (see Figure 3.3) of its identified problems, short-term (quick-wins), and long-term student learning goals (ambitious and complex long-term challenges).

Figure 3.3. South Central Short- and Long-Term Goals in Mathematics

Problems	*Quick-Wins/ Short-Term Goals*	*Ambitious and Complex Challenges/Long-Term Goals*
1. On-task Learning—students were receiving variable amounts of instruction ranging from 23 to 90 minutes.	1. Teach math 60 minutes a day.	1. Create a math lab in which parents trained in hands-on teaching activities work with approximately half the class, freeing up the teacher to work with smaller groups of students.
2. Understanding the meaning of key concepts such as place value, fractions, decimals, ratios, proportions, and percents— many students spoke English as a second language.	2. Review state assessments and create a math vocabulary list. Teach the list to students.	2. Align curriculum with state assessments.
3. Problems and applications— much of math instruction was remedial and textbook driven	3. Initiate a problem of the week program.	3. Sequence the curriculum so that what's assessed is taught.
4. Principles of learning. Moving from "concrete to semi-abstract to abstract—much of instruction was based on algorithms and paper and pencil practice. Teachers had been trained in the use of concept boards, but needed to simply recommit to using them. Parents had raised $10,000 to purchase math manipulatives.	4. Use concept boards and manipulatives for graphic and visual representation of math concepts.	4. Determine staff development needs and plan for appropriate workshops, school visits, and conferences.
5. Extended school day—students typically went home after school. A tutoring program was not an option for students not meeting state standards	5. Pilot an after-school tutoring program	5. Create a school-wide after-school tutoring program and a summer enrichment program.
6. Curriculum integration—instruction was textbook driven and taught in isolation from other content areas.	6. Keep Math Journals	6. Plan integrated units of study including all of the state-assessed curriculum areas.

The point we wish to make is that schools can begin implementing research-based best practices relatively quickly. Above all, however, the student learning goals must be measurable and capable of demonstrating student progress. In this process, the leadership team serves as a clearinghouse and feedback loop for all of the task groups, ensuring that the school as a whole endorses the plans before they are implemented. If these plans are reasonable, make sense, and are doable, they are less likely to be met with resistance. With minor adjustments, your school can get a head start on its path to improving student achievement, increasing student engagement, promoting active learning, and ultimately meeting state standards.

Schools can begin implementing research-based best practices relatively quickly.

Introducing an Enrichment Model of Teaching and Learning and Building on Strengths

In most schools, we identify gifted and talented students and then provide them with programs that accelerate their learning. At the same time, we also identify students who are at risk of not succeeding and place them in remedial programs that often further retard their rate of learning. The focus of our work, then, is to eliminate this inequity. It goes to the heart of the proverbial gap between the achievement rate of high-achieving and lower-achieving students. It recognizes that a prime determinant of students' success is the instructional opportunities to which they have access. It involves all students learning to learn!

Conley,[28] Lambert,[29] and many others view constructivism as the overarching instructional concept driving current school reform efforts. The learner actively constructs knowledge. Learners are increasingly responsible for their own learning that is built around their life experiences, interests, and strengths. Learning activities are authentic, relevant, and meaningful. Major national school restructuring initiatives and projects like Accelerated Schools (Hepfenberg & Levin,[30] Finnan, et al.[31]) also view constructivism or powerful learning at the core or center of their efforts. Such an approach is not laissez-faire teaching and learning, but requires that teachers become accomplished planners and skilled diagnosticians. Lesson planning needs to become more mindful and developed around genuine student interests and relevant experiences.

A prime determinant of students' success is the instructional opportunities to which they have access.

There are five descriptive components in the Accelerated Schools powerful learning framework:[32]

1. **Authentic:** Students can relate what they are experiencing in the classroom to real issues and situations. Lessons are relevant to the learner, have recognizable goals, and build connections.

2. **Interactive:** Students participate in interactive opportunities. Individuals collaborate with others in the learning process and work together toward a common purpose. Through this interaction, students are able to share their experience.

3. **Learner-Centered:** Student exploration and continual discovery are essential in the powerful learning process. The learners' experiences and interests help shape the direction and content of the lessons. Students become enabled to take charge of their own learning.

4. **Continuous:** Students perceive knowledge in a more holistic manner to strengthen connections between different contexts. Students can apply existing knowledge to what they have already learned and make connections between different subject areas.

5. **Inclusive:** Powerful learning focuses on giving all students equal access to learning opportunities. Challenges are structured to encourage the class to draw upon the expertise of students who may not be as vocal or perceived of as "smart."

How do we introduce the concept of powerful learning to staff? In our work with teachers we ask them to think of a positive powerful learning experience in their own lives. The learning experience could have happened anywhere in or out of their formal schooling process. We then ask them to reflect and write down the characteristics of that learning experience. What happened? How did it happen? Where did it happen? Then, in small groups, we ask them to share their experiences. We ask for some examples to share with the group as a whole. As these experiences are shared we ask, "What do they have in common with the characteristics of powerful learning?" What we discover together is that many of the five components noted above were also part of the powerful learning experiences of the participants. We then point out that we all intuitively know the ingredients of powerful learning and have experienced it ourselves.

We all intuitively know the ingredients of powerful learning and have experienced it ourselves.

Next, we develop creative tension or cognitive dissonance by asking, "Why don't we see more powerful learning in our schools?" The answers usually focus on lack of planning-time, an obsession with state achievement tests, a perceived need to cover the basic or remedial skills first, lack of professional development and follow-up, etc. We conclude by asking the teachers to make a formal commitment to increase the number of powerful learning experiences for students. We ask them to write down on an index card what they will do in the coming weeks to create a powerful learning experience in their classroom. The index cards are

then sealed in an envelope with their name and given to the leadership team for future follow-up, recognition, and feedback.

Chapter Summary

It is important to realize that building commitment to school change can be facilitated by
building dissatisfaction with the current condition of your school and dissatisfaction with the
present life chances for the success of your students. Furthermore, thinking of the school,
rather than the students, as being "at-risk" will help to redefine the meaning of "at-risk" and
liberate your school community to make significant changes within its reach. Also, the identification of a high-stakes problem such as that delineated by a state report card can help further
define the problem and help staff make a commitment to doing something about it. Finally,
there is no substitution for knowing your students well and forming caring relationships with
them. Having a vision or positive picture of what your school can become is both motivating
and uplifting. Building commitment to school change will be most effective if there is a central focus on improving teaching and learning.

In the following chapter we turn to issues in the successful implementation of change.
Your leadership team will need to adjust its behavior from learning and thinking about change
to one of doing something to effect change.

Reculturing Map

How do you know if you are building commitment to school change?

Increase:	*Decrease:*
☐ Thinking of the school as "at-risk"	☐ Thinking of the student as "at-risk"
☐ Understanding and appreciation of student life circumstances	☐ Trying to change students and make them fit the school
☐ Working on a clearly defined problem within the school's reach	☐ Stuck on an externalized and vaguely defined problem beyond the control of the school to solve
☐ Guided by a shared and meaningful vision focused on the improvement of teaching and learning	☐ Token acknowledgement of a meaningless vision created by a subgroup of the school community
☐ A focus on state-assessed curricular content areas	☐ A focus on areas not directly linked to learning, such as climate or resources
☐ The development of both short-term and long-term learning goals	☐ A preoccupation with either short-term or long-term learning goals
☐ Early quick-wins and accomplishment related to student learning	☐ Trying to figure out what to do and getting bogged down
☐ An enrichment approach to instruction	☐ A basic skills approach to instruction
☐ Building on student strengths	☐ Working on student deficiencies

References

1. Rogers, E. (1962). *The diffusion of innovations*. New York: Free Press.

2. Johnson, R. S. (1996). *Setting our sights: Measuring equity in school change*. Los Angeles: The Achievement Council.

3. Olson, L. (September 27, 2000). Children of change. *Education Week, 20*(4).

4. We wish to acknowledge the work of Dr. Jane McCarthy at the University of Nevada, Las Vegas, for stimulating our thinking about who's coming to school.

5. Sobol, T. (November 1990). Understanding diversity. *Educational Leadership*, 27–30.

6. Henry, W. A., III. (April 19, 1990). Beyond the melting pot. *Time*, 28–31.

7. Bridges, W. (1991). *Managing transitions: Making the most of change*. Reading, MA: Addison-Wesley.

8. Ibid., p. 53.

9. Means, B., & Knapp, M. (1991). Introduction: Rethinking teaching for disadvantaged students. In Means, B., Chelemer, C., & Knapp, M. S. (Eds.), *Teaching advanced skills to at-risk students: Views from the research*. San Francisco: Jossey-Bass, p. 9.

10. Schorr, L. B., & Schorr, D. (1988). *Within our reach: Breaking the cycle of disadvantage*. New York: Anchor Press/Doubleday.

11. Ibid., p. 28.

12. Olson, L. (September 27, 2000). High poverty among young makes schools' job harder. *Education Week, 20*(4), 40–41.

13. Hill, P., Campbell, C., & Havey, J. (2000). *It takes a city: Getting serious about urban school reform*. Washington, DC: Brookings Institute, pp. 3–4.

14. Haberman, M. (1995). *Star teachers of children in poverty*. West Lafayette, IN: Kappa Delta Pi, p. 1.

15. Payne, R. K. (1998). *A framework for understanding poverty*. Highlands, TX: RFT Publishing.

16. Delpit, L. (1995). *Educating other peoples children*. New York: The New Press.

17. Menéndez, R. (Director). (1998). *Stand and deliver* [videotape]. Available: http://www.amazon.com.

18. Meier, D. (1995). *The power of their ideas: Lessons from a small school in harlem*. Boston: Beacon Press.

19. McCarthy, J., & Still, S. (1993). Holibrook accelerated elementary school. In J. Murphy & P. Hallinger (Eds.), *Restructuring schooling: Learning from ongoing efforts*. Newbury Park, CA: Corwin Press, pp. 63–83.

20. Cawelti, G. (1999). *Portraits of six benchmark schools: Diverse approaches to improving student achievement*. Arlington, VA: Educational Resources Service.

21. Edmonds, R. (October 1979). Effective schools for the urban poor. *Edcuational Leadership,* 15–27.

22. Senge, P. M. (1990). *The fifth discipline*. New York: Doubleday, p. 206.

23. Hopfenberg, W. S., & Levin, H. M. (1993). *The accelerated schools resource guide*. San Francisco: Jossey-Bass, p.74.

24. Schmoker, M. (1996). *Results: The key to continuous school improvement*. Alexandria, VA: ASCD, pp. 56–57.

25. Joyce, B., Wolf, J., & Calhoun, E. (1993). *The self-renewing school*. Alexandria, VA: ASCD, p. 52.

26. Schmoker. *Results: The key to continuous school improvement,* op. cit.

27. Schaffer, R. H. (1988). *The breakthrough strategy: Using short-term successes to build high performance organizations*. New York: Harper Business, p. 13.

28. Conley, D. (1993). *Roadmap to restructuring*. University of Oregon: ERIC Clearinghouse on Educational Management.

29. Lambert, L. (1995). *The constructivist leader*. New York: Teachers College Press.

30. Hopfenberg, W. S., & Levin, H. M. *The accelerated schools resource guide*, op. cit.

31. Finnan, C., St. John, E., McCarthy, J., Slovacek, S. (Eds.). (1996). *Accelerated schools in action: Lessons from the field*. Thousand Oaks, CA: Corwin Press.

32. Levin, H. M., Koerschen, C., & Reguerin, P. G. (Fall 1999). Building strengths through powerful learning laboratories. *Accelerated Schools Newsletter, 8*(2); Finnan, C., & Swanson, J. D. (2000). *Accelerating the learning of all students: Cultivating culture change in schools, classrooms, and individuals*. Boulder, CO: Westview Press

DID YOU SAY TO TURN PORT OR STARBOARD?
Implementation

Chapter Highlights

♦ *Follow a systematic approach for problem solving.* A few key strategies will help you jump-start the implementation process.

    ☐ Adopt an inquiry approach to problems that present themselves.

    ☐ Develop shared leadership for implementation.

    ☐ Obtain the resources to support implementation.

♦ *Develop strategies to "jump-start" the implementation process (early stage).* Implementation involves an evaluation toward carefully identified new practices.

    ☐ Help staff make the transition from time-honored but outdated practices

    ☐ Develop different management strategies for putting new ideas into practice.

    ☐ Seek out linkages and assistance from those who can help

♦ *Reculture by aligning practices with beliefs (mid stage).* This is where change really begins to take root. Focus on aligning your new practices with beliefs about effective schooling.

    ☐ Create symbols that show a new culture is in place.

    ☐ Examine data that inform if the desired changes are being made.

    ☐ Establish reasonable timelines for implementation.

    ☐ Expect setbacks and don't be thrown off-course.

♦ *Monitor progress and maintain momentum (mature stage).* It's critical to begin tracking progress as you make changes.

    ☐ Maintain your vision and be sure you're heading in the right direction.

    ☐ Move beyond state standards and define what effective learning means in your school.

    ☐ Accelerate the evaluation and assessment process..

After reading this chapter, you will understand that the process of implementation consists of three connected stages (early, mid-level, and mature). You will learn that the skills necessary for effective implementation of change are somewhat different than those required in the initiation of change. Especially important in the earliest stages of implementation is being attentive to the fact that there is a normal transition from the old ways of doing things to new ways, and that you need to help your staff make this transition without dismissing the practices of the past. As you continue your change efforts, you'll find that of utmost importance is a good alignment between your school's beliefs about what needs to be changed and the behavior that supports those beliefs. Again, the leadership team can facilitate the staff's change in behaviors in a manner that is positive and encouraging. As your school grows more accustomed to new patterns, you'll learn that revisiting your school vision and purpose helps to maintain alignment between beliefs and practices. Finally, you'll want to consider a more sophisticated evaluation and assessment strategy that helps inform you how well implementation is going.

Implementation at South Central School

After a year of discussion and pre-initiation activities, Mary and her staff decided that during this second year of Project Improve they would officially announce that South Central School would , through Project Improve, be engaged in a number of new directions. A community-wide meeting was scheduled for Tuesday evening of the first week of school, the purpose of which was to inform the general community of the overall commitment of the staff to increase the academic learning of all students at the school. As technical support providers, both of us believed we had prepared the leadership team as well as we could for this significant occasion. They'd done their homework, involved the right constituencies in the process, and had carefully thought through how they wanted to begin Project Improve.

Mary and her team members arrived at 6:30 in the evening to ensure that the school library was ready for what they hoped would be a large crowd. Bill tested the computer one more time to be sure that the Powerpoint presentation would work. Joan arranged the items on the table near the entrance to the li-

brary so that people could more easily create their own nametags. Mary stationed herself at the entryway to the library, greeting parents and community residents as they filed in.

Both of us sat in the audience to get a sense of how the presentation would go from the point of view of a person new to the ideas of Project Improve. Although a little nervous at first, Mary and Bill provided just enough detail about the project, but not so much that it overwhelmed the audience. They summarized the essential issues involved in initiation, building commitment, implementation, sustaining change, and evaluation and assessment. Jargon was kept to a minimum, and the vision underlying the Project was evident throughout. The overall goal of the project was to increase student learning, increase student commitment to the learning process, and to improve the involvement of the entire community in the life of South Central. The focus on heightened participation of parents and nonparents, teachers and staff, and students in creating a culture of success at South Central was emphasized. Integral was the reorganization of the school into smaller communities where three teachers and an instructional assistant would work with 80 students for half the day on math, language, and science skills. This was presented as a specific vehicle to provide closer contact between students and teachers. In addition, the teaching strategy of "building on strengths" involved many active-learning activities in the core curriculum as well as the addition of enrichment electives in the afternoon. Finally, linkage with Project Improve would connect South Central with a national network of schools that shared similar objectives and could learn from each other. It was a package designed to appeal to virtually anyone in the audience.

Of the 50 to 60 people in the audience, only six asked questions. One question focused on how these changes would be funded. Mary explained that creative "resourcing" involved bringing Title One funds, some internal reallocations, and $75,000 a year for three years from the Comprehensive School Reform Design(CSRD) program to support Project Improve. A woman asked if the presence of the students with the same teachers for half the day might lead to too much group work, which she believed was largely a waste of time and which she saw as the "smarter

students (obviously like hers) teaching the slow learners." Joan handled this question well, citing research indicating that groups that are properly constituted benefit the performance of all students. Then there were some questions about how students would be assigned to a "community," a complaint from a parent who didn't like the mathematics text that his son had been using at South Central, a statement of praise from a woman who said that, as a one-time middle school teacher herself, she was pleased that at "long last, somebody's taking seriously the fact that early adolescence is a critical period in a youngster's life and it was about time the schools did something different."

After the crowd filed out, both of us congratulated Mary and her team for a job well-done. They were pleased with what they had accomplished in the past year and seemed on their way in this, the first year of implementation of Project Improve. It was a good beginning to the implementation process, and now the really hard work was before them.

Follow a Systematic Approach for Problem Solving

The issues that you emphasize as you take on the implementation of change are important to your future success. What needs to be in place when you begin to actually "do it?" How will you deal with efforts that don't work out as you expect? What does your management team need to do differently than before? How much support will you need and how will you obtain it? Although many other questions could be posed, we believe that planning to implement democratically-based comprehensive school improvement can be narrowed down to three issues:

Key Issues in Implementation

♦ Your team's attitude about problem solving

♦ The process of developing shared leadership

♦ Obtaining the resources needed to support the emerging changes

---

In this section, we discuss some important issues in each of these three areas.

Adopt an Inquiry Approach to Implementation Problems

How do you approach change in your life? Do you like to take a vacation where you know your daily itinerary down to the hour, or are you the type that buys a ticket to and from a destination, takes a good guidebook, and then fills in the time as you go? And how about your professional life? As a teacher, are you a "cover the material" type or a "teach to the situation" type? And as an administrator, do you thrive most under conditions of certainty or uncertainty? Do you feel best when you solve smaller problems by finding predictable solutions or do you enjoy taking on the larger tasks by jumping into the swamp and then find ways to work yourself out of it?

Try to honestly answer the 10 questions in Tool 4.1 (p. 94), rating each on a five-point scale from *true almost always* (5) to *hardly ever true* (0).

Although most of us adopt a variety of stances depending on the type of change we encounter, the fact is that we also exhibit patterns in our attitude and our behavior. Some of us are out-and-out resisters to change, believing that unless there is a compelling reason to change, we won't try something new. You may be closer to this description if you scored 25 or below on these 10 questions. Others are always trying something new, and in the process might be discounting patterns from the past that ought to be maintained. Those of you who scored 45 or above are probably in this category. Most of us, however, normally score between 20 and 40. This is not to say that a low number necessarily means you're a foot-dragger and that a high number necessarily means that you are a creative change-maker. After all, there are many changes that deserve to

Your perspective about the change process influences how effective implementation will be.

be resisted and many that cause us to hastily throw out past practices that could have been valuable. It is to say, however, that your attitude toward change will, to a great degree, influence how you approach the change agenda.

Tool 4.1. How Open Is Your School to Change?

A Quiz:

Schools vary widely in the willingness to take on change. Here's a test to see where your school stands. Scoring. If the item is "generally true for you and your staff," score 5 marks; if you feel it is "true some of the time," score 3 marks; if you response is "never in a million years," score zero. You can adjust for marks in between. Add the totals and look below for results.

1   My colleagues and I are given time to talk about changes in the school (3-point bonus if the principal provides donuts)

2   My principal invites the staff to share decision making on items much more important than who's assigned to clean the coffee machine on Tuesdays.

3   My staff enjoys working together on new ideas almost as much as it enjoys potluck suppers.

4   We've been involved in transition years, writing folders, mission definitions, safe schools and recently sold advertising rights on our soccer team jerseys to a major beverage company.

5   My staff takes time to talk at the end of the year, not just about promoting or holding back students, but about how well our program works for students.

6   Our school has a real mission or vision which is a lot more meaningful to me than the official "mission statement" framed on the wall outside the office.

7   Teachers frequently visit each other's classrooms, not just to borrow crayons. They like to see what is going on and borrow ideas.

8   When I've had a lousy day in the classroom, I don't feel awkward telling other teachers and administrators about it, and sometimes I even get sympathy. (3 point bonus if somebody will offer to buy you a liquid refreshment)

9   Experienced teachers help out new teachers, both in informal ways and in official "mentoring" positions.

10 Risk-taking at my school is encouraged at least as much as contributions to the United Way.

Marking your school:

45–56   Bandwagon Boomers. Your staff is so open to change that you may not even take time to think about what's needed, or analyze the problems that you students really face. Maybe your principal is bucking for a promotion or half your staff (not your half, of course) is a bit wingy, but in either event it's time to do some deep thinking before the next bandwagon comes along.

32–45   Change Creatures. Your school and staff enjoy change, understand why it has to keep happening in our schools and are ready to look for new ideas. Congratulations. Call us at 1-800-268-7061 if you want some help.

20–32   Willing Wallflowers. Your staff has a hunch that change is important, has a vague sense that your school could be doing something different and better, but is a bit fearful of giving change a try.

Under 20   Granite Grinds. Your staff has been so burned by the press, curriculum initiatives and frequent policy turnarounds that it's lost the capacity to change. Your school, procedures and courses are carved in stone. Your poor students will still be learning radio repair and Palmer penmanship in the year 2020. Accept our sympathy.

Once your school or district has made a decision to embark on an improvement process and indeed has begun that process, you and your team are faced with a daunting task—facilitating human behavior. You become part of a vanguard, assisting your colleagues as well as yourself to change patterns of behavior from what was to what all of you want it to be. This, as we know, is difficult in general, and doubly difficult in schools because we can't suspend what we are doing in order to "gear up" to where we want to go. Students will continue to walk through your doors, parents will still expect that you accomplish quality learning with their children, and the citizens of your district will maintain high expectations about the nature of your job which, for the most part, does NOT include much time for "professional development." Given these constraints, the attitude you and your staff develop to improve the learning of your students is critical.

Probably one of the most important attitude shifts which you want to encourage (and model) during the implementation phase of school change is that of learning from problems. As we discuss later in this chapter, you'll have more problems than solutions in the earliest stages of the implementation process, and your team's attitude toward those problems will make a considerable difference in your journey.

What do we mean by the phrase, "learning from problems?" Fullan uses the catchy phrase (which we like): "problems are our friends."[1] By this he means that the way we learn is through our ability to be successful at something we haven't done before. Therefore, successful organizations are those that embrace problems rather than hiding from them, that examine deep ways of solving problems rather than taking the path of least resistance by searching for quick fixes. In other words, when problems present themselves, they should be seen as learning opportunities and not just barriers in need of removing.

True learning involves solving a problem not encountered before.

The implementation process is complicated in part because there are so many factors that affect its evolution (e.g., the mix of people both in and out of your school, local politics, resource availability, timing, and even luck!). Because of these complexities, there are many challenges to the ideal of facing problems as opportunities. The classic challenge is found in the earliest stages of implementation when programmatic changes incur resistance, which they inevitably do. Some years ago, we worked in a school district undergoing "comprehensive change," an ill-defined end goal that the superintendent and his cabinet supported and for which the district had received a large amount of outside funding. Once the funds had been obtained, the district then had five years to "implement" comprehensive change and to demonstrate regular progress toward that goal. The implementation problem, however, was that many, if not most, teachers and indeed building principals were not clear as to what it was they were to change in order to change "comprehensively." Because staff had been only marginally involved in the initiation process, and therefore had little commitment to it, it was not surprising that confusion existed.

Here was a problem begging to be embraced and discussed. Yet, the district administration viewed this conceptual confusion as blocking the implementation process, and thus in need of a quick resolution. The resolutions amounted to a series of regular pronouncements from the central office as to the nature of comprehensive change. Because of the minimal involvement of the staff in deliberating comprehensive change as it applied to their own professional roles, these top-down pronouncements never "took" and comprehensive change faltered for the duration of the project.

Too often, problems are avoided rather than faced.

Viewing problems as a learning opportunity may seem, at first blush, to be a naïve viewpoint to adopt. After all, problems *are* the norm and not the exception in school life. Teachers and administrators are continually faced with problem after problem (indeed, a principal whom we know once said that she could come to work at 7:30 in the morning with no appointments scheduled and by the time it was 8:30, her day was completely booked). We aren't suggesting that every unanticipated problem that you confront in the implementation of change can be examined deliberately and reflectively. We're talking, however, of the seemingly intractable problems that regularly confront implementation—problems such as knowing what to implement, developing continual commitment to student learning in any change effort, and being aware of the reasons why resistance to change occurs. These are the kind of "big-picture" issues that are endemic to the implementation process, and are the issues that must be worked through again and again.

What happens when change is not approached in this manner? Fullan and Miles are right on target when they note that, in their experience, the schools that are the least successful at implementing change are the ones that develop superficial solutions to major problems.[2] Unwilling, or unable, to take the time to work through these problems(such as those mentioned above) too many schools try to shortcut them. Interestingly enough, as Fullan and Miles report, it isn't that successful schools have fewer problems; they don't. Rather, they are more successful in part because they develop the "deep" strategies to work through those problems (this is one reason that we emphasize the importance of a design model such as Project Improve as well as an inquiry process as presented in Chapter 2).

Successful schools don't have fewer problems, they just deal with them better.

The lesson learned here is that attitude towards bumps in the road in implementation makes a difference. You'll want to help your staff understand that setbacks can be useful in teaching lessons, and that a setback in and of itself doesn't mean failure. Here is where your approach to problem solving is important, and we invite you to review again the inquiry model, which we presented earlier in Chapter 2.

Develop Shared Leadership in the Implementation Process

We believe that whereas change must be successfully managed, such management does not happen naturally. To be successful, implementation strategies need to be continually monitored, invented, reinvented, and shared. Developing shared leadership is the second major issue for successful implementation.

The process of successfully implementing change is so complex and dependent upon the right decisions at just the right time one could conclude that only a deity could pull it off. Please don't take this to mean that implementation is impossible, because it isn't. But because we are all mortals and not gods, it's unlikely that any one of us alone has the skills and capacity to single-handedly direct a major change effort in a school. This takes us, then, to the obvious conclusion that finding the right mix of people—a mix of people with complementary skills and personalities—is absolutely essential in order to make significant changes.

We hope that by this time in the change process, you feel comfortable with the members of your leadership team. But now that you're beginning the process of actually putting the changes you've proposed into action, how you work as a team will change. Up to this point, you've undoubtedly been involved in many discussions with your staff as to the directions for your school. Putting those ideas and thoughts into practice, however, requires different skills. As Senge notes, "shared vision and talent are not enough...the great jazz ensemble has talent and a shared vision, but what really matters is that the musicians know how to play together." In the implementation phase of change, playing well together is critical. This is what Senge calls "team learning."[3]

In the implementation game, it's important to play well with others.

It's been our experience that creating leadership teams that are truly engaged in learning will need to overcome common impediments:

Impediments to Team Learning

♦ Efforts of the team are not aligned

♦ Efforts of the team are not coordinated

♦ Efforts of the team are not connected to constituent needs

First, often the efforts of the team are not aligned, resulting in too much wheel-spinning, time spent on low-priority issues, and the absence of collective understanding regarding the goals of the team. Second, even if purpose and ideas are well aligned, the team may be unable to coordinate its activities as a result of leadership problems within. A team must delegate to its members the authority to coordinate activities and to garner the resources needed to operate effectively and efficiently. In the absence of designating those responsibilities, the team can flounder. Finally, the leadership team often loses touch with its constituency—it becomes removed from the very people and concerns that it was designed to lead. Teams often create their own "group-think"—their own perception of the way things "are," and in so doing, fail to test those assumptions with reality.

It would be nice if we could offer some quick fixes as to how to avoid these pitfalls, but we can't. We can, however, alert you to the important strategy of self-monitoring the process by which your team is working. On the one hand, teams are critical to the success of the change effort because only a team (and its constituent members) has the multiple skills and relationships to guide the implementation process. But if the team does not "track" what it is doing—if the team does not consciously test its assumptions, check its internal processes for getting work done, and avoid being defensive if implementation bogs down—then it will not reach its true and necessary potential in the implementation process. Some of the common obstacles to effective groups include issues such as a lack of time for meetings, insufficient training or practice, and a lack of effective leadership at the site level. Tool 4.2, *Team Self-Assessment of Strengths and Needs*, pages 99–100, is a tool we have found useful in helping teams to monitor how well they are functioning.

The effective team is one that tracks its progress.

Another useful guide is provided by Murphy and Lick, who note 16 issues to address in order to "unstick" a "stuck" group.[4] Those that we believe are particularly important and deserve your attention are noted below:

Issues Associated with Stuck Groups

♦ Clarity and complexity of the problem. Teams can get stuck when there is confusion about the nature of the change.

♦ Contributors to the problem are superficial and not fundamental. Too often, teams focus on symptoms and not the core nature of the problem.

♦ There is information overload. Teams need to be able to see the forest through the trees and not feel overwhelmed about either the problem or possible solutions.

♦ Awareness that regressions are a natural part of the "implementation dip." Teams need to view change as a process of ups and downs—the goal being more frequent ups than downs.

♦ Establishment and revisiting of group norms about how the team will function. Once these norms have been established, the team needs to respect them and "enforce" them.

Tool 4.2. Team Self-Assessment of Strengths and Needs

Team Self-Assessment of Strengths and Needs

A. RATING

Direction: Working independently, in the sections below use the 1-5 scale to rate each item in reference to the team's performance or to your individual performance as a team member. Use the "TEAM" column first. Then fold this column under and use the "SELF" column.

NEED				STRENGTH
Immediate Need	Somewhat Need	On the Way	Somewhat a Strength	Great Strength
1	2	3	4	5

STRUCTURE AND LOGISTICS	TEAM
Representation	
Size	
Clear focus on improving student achievement	
Where the team fits in the organization of the school	
Clear delineation of: • team's leadership role, function • team's responsibilities, rights, authority • each team member's role, responsibilities	
Team meetings: • schedule—adherence to • location • formats and agenda	
System for accountability: • internally • with school community	
Other	
Other	

RELATIONSHIPS AND INTERACTION	SELF	TEAM
Team-building trust		
Commitments—long-term		
Group dynamics—communication skills, participation, inclusion/exclusion, power-sharing, interdependence		
Group diversity factors—race, ethnicity, occupation, language, gender, schooling, age, work styles, behavioral styles		
Candor, risk-taking, energy, enthusiasm, humor		

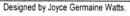

Designed by Joyce Germaine Watts.

Tool 4.2. Team Self-Assessment of Strengths and Needs (continued)

RELATIONSHIPS AND INTERACTION	SELF	TEAM
Meeting agendas—setting and following		
Meeting facilitation		
Ground rules—shared responsibility for respecting differences		
Decision making: collaboration, consensus-building, synergy		
Problem solving		
Collecting and using data for multiple purposes		
Using research and professional literature		
Strategic planning, *implementation, evaluation		
Following through according to time-task sequence		
Engaging the school community		
Using tension creatively and constructively		
Receiving and offering feedback: • internally • with school community		
Evaluating individual and team		
Other		
Other		

*Includes vision/mission, principles, assessment, goals/objectives, strategies/tasks, resource identification/alignment, roles/responsibilities, timelines

B.   PRIORITIES FOR DEVELOPMENT

STRUCTURE AND LOGISTICS

TEAM
1.
2.

RELATIONSHIPS AND INTERACTION

SELF	TEAM
1.	1.
2.	2.

PROCESS

SELF	TEAM
1.	1.
2.	2.

Obtain the Resources to Support
the Emerging Implementation Process

School boards and legislators often believe that major instructional changes can occur in schools with nary an extra dollar being provided. As one business leader in our community told us recently, changing to meet new conditions is what every organization does as part of its everyday life.

Well, the literature on school change doesn't support this premise and neither do we. If your team begins the implementation process with an empty bank, chances are that the school will get what the lack of investment usually produces—little or no change. As Firestone and Corbett conclude, resources make a great difference and those who argue that significant change can come about merely through internal reallocation are wrong.[5]

Despite what some say, resources are key to effective implementation.

Be aware, however, that resources come in all shapes and sizes. One place where extra support is essential in the implementation process is via the external facilitation, such as that being provided by outside consultants like both of us (authors) in the story of South Central. Certainly, outside support is valuable at all phases of change, but it's particularly crucial during implementation because of the complex challenges of building a new culture within an existing culture, all the while serving the students who attend the school. It's so easy for all of us, despite our best intentions, to stay within the routine to which we are accustomed if for no other reason than it is a routine that we know. External assistance facilitates the reculturing process by pointing to the essentials which must demand our attention if change is to be successful. The New American Schools, a consortium of comprehensive change-oriented programs (including Success for All, Expeditionary Learning, and others) has recently issued a set of guidelines (in the form of questions to address) to use in choosing the kind of support you will need for effective change.[6] These guidelines, shown on the next page, are a valuable resource as you make decisions about the resources you need and to what end they might be used.

As we infer above, change requires not only resources but "resourcing." Fullan and Miles use this term to mean that your team needs to proactively look for ways to support the change effort on an ongoing basis, and to utilize those resources in ways that apply directly to the improved learning of students. Resourcing means more than just searching for grants and gifts to support implementation, although that, too, is important. Rather, it means that the team needs to think creatively about how funds can be leveraged in such a way to provide the resources necessary.

Think "resourcing" as well as resources.

For example, the Comprehensive School Restructuring and Development Grants (CSRD) are awarded to schools proposing to make systemic changes in order to improve student learning. Although the grants can provide up to $75,000 a year for three years, they can also be con-

New American School Guidelines for Implementation

♦ How has your school implemented the Comprehensive School Reform Model? Does it follow design specifications outlined in the model? Is there program fidelity?

♦ Is there a comprehensive approach to aligning programs and resources? Is instruction, curriculum, technology, professional development, and parental involvement aligned to improve student achievement?

♦ Is there a continuous and appropriate professional development component? Has your school determined if professional development activities have produced change in classroom practices?

♦ Is there the necessary external support to facilitate the reform effort? Has the school/district management taken steps to ensure the long-term commitment to the change effort?

♦ How has the school utilized technical support to enhance the change efforts? Is the technical support appropriate and useful to achieve the ends of increased student achievement?

♦ Has a comprehensive evaluation plan been designed and is it being utilized? Does the school show evidence of adjusting its practices based on the evaluation results?

♦ Have resources from a variety of sources been coordinated to maximize the scope of reform?

nected to other funding sources . One example of the benefits of this coordinated effort is the manner in which ESEA funding categories are congruent with categories for comprehensive reform programs such as Accelerated Schools (see Figure 4.1).[7]

Another proposal focuses on restructuring in order to free up existing resources. Odden and Busch argue that school districts and the schools within them can free up dollars by redefining what the core district functions and core school functions are, the result of which can send more dollars to school sites to handle some of the tasks previously carried out by the central office.[8] In the same way, schools can restructure certain functions(especially those carried out by "specialists"), and by so doing provide funds to underwrite the costs of an external facilitation network such as the Coalition for Essential Schools or Accelerated Schools. This is in part what happened at South Central when Superintendent Jennifer Craig created funds from central office budgets to allocate money to schools for targeted school improvement.

Figure 4.1. Allowable Distributions for
ASP Implementation within ESEA Policies

Distribution category for ASP ESEA policy	Salary & benefits for personnel (coach)	Professional development & technical assistance	Staff release time (salary & benefits)	Substitute pay	Materials	Travel
Title I	yes	yes	yes	yes	yes	yes
Title II		yes	yes	yes		yes
Title III		yes			yes	
Title IV	yes	yes	yes	yes	yes	yes
Title VI	yes	yes	yes	yes	yes	yes
Title VII	yes	yes	yes	yes	yes	yes
Title VIII	yes				yes	
Title IX	yes	yes	yes	yes	yes	yes
Title X		yes	yes	yes		
CSRD	yes	yes	yes	yes	yes	yes
Goals 2000		yes	yes	yes	yes	

The resourcing process is a responsibility assumed by the principal but is not normally taken on by leadership teams. However, we believe that the leadership team must broaden its agenda and become actively involved in finding the resources to support implementation. As we've noted consistently, the job of change is just too complex to be carried out by one or two administrators.

We next examine how these conditions for successful implementation play out through the stages of the implementation process.

Develop Strategies to "Jump-Start" Implementation (Early Stage)

It's difficult to say when implementation really begins. Rarely is there a specific time that one can point to and say, "this is when we began to implement our change effort." Indeed, what we've referred to as the pre-initiation phase and the implementation phase often fold together so that planning and doing seem to be one and the same.

However, there is a time when the changes your team has spent so long preparing for begin to take shape, and be shaped, in such a manner that slowly, but inexorably, they begin to replace practices and patterns that were in place before. When that happens (and you will know when this is) you will find that the early stages of implementation have begun. We believe that these early stages are characterized by:

Key Issues in Early Stages of Implementation

♦ Attention to transitions from the old to the new

♦ Developing appropriate strategies for managing change

♦ Building linkages with others to better support change.

Focus on Transitions from the Old to the New

You and your team members are likely proud that you have come this far, as well you should be. Quite often in these early stages of implementation, it's not uncommon to think that most of the major obstacles have been overcome and that there is no turning back. This may be the way that those of you who were most involved from the beginning think, but it's not necessarily how everyone thinks.

As we reviewed in Chapter 2, the literature is clear that change implemented is not always change made. Indeed, it is in this earliest stage of implementation that what we call "non-implementation" becomes apparent. Changes anticipated are not easily made and there is often a continual trajectory back to what was, rather than toward what was intended. Things are not done as easily as was thought and resistance to the change becomes more obvious.

We note these factors not to dampen your enthusiasm for the work you've done to date, but to help make you aware of what statisticians call "regression to the mean"—the tendency of any change to encounter pressures that move it back to a steady-state—is commonplace. Others, such as Fullan, refer to this as the "implementation dip." It's a natural part of most changes, and one that can be understood and dealt with if you are prepared to do so.

Somewhere along the line, implementation will begin to regress back to past practices.

William Bridges has argued that often in the process of moving from something with which we're comfortable to something which is unknown, people experience a sense of loss.[9] This sense of loss is much like that which we experience in the death of a friend or relative, divorce or separation, or when we move from a long-time residence to a new town. When we experience this loss, our emotions become increasingly brittle and we often "hang on" to the past because of the comfort provided by what is familiar. Indeed, as Bridges notes, quite often the past becomes romanticized as better than it actually was, leading people to downplay such realities as an abusive partner, a conflicted relationship, or a home that was not as attractive as it is now perceived to be.

We mention the work of Bridges because the notion of "transitions" is important for your leadership team to understand. Imagine that you are an employer and one of your employees has just lost a loved one. Knowing what they are going through, you would probably understand if that employee's job performance was a bit sub-par for some time as the employee went through a grieving process. In turn, most likely you would try to do what you could to help that employee, including possibly referring him or her to the employee assistance program provided by many health care providers. You certainly wouldn't blame the individual for feeling the way they do.

Accepting the "new" can mean leaving the comfortable world of the "old."

Yet, in the implementation process, blame is often placed on those who aren't as enthusiastic about change as the change agents would like. Often those who are slow to jump on board are viewed as spoilers and treated in a manner that isolates them from the new emerging culture. The more they are isolated, the more they express their anxiety about the transition to the new culture and can feel punished for the difficulty they are having in forgetting the past. The end result is that resistance deepens—a phenomenon that we saw happen at South Central as well as other schools where we've worked.

Feeling a sense of loss about the old can create resistance to the new.

If the team can understand what happens as organizations undergo transitions, they can do much to ease this process by working with individuals and groups who are experiencing such transitions. We come back to this topic later in this chapter, but we can say that in the earliest phases of implementation, it's important to practice good listening skills, and a good way of practicing these skills is to encourage your school faculty to recount their stories of their role in the past history of the school. By doing so, you are honoring the contributions of everyone, even those who may be reluctant to be involved in the change process. The development of such an oral history can occur along the lines presented in Tool 4.3 (p. 106).

Develop Strategies and Skills for Managing Implementation

A second important component of the early stages of implementation involves establishing a strategy to manage putting ideas into action. Your first reaction to this suggestion is likely to be: "we've already developed a strategy to initiate our desired changes; why don't we just continue with what's worked to date?"

A simple answer to this question is: things are different. When you were creating the vision of change for your school, you spent considerable time working on defining the destina-

---

Tool 4.3. Chronicling Your Journey

Chronicling your journey is a way to record events from the past in a visual or graphic format. Using art and graphics, the school staff and community provide answers to some of the following questions:

♦ What are the key events and milestones that have brought us to the present?

♦ What obstacles have we overcome?

♦ What support have we had?

♦ What influences (positive and negative) have there been?

♦ What are we proud of?

Use this information to generate a series of conversations about how a school community has come to a specific point in time. Especially useful is to ask small groups of four to six people to choose one of the questions and present it to the larger group through a story, drama, or pictorial presentation.

---

tion you wanted to reach. This resulted in your vision statement, a product that not only set direction but also (hopefully) inspired members of your school community. Then you worked

Implementation demands effective management strategies.

hard to build commitment and establish the basis on which the proposed changes could be launched. Now you are in the earliest stages of implementation of those changes. Your team isn't as heavily involved in conceptualizing and planning as they were earlier. Your time now is more centered on the management of change itself, and such a role requires a different set of strategies and skills. We believe that you are now more actively involved in developing specific management strategies during the earliest stages of the implementation of change.

What strategies and skills are particularly important at this stage? Consider the following:

Management Strategies for Moving Ideas into Practice

♦ Keeping and maintaining the vision—regular and consistent emphasis on the vision underlying the change.

♦ Extending commitment—broadening the level of involvement of staff and community members.

♦ Evaluation and assessment—beginning to identify the data to chart how well you are doing.

Let us look at each of these in order.

As discussed earlier, establishing a vision is an important component during the initiation stage of change. However, don't think for a moment that once you have voted on your change initiative, and you have reached what appears to be consensus with the vision appropriately framed in the hallway entrance to the school and on school letterhead, that you are done with this phase. Indeed, during the earliest stages of implementation, it's important to return again to the root purposes of your change effort, or else the vision becomes lost during the daily school routine.

We want to emphasize this point in part because of the fundamental conclusions drawn by the RAND studies as discussed in Chapter 2. To refresh your memory, a major conclusion of those studies was that educational changes are not so much implemented as they are adapted by schools. This is to say that, at least for change efforts designed externally to the school, the school culture has a fundamental effect on shaping that effort. Although there is nothing "wrong" with this (insofar as mutual adaptation may be somewhat of a natural process), too much adaptation dilutes the intent of the change and often does not result in the kinds of reculturing necessary to bring about the desired effects. So, as a management team, you'll want to keep asking yourselves and your colleagues the key question: "are the activities we are implementing true to the vision that we established for our school?"

Too much adaptation can dilute the direction of change.

One simple but useful activity you can engage in is "vision anchoring." This is something that the leadership team can help groups of teachers address as they consider a wide array of specific issues, such as which reading curriculum to use or how to group students for instruction.

Vision Anchoring

♦ What are the vision components?

♦ What activities are proposed to meet the vision and are they consistent with the vision?

♦ What is the rationale for these activities?

♦ What is the intended effect on student learning?

A second management imperative of importance during the early stages of implementation involves extending the base of commitment to, and by, those within your school community. Prior to implementation (and in the process of forming your leadership team) most likely you put together a small group of dedicated educators and community members who understood the merits of the changes you were proposing and wanted to play a part in their further development. Now, as you begin implementation, you'll need the commitment of the overwhelming majority of your school community.

Again, research on implementation sheds some light on this issue. Many years ago, Everett Rogers, in his studies of the adoption of innovations in agriculture, discovered that the adoption of change occurs through a somewhat "normal distribution"—the bell-shaped curve.[10] Thus there are what he called "early adopters," a small percentage of people who try a new product early; "middle adopters," the larger percentage who jump on the bandwagon after someone else has tested it; and "late adopters," or those that come in at the very end when most of the serious issues have been worked out. In general, these same patterns seem to occur in educational change as well. Yet, this "natural" change process can be problematic because successful implementation might occur too slowly and thus stall as a result of a lack of momentum.

The challenge for your team is to speed up the implementation process so that you reach a larger mass of committed participants earlier than might occur "naturally." Accelerating this process is not easy, especially in organizations such as schools, where the old way of doing things occurs simultaneously with new initiatives.

Successful implementation requires accelerating the number of early adopters.

For example, in comprehensive school change programs such as Accelerated Schools, we work with school teams to develop what we call "powerful learning"—learning that is constructivist in nature and that builds on students analytical skills. Yet, developing powerful learning must be done across the entire school, and with teachers who vary in terms of possessing those skills. We strive to speed up the number of early adopters (to use Rogers' term) by working across the school to provide the assistance to help the entire staff translate earlier commitment into full-scale implementation. This assistance focuses on the main goal of improving the learning of students in their school—and ensuring that everyone is aware of that goal. Generally speaking, you will want to do the same by creating an atmosphere wherein the improvement of student learning is a collective responsibility. If your leadership team focuses on this specific goal, it will pay dividends in the long run through a process of changing the culture of your school to one where everyone centers their efforts on the improved learning of all students.

A useful strategy is to invite additional community members, school staff, and students to meet regularly with your leadership team and provide input about the progress of the implementation process. Choosing representatives from constituent groups who are most likely to be impacted by implementation, and encouraging them to offer feedback can provide useful and timely information as to how the implementation process is proceeding. We believe strongly that you can't do enough solicitation of perspective and advice from multiple sources, and that this is a good way of extending commitment to the change agenda.

Finally, the earliest stage of implementation is the perfect time for the team to begin developing a plan for collecting the data your school will need in order to assess the direction and impact of your change agenda. All too often, systematic evaluation and assessment are little more than an afterthought, and are undertaken primarily to fulfill a mandate from an external agency such as a foundation or a state education department. This is not the way in which evaluation and assessment should be carried out. Rather, as we note in Chapter 1, they need to be embedded in the entire change process rather than appearing episodically. If this is to occur, steps need to be taken early and consistently built upon. Tool 4.4 is an excellent way to gather useful and appropriate data from your staff early in the change process. When data are collected in this manner, assessment results stand a better chance of becoming a useful tool for implementation rather than just a passing thought at the most inopportune of moments.

Successful implementation requires knowing where you are.

Tool 4.4. New Project/Program Implementation Success Feedback Form

Please let me know your perceptions on these items regarding our efforts to implement
_____.

		absolutely					*afraid not*
1.	Have the necessary resources to support the new effort or project consistently been made available?	1	2	3	4	5	6
2.	Do you believe this effort/project is doable?	1	2	3	4	5	6
3.	Is it usable?	1	2	3	4	5	6
4.	Has training and continued development of necessary knowledge and skills been ongoing?	1	2	3	4	5	6
5.	Are progress checks being done on a continuous basis?	1	2	3	4	5	6
6.	Have you been given frequent feedback based on the progress checks?	1	2	3	4	5	6
7.	Are there people who are serving as cheerleaders and coaches for this project/program?	1	2	3	4	5	6
8.	Are the purposes and direction of the project/program clear?	1	2	3	4	5	6

Build Linkages to
Those Who Can Help

Implementation can be a daunting process, one in which schools that are pressing to dramatically improve the learning of all students may feel as if they are not only rowing upstream but also are the only boat in the water. In part, this may be true, but often this is so only if you don't seek out other rowers who are in the same water as you. We believe that building linkages with important constituencies is critical to the early stages of the implementation process. It's also a management function, which your team needs to address early and often.

It's easy to ignore linkages that exist in your own back yard, but often they are the most important. First and foremost build linkages with your district office and school board. You

Look for linkages, both nearby and over the next hill.

need your central office and board to be committed to your change activities in a way that they will continue to support you in the implementation process. Some research indicates that change is more likely in schools wherein the change agenda is one of the district's top two priorities and has long-term support (see Chapter 8). When such support exists, implementation is less likely to be disrupted if revenues become limited or when there is a turnover in leadership.

As we discussed in Chapter 3, of special importance are the linkages with organizations and schools pursuing the same agendas as your school. These are significant partnerships that can materially add to the success of your efforts, especially during this period of early implementation. Lieberman and Grolnick illustrate the many purposes that school networks can serve, and we're confident that your school or district would discover the value of being a member of one or more of these networks.[11] Some of those networks, with goals similar to those of Project Improve, include: The Program for School Development—League of Professional Schools, the Center for Collaborative Education, and Center for Educational Leadership. The addresses of these as well as other networks are available in the *Ports of Call* section at the end of this book.

One of the benefits of being part of an externally derived change process such as Accelerated Schools, Coalition of Essential Schools, or any of the variety of school networks, is the access it gives you to the rich expertise within the larger educational community. As you face up to issues you never even imagine existed, your school community benefits when its members feel free to talk to educators at other schools who have similar experiences to yours. Because these networks and the organizations that comprise them also have both national and regional meetings, the information and perspectives gathered at these sessions can be extremely useful. We know from our own experience as external facilitators that the information shared and assistance provided among the members of the Accelerated Schools network does much to aid the continuing development of schools in the project. Linda Darling Hammond gets to the heart of the benefits of linkages to other professional organizations by noting that professional development strategies that end up improving teaching are those wherein teachers regularly attend to problems of practice—"using their colleagues for mutual assistance.[12]

Reculture by Aligning Practices with Beliefs (Mid Stage)

As part of Project Improve, Mary's goal was to have a Leadership Team that would assume collective responsibility for the project. Meeting this goal was difficult at first. After all, the teaching culture is not characterized by differentiation of role and status among its members, and teachers at South Central felt a bit uncomfortable seeing their colleagues as having specialized skills that could help move the project along. Yet, the more that teachers actually benefited from the role of leadership team members, the more they came to see the team as a resource to help improve their practice.

Project Improve placed an emphasis on better diagnosis of each student's learning needs and an attempt to match that need with a specific teaching/instructional strategy. The assumption underlying the Project was that teachers cannot use the same methods with every student, but must try to root the child's learning to an activity or topic of interest to that child. The best evidence of change happening at South Central was the different ways of thinking about student learning. Mary heard much more discussion of this issue among more of the staff, and if the presence of this language indeed was indicative of changes in practice, then Mary and the team had reason to be optimistic.

Apparently teachers and administrators at other schools had heard about some of the early successes at South Central and were now inquiring into visits to the school. The fact that the word was out that South Central was constructing a culture focused on student learning became an ego-booster for many of the staff, and was especially welcome after years of bad press and negative community perceptions. The staff felt special, and for good reason. It was an honor that others wanted to learn from the South Central staff. Mary knew from past experience, however, that such visits had their downside, the most notable of which was the possibility of too much rhetoric and too little attention to reality. However, outside interest in South Central and its changes was an interesting problem to have.

At South Central, then, implementation was beginning to show results. The Leadership Team was instrumental in facilitating the evolution of Project Improve and increasingly saw itself as a multifaceted team of professional colleagues who served as a catalyst to improve the conditions of learning at the school. A major impetus of the team was to translate vision and policy talk into action. Teachers were now talking about which of those instructional practices were appropriate for certain learning

A major role of leadership in implementation is to help translate talk into action.

needs and under what conditions—a sign that teachers were beginning conversations among each other about the nature of their craft and how that translated into new experiences for students.

As the implementation process develops and begins to become "regularized," it is useful to view it as the changing of a culture. Firestone and Corbett have a way of thinking about organizational culture—as "the wellspring from which flow recurrent and predictable behavior patterns."[13] Because behavior is derived from socially shared knowledge and beliefs of what is and what should be, then that behavior can change to the extent that the knowledge and beliefs behind that behavior change. When it does, then we can say that reculturing is occurring. Reculturing is the major work that occurs when implementation is in mid-stream.

How can your team enhance the reculturing process? We suggest four characteristics:

**How Do You Know When Implementation
Is Changing the Culture of Your School?**

♦ There are visible symbols of a changed culture.

♦ Data are available that show changes in behaviors

♦ Timelines are reasonable and regularly monitored.

♦ Setbacks are successfully handled.

Create Visible Symbols of a Changed Culture

What are the symbols of change in your school?

An important part of reculturing involves establishing the visible symbols of cultural change. Much of this involves creating a meaning system around the change effort that signals the school is indeed in the process of constituting something different. Herein, symbols play a key role in the implementation process.

Have you ever been in a school where unity of purpose permeates everywhere, yet still in a tasteful manner? One of us spent a week in a school just like that. In this elementary school in a low-income neighborhood, visitors were first treated to an exhibition of student work displayed in the entry hallway. It wasn't a normal potpourri of paintings and drawings from an art class, but rather a project clearly linked toward one or more key academic standards. In the hallway, there was a also a tripod on which was placed a nicely crafted artistic presentation of the school's mission plus an invitation to visit the school office and to view a five-minute videotape of the school and it's programs. Also in the office there was a handout that provided an overview of the specific focus of each classroom teacher insofar as the learning standards were concerned. On the hall wall there was a well-designed bulletin board noting the schedule of the bi-weekly "learning celebrations" that were held in the school cafeteria on Fridays during an extended lunch period. All teachers and staff members wore a large nametag with the slogan "Learning and Growing" prominently displayed. Symbols such as these were designed so that a visitor to that school would come away believing that this was a school that was "different" from the typical elementary school. Here was a school that had its act together in terms of being serious about improved student learning. This was a school that was proud of the work it was doing, and there were visible representations pointing to active implementation.

Are these symbols artificial and thus "unreal?" Hopefully, they are not. Bolman and Deal tell us that an organization's character is revealed and communicated most clearly through its symbols.[14] To this degree, then, the symbols such as those described above were part of the school's character and not just empty symbols made up to impress visitors. This is why it's important to recognize that reculturing involves a complex relationship and interaction between structural and behavioral changes on the one hand and ways of understanding and representation on the other hand. Schein terms this as the striving between patterning and integration.[15] Reculturing takes place when this patterning and integration is pervasive enough so that a new set of shared assumptions about how the school will work begins to operate outside of everyday awareness.

Are the symbols of change effectively communicated?

We believe that a leadership team must work diligently to integrate the appropriate symbols into the tapestry of implementation. These symbols can take a number of forms, and, as Bolman and Deal note, might include rituals, stories, visual representations, and celebrations. Through such symbols, your entire educational community can begin to play out the elements of a new school culture. The more that this drama is played out, the more real it becomes.

Examine Data That Demonstrate Changes in Behavior

It is important also that such symbols become translated into real changes in student learning. Our second characteristic of effective reculturing, then, is the availability of data that show evidence of actual changes of behavior in your school.

At South Central, Mary and her team used the school's vision to develop a fairly specific baseline against which to evaluate the implementation of Project Improve. They asked each teacher to enumerate the variety of learning environments typically used in their class (e.g., whole group instruction, small group instruction, differentiated instruction, project-based instruction, etc.), how the teacher decided which students were to be assigned to that mode of instruction, and on what basis they decided to maintain or change that learning environment for the students who were assigned to it. As Project Improve became implemented, Mary asked the Leadership Team to query the staff, on a regular basis, whether or not there were any changes in the nature of these environments and why. The point of these questions was not to evaluate teacher performance; rather, it was to use the vision and its manifestation as the focus of continuing dialog about the nature of classroom practices.

Thinking about what is supposed to change and monitoring the degree to which it is changing is not something to which classroom teachers are accustomed. The press of the classroom and the need to be attentive to the needs of students often takes away from time for reflection and assessment. We know, however, that in the absence of careful monitoring, successful implementation is less likely to occur. Figure 4.2 indicates some of the characteristics on which data could be collected as a school moves toward comprehensive change.

Establish and Monitor Implementation Timelines

Our third characteristic of successful reculturing focuses upon establishing and monitoring timelines. Any examination of the literature on school change reveals that it is almost axiomatic that change occurs over a longer, rather than shorter period of time. When we say "longer rather than shorter" we don't mean that there is a magical number (four years, six years, or longer?) that you can select in order to expect the desired results. We do mean, however, that because change in schools is complex and multifaceted, and because it occurs within an existing culture at the same time that this culture is undergoing transformations, the time lines must go far into the future.

Your change calendar has to be multi-year.

Consider the story of one of the most innovative schools in the country, Central Park East in New York City.[16] The school began in 1974, in the midst of a New York City teacher's strike, during an era of incredible conflict. The conflict was between the school system and its various and diversified communities, and was over whose needs were being served (or not being served). It occurred in a part of the city where most of the students were either African American or Latino, and whose performance on standardized tests was at rock bottom.

Some 11 years later (in 1985), the ideas of Central Park East had expanded to three elementary schools and a secondary school. Students who finished the elementary school (and eighty-five percent did) were well prepared for entrance into any secondary school. Ninety-five percent of those who entered the Central Park East Secondary School graduated from that school, and 90 percent of those went on to postsecondary education. These are amazing statistics for a school where, a decade earlier, even average performance (let alone superior performance) of students was neither expected nor achieved.

Notice the time frame here: 10 years, and the first few were very challenging. As Meier notes (and some of this will sound familiar): "we stumbled a lot in those early years...we fought among ourselves. Personal autonomy and communal decision-making didn't always go well together. We were teachers with strong personalities, used to going our own way and annoyed at having to convince others about pedagogical issues—colleagues or parents."[17] The point is that change came neither easily nor quickly, something that should come as no surprise, considering the scope of changes which Meier and her staff brought about.

Before the famous Central Park East was discovered by the media, it had a 10-year incubation period.

Figure 4.2. Characteristics of a Traditional and an Accelerated School

The Traditional School	*The Accelerated School*
Organization	Organization
Hierarchical, top-down structure	Empowerment coupled with responsibility
Bureaucratic, remote-control changes	Formal Accelerated Schools process
Teacher isolation/autonomy	Total staff involved in each level of governance:
Subject area departments	cadres, steering committee, faculty
Isolated classes/departments	Cross-department cadres
Fixed scheduling	Flexible scheduling
Separation of all staff	Building on strengths of all school members
Principal as manager	Principal as one of the facilitators
Limited parent/community involvement	Active involvement of parent/community
Maintenance oriented	The inquiry process
Central office monitoring compliance	District is part of school groups
Age-graded institution	Student-centered vision
Little/negative attention to school-wide goals	School-wide vision, unity of purpose
Cosmetic piecemeal changes	Long-term/short-term goals
Staff development from outside	Open to new ideas and adventures
	Total staff decides on programs
Curriculum	Curriculum
Standardized curriculum	Equal access to all courses by all
Basic core classes for all	Integrated curriculum
Standardized testing	Assessment integral to inquiry process
Stress on facts, abstract concepts	Real-world curriculum
Remediation for lower-level students	Inquiry process part of curriculum
Acceleration for upper-level students	Student participation on cadres and committees
Tracking	No tracking
Textbook serves as primary source	Multiple primary sources
Electives and extra activities for gifted	Cocurricular and extracurricular activities for all
Isolated subject areas	Equity in course content
"Traditional" content	Cadres and faculty determine curriculum
Controlled/mandated by outside	
Instruction	Instruction
Homogeneous grouping	Heterogeneous grouping
Conventional techniques (lectures, rote learning, drill, worksheets, etc.)	Active, powerful learning techniques and strategies
Teacher's guide serves as primary source for lesson development and presentation	Real-world experiences as primary sources
Teacher-centered classrooms	Student-centered vision of school
Students work independently of each other	School is seen as center of expertise
Reliance on standardized tests and external assessment for evaluating progress	Group activities and cooperative learning
	Open-ended activities
	Multiple ability learning opportunities
	Alternative assessment and self-assessment

Unfortunately, it is difficult to gain a perspective of such an extended period of time for change unless you are focused, strategic, and even a bit lucky. And you can't wait 10 years for a total change to occur; you have to build a series of smaller successes—what we term "quick wins"—into the goal of reculturing your school. We've already talked about the need to continually revisit your vision of what your school should be doing in order to change the culture. Certainly, Meier and her staff knew that improving the educational success of their students was the top priority, and all changes that were proposed were held up to that mirror. The staff was also strategic because staff members were willing to adjust their ideas when the evidence didn't support what they wanted to do. Your team must understand that in implementation of a change, good ideas may not bear fruit or that unanticipated consequences may arise. We suggest that you attend to these consequences because, if you don't, they'll come back to visit you when you least expect it.

Change requires some "quick-wins."

Expect Setbacks

Finally, the ability to effectively handle the setbacks that inevitably arise is a crucial element of continuing to change the culture of your school. As we noted earlier, setbacks are bound to occur, even when you believe that change is moving along at a good clip. How you handle this is an essential key to continued progress.

At South Central, Project Improve had become the focal point of the school curriculum and the keystone of teaching strategies in virtually every classroom. Because there were statewide assessments of student performance at the eighth grade, everyone was aware of the student performances necessary to meet those benchmarks. In addition, community expectations were high for continued school improvement.

In the middle of the first year of Project Improve the leadership team, in an effort to provide more assistance to students struggling with math, recommended that in the following year that the art teacher's position be shared with another elementary school. This would reduce that teacher's time at South Central by some 50 percent. The funds released by this change would then be used to employ a half-time math teacher to assist those students not meeting the standards.

As you can imagine, when those parents who were interested in the arts heard about this proposal, they were on the phone to Mary demanding a meeting. They believed not only that this was a blow to the arts program at South Central, but also was indicative of what they had warned about earlier—that preoccupation with meeting the standards would change the culture of the school to one based purely on a narrow definition of learning. In other words, South Central decisions were being dictated by the presence of state tests.

It's a situation such as this, if it isn't handled properly, that stands the chance of turning progress on implementation into a threat to its continuation. Much about the way it is handled depends on the attitude your team brings to the problems as they develop. Let's return to Fullan's belief that we treat problems as "friends."

Too often in the implementation process, problems are seen as something to avoid. If they can't be avoided, then often they are swept aside, ignored, or put off as long as possible. It's not that educators are preordained to deflect problems, but more because we come to the change effort with a mental set that a problem is a sign that somebody goofed—otherwise, why would the problem be present? We seem to have difficulty in viewing a dilemma as something from which we can learn (as we encourage our students to do). Fullan, however, comments that his research shows that schools that are successful in the innovation process are those that engage in a deep probing of the problem and are then more likely to make "substantial interventions such as comprehensive restaffing, continuous training, redesigning programs, and the like."[18] It isn't that successful schools do a better job of planning ahead or have better leadership and thus have fewer problems. Rather, the way they deal with their problems is instrumental in contributing to their success.

Let's return briefly to South Central and the parents' objections to the proposed reduction in the arts offerings. The school leadership team was convinced it needed to find a source of revenue for math tutoring because its members believed that the additional assistance would increase the performance of a number of the students. Although the team, like the parents, also valued the arts, the reality was that art was not on the statewide assessments. Consequently, hard choices had to be made.

In part as a result of that input, Mary asked the team to consider some other options because she didn't want to devalue the arts regardless of whether that subject was "measurable" on any standardized test. Because adding back the half-time position for the arts would cost $25,000 (including benefits), she proposed that the school reduce its expenditures for field trips by 50 percent, thus freeing $10,000. Then she asked the leadership team to participate in discussions with the parents who were promoting the arts. These discussions led to an agreement to submit a proposal to the city Arts Council for an Artist-in-Resident program for two years at a cost of $10,000 a year. The balance of $5,000/year could be raised through a South Central Festival for which local artists would be asked to donate work which would be auctioned to benefit the school.

Here was a solution that could work because it was generated collaboratively with the entire school community. It required that every party "give" something in hopes of establishing a long-term solution to both the math as well as the arts dilemma. It demonstrated commitment to the school's vision of helping all students to meet state standards as well as to the well-articulated goal of some parents (a goal shared by the staff) that South Central needed to be more than just a school whose purpose was defined by test scores. Successful adaptation to this and other problems helped South Central to continue the implementation process to the next level.

Monitor Progress and Maintain Momentum (Mature Stage)

South Central School was now well into implementing Project Improve. The staff had made significant changes in the organization of the school and the core teaching and learning strategies that defined the school. The most significant changes in the Project involved the creation of teaching teams of three people, each team being responsible for a group of 80 to 90 students who remained with the team for two years. Because the district was focused on increasing the percentage of students who meet the eighth grade standards, teaching teams permitted a more flexible grouping of students as well as allowing each team member to develop specialized competency in an area assessed by the standards (e.g., reading, writing, mathematics).

South Central was now in what might be called the late or mature stages of implementation. For our purposes, this means that there should be an increasingly close alignment between values and beliefs and the activities that define those values and beliefs. As we noted earlier, implementation is not a linear process through which a school marches on its way to completion. Yet, there are still some important issues that demand special attention when implementation has reached a mature stage. We present below three of those issues, which we discuss in this section:

Key Issues as Implementation Matures

♦ Maintaining the commitment to the vision.

♦ Moving beyond standard testing into an authentic and enriched learning environment.

♦ Accelerating the evaluation and assessment process.

Maintain Commitment to the Vision

Precisely at this stage of the change process is where " vision fatigue" becomes commonplace. You've fought a lot of battles, struggled during the process of reculturing, and have in place some worthy changes, proving that indeed there have been real improvements in the manner in which your school operates. That's the good news. Lurking in the background, however, you realize that the accomplishments, as notable as they are, don't always meet up with the expectations encoded in your vision. There is a gap between the real and the ideal, and your knowledge about this gap creates an

Late in the implementation cycle, "vision fatigue" often sets in.

underlying tension for you. Does the gap in performance indicate some degree of failure, or have you done the best you can under the circumstances? Should you be working harder to minimize the gap so that the ideals of the vision are better manifested in reality? These are tough questions, and answers to them often come at a stage of implementation when what we call "vision fatigue" sets in.

Senge and Lannon-Kim argue that the tension between the real and the ideal is a "creative" tension and one that is natural in all change processes.[19] We can never eliminate the tension because what we want to do and what we have done are always two different things. The real issue, however, is how we handle this tension, which is fundamental to the implementation process.

The natural tendency is to accept the reality of where you are and then scale the vision back to meet that reality. It might appear in the form of something like: "we wanted to increase the percentage of kids meeting the standards to 50 percent, we only got it to 40 percent, and that's about as good as it's going to get in a school with so many poor kids." This, then, is the way in which the vision is scaled down to meet *Scale up; don't scale back.* reality, and it's the path normally taken. That's somewhat understandable when, late in the implementation process, fatigue begins to set in.

But another approach is to continue to view your vision as attainable and to strive for it. An increase to only 40 percent of students who met benchmarks still leaves over half the students behind, and you need to ask what level of attainment your school is willing to accept. If Central Park East, drawing from a poor and ethnically diverse section of New York City, can graduate 95 percent of it's students from high school, then why can't South Central School aspire to increase the number of its students meeting standards from 30 to 50 percent over three years? And if you aren't successful at reaching that goal, why should you assume that you were too idealistic? You want your school to have the leadership where everyone (and not just the principal or leadership team) asks that question. It takes considerable focus and dedication to do so, especially when the implementation process has matured, some complacency has set in, and nobody wants to rock the boat.

Move Beyond State Standards into an Authentic and Enriched Learning Environment

A second important issue to your school as it moves through the implementation process concerns the manner in which your school change effort is part of an overall movement of educational change. An example from South Central illustrates what we mean.

South Central, like most schools today, is part of a larger social movement demanding higher performance of students as well as greater accountability for schools. One of the reasons Mary was appointed principal was to accomplish those two goals, and Project Improve was adopted in part to reach those objectives. But the improvement of student performance on statewide assessments was not the only goal of Project Improve. The project also placed a premium on students' enhanced learning of problem-solving skills, the ability to work cooperatively with other students in an active learning environment, the demonstration of learning through projects and exhibitions, and students learning about their roles as citizens in a multicultural and democratic society. In sum, Project Improve was intended to create a school *context* within which all of these dimensions reinforced each other, and improved student performance on statewide assessments was just one of these dimensions.

Yet, every day, what the school staff heard most about in the media and, indeed, often from the district office, was the fundamental need to increase student performance on statewide tests. The fact that this responsibility was so explicit and consistent was a challenge for the school because student performance on norm-referenced tests could have easily become the primary activity within the school. Therefore the leadership team at South Central had to be especially vigilant so that the implementation of Project Improve did not become solely devoted to teaching to the tests.

A major challenge is not to be ruled only by standardized tests.

In an era of state standards, it's easy for "number magic" (what gets counted) to drive the implementation process. School boards, Superintendents, and outside groups (many well-intentioned) beat the improved performance war drum so much that it can drown out other activities that are important for student learning. Your team must have the vision and the courage to resist too specific of a focus on one dimension of student learning so that it obscures other dimensions. You will need to understand how different components of your change agenda weave together to constitute a whole, thereby helping to keep your staff, as well as the larger school community, focused on the context within which any one change dimension exists. As Fullan and Miles tell us: "because education reform is so complex, we cannot know in advance exactly which new structures and behavioral patterns should go together or how they should mesh. But we do know that neglecting one or the other is a surefire recipe for failure."[20]

Accelerate the Evaluation and Assessment Process

Finally, how's your evaluation and assessment work coming? We raise the question because, in order for implementation to reach a level of maturity so that it becomes sustained, it's critical that you begin to have useful information about how well you're progressing. We suggest a careful read of the book by Garmston and Wellman, and in Chapter 6 we discuss at considerable length the topic of evaluation and assessment.[21] However, it's important to understand that evaluation(which focuses on the fidelity of implementation) and assessment (focusing on improved student learning)

There's a difference between evaluation and assessment.

must be integrated into the entire change process and not be relegated to an afterthought or something done after the important work has been completed.

Evaluation and assessment are important to implementation for two reasons. The first reason is one of necessity. Most likely, you are working in an environment where your school is expected to demonstrate improvements in student performances. Many of you work in a state like Oregon where your school is "graded" every year on a number of measures (including the percentage of students meeting state standards in designated subject areas) and where those evaluations are public information. Others of you may work in an inner city district (such as Newark, New Jersey) where failure to produce results can and has led to such dire consequences as an entire district being placed into receivership. In public education now, whether we agree with it or not, assessment is integral to what we do. Thus we cannot escape the heavy-handedness of top-down assessment criteria.

Second, valid assessment data are critical if you don't want to be totally at the mercy of these externally developed assessments, under which most educators bristle. One of the reasons state-mandated assessments have become so pervasive is because the education profession has not developed many assessment strategies, which demonstrate valid student learning gains that can be used to make school/district policy decisions. State-mandated assessments thus fill a large vacuum, one that continues to expand as the need for information to drive decisions expands.

The implementation process, then, is enhanced by valid evaluation/assessment procedures that produce information that teachers can use to improve their teaching and the performance of their students. If the evidence to which teachers and administrators have access shows reasonable progress towards meeting expectations, the school then has the data to continue the efforts that contribute toward that end. Where the evidence shows that the value-added by classroom strategies is below expectations, the school has the information it needs to make the collective decision to make targeted changes. In either case, the staff is empowered because they, and not somebody else, have the means of control over the situation. Evaluation and assessment then become sharp surgical tools dedicated toward improvement rather than a pile driver intended to club schools into submission.

Evaluation and assessment are not restrictive. They're empowering!

Chapter Summary

Implementation is the heart of the change process. All of the work that your school has done to date doesn't amount to much if the change you intended doesn't materialize. Yet, the literature is replete with stories of change efforts that were begun but never effectively implemented. It's important that you have the right tools and strategies to successfully implement your change effort.

In the earliest stages of implementation, the leadership team will begin to see that the approaches used in the initiation and commitment-building phases need to evolve into a set of different responsibilities. In implementation, you're moving from talking about change to actually "doing" change, and, consequently, you'll be more actively involved in helping your colleagues change the way they work. This is bound to create misgivings and anxiety on the part of your staff, and you'll need to be sensitive to these matters of transitions. One way of facilitating the change process is through the involvement of constituent groups within your district so that the base of ownership is broadened. In addition, it's also useful to create linkages and networks with other educators, both in and out of your district, so you can learn from their experiences.

As implementation reaches the mid-course, you'll be working hard to move from ideas and beliefs to a change in behaviors of teachers and students. This is what we call the "reculturing" process and is central to successful implementation. You'll want to pay particular attention to the symbols and actual data that tells you the extent to which real behavioral change is occurring.

In the mature phases of implementation, you'll find yourselves reexamining your vision and calibrating the direction of change to remain true to your change agenda. This is key to your ability to sustain your change effort over the long haul, a topic which we explore in detail in the next chapter.

Reculturing Map

How do you know if implementation is successful?

Increase:	*Decrease:*
☐ Using a problem solving approach	☐ "Winging it"
☐ Team decisions about responsibilities	☐ Individuals deciding about responsibilities
☐ Resourcing	☐ Using scant resources as an excuse
☐ Learning from problems	☐ Denying problems
☐ Honoring school history	☐ Ignoring school history
☐ Understanding resistance	☐ Powering through resistance
☐ Links with other educators	☐ Going it alone
☐ Returning to the vision	☐ Asking what the vision is
☐ Changing behaviors	☐ Talking about changing behaviors
☐ Use of information to assess change	☐ Making assumptions that change is happening

References

1. Fullan, M. (1994). *Change forces*. London: Falmer Press.
2. Fullan, M., & Miles, M. B. (June 1992). Getting reform right: What works and what doesn't. *Kappan, 73*(10), 745–752.
3. Senge, P. (1990). *The fifth discipline*. New York: Doubleday, p. 236.
4. Murphy, C. U., & Lick, D. W. (1998). *Whole faculty study groups: A powerful way to change schools and enhance learning*. Thousand Oaks, CA: Corwin Press.
5. Firestone, W. A., & Corbett, H. D. (1988). Planned educational change. In N. J. Boyan (Ed.), *Handbook of research on educational administration*. New York: Longman, pp. 321–340.
6. Available: http://www.newamericanschools.org.
7. Petti, A. D (March 1, 1999). *Show me the money: Funding school reform*. Unpublished paper presented in EPFA 651—Educational Policy, Portland State University, Portland, OR.
8. Odden, A., & Busch, C. (1998). *Financing schools for high performance*. San Francisco: Jossey-Bass.
9. Bridges, W. (1991). *Managing transitions: Making the most of change*. Reading, MA: Addison-Wesley.
10. Rogers, E. M. (1962). *Diffusion of innovations*. New York: Free Press.
11. Lieberman, A., & Grolnick, M. (1998). Educational reform networks: Changes in the reform of reform. In A. Hargreaves, A., Lieberman, A., Fullan, M., & Hopkins, D. (Eds.), *International handbook of educational change*. London: Kluwer Academic Publishers, pp. 710–729.
12. Darling-Hammond, L. (1997). *The right to learn*. San Francisco: Jossey-Bass, p. 326.
13. Firestone, W. A., & Corbett, H. D. (1988). Planned educational change. In N. J. Boyan (Ed.), *Handbook of research on educational administration*. New York: Longman, 1988, p.335.
14. Bolman, L. G., & Deal, T. E. (1997). *Reframing organizations*. San Francisco: Jossey-Bass, p. 326.
15. Schein, E. H. (1992). *Organizational culture & leadership*. San Francisco: Jossey-Bass, p. 11.
16. Meier, D. (1995). *The power of their ideas*. Boston: Beacon Press.
17. Ibid., p. 24.
18. Fullan, *Change forces*, op. cit., p. 26.
19. Senge, P., & Lammo-Kim, C. (November 1991). Recapturing the spirit of learning through a systems approach. *The School Administrator, 48*(9), 13.

20. Fullan, M., & Miles, M. Getting reform right: What works and what doesn't, op. cit., p. 748.

21. Garmston, R. J., & Wellman, B. M. (1999). *The adaptive school: A sourcebook for developing collaborative groups*. Norwood, MA: Christopher Gordon.

WAS THIS ROCK ON THE CHART?
Sustaining Change

Chapter Highlights

♦ *Guard against slipping backwards.* No matter how successful the implementations may be, there is often a counter-momentum back to the past.

   ☐ Identify the signs of "regression to the mean."

   ☐ Take action to assure that change is sustained.

♦ *Prepare for project fade-out and the consequences of staff turnover.* Your organization changes in many different ways, one of which is through the departure of some staff and the arrival of others.

   ☐ Honor the efforts of those who leave.

   ☐ Assist those who are new in the roles they will play.

♦ *Refocus on student learning.* Despite the best efforts of everyone, goal implementation can change so that the original intentions become obscured.

   ☐ Assure that the improvement of student learning is a top priority.

   ☐ Provide credible evidence that student learning is improving

♦ *Create a learning organization dedicated to continuous improvement.* Regular adjustments in your school's functioning will emerge from a process of continuous improvement.

   ☐ Use the characteristics of a learning organization to sustain your change.

   ☐ Systematically gather information that tells you how well you are doing.

After reading this chapter, you'll better understand that the change process is not linear, but, rather, often consists of two steps forward and one step backward. Indeed, some changes wither on the vine and die. We provide some simple guidelines for effectively coping with this often-frustrating pattern. You'll also learn how to keep the change effort moving ahead in the face of the inevitable changeover in staff and families in your school. Recognizing the need to honor those who are leaving and to effectively socialize newcomers is critical. Next, keeping your collective eyes on the "prize" (i.e., improved student learning) is critical, and you will want to become better prepared to re-center yourselves on student learning. Finally, working towards continuous improvement is important, and we presage the next chapter of the book as we encourage you to ensure that your school is using the data frameworks developed earlier to evaluate its progress.

Sustaining Change at South Central School

Mary and the staff at South Central School felt confident as Project Improve matured. After all, parents seemed genuinely positive about the change of environment within the school and the number of parents who volunteered to assist in the school had increased significantly. The school had received considerable favorable publicity in the community newspapers and television stations, with one news story appearing in the statewide newspaper. The number of visitors who wanted to learn firsthand about Project Improve had risen dramatically, so much so, that at a staff meeting the faculty asked Mary to consider restricting the number of visitors beginning in the fall.

Mary and the team's ebullience was quickly erased upon receipt in late July of the results of the statewide assessments for eighth graders. Reading scores had flattened and, of most concern, overall math scores had declined appreciably. Some of the sub-tests within the overall math test indicated particularly troublesome trends. After three years of hard work and two years wherein student performance had actually slightly increased, this was the first indicator that the bold initiatives of Project Improve were not being achieved as expected. Mary notified the members of the Leadership Team that there would be a special meeting next week (before two of the team members departed for vacation) to discuss how the change effort could be sustained.

At the meeting, team members were clearly in a somber mood. Charles commented that the goals of Project Improve were unrealistic to begin with and should be scaled back. Joanne commented that the district office wasn't providing enough resources for South Central to hire all of the instructional assistants that were needed, especially considering the increased number of LEP students attending the school. Then Fran said something that Mary hadn't heard at Central for the past three years, commenting that "with all of the minority students we now have, what would anyone expect? Of course our test scores are going to drop—after all, most of these kids don't have parents to supervise them when they come home." Mary thought to herself: "I can't believe it; we're back to looking for excuses." Here it was, early August, and Mary realized that unless the team members could change their perspective prior to September, the school was in danger of losing many of the gains made to date.

Slipping Backward to the Way Things Were

The above scenario at South Central School is not at all unusual. Just when you think that the changes you're trying to make have taken root, and you've emerged out of the tunnel and set a course that is irreversible, ghosts from the past reappear. With South Central, these ghosts weren't represented only by the performance of students on the statewide assessments. Indeed, at this point Mary hadn't the time to figure out the possible causes for the decline. Rather, most troublesome to Mary was the attitude reflected in the comments from members of her own leadership team. What she heard was too similar to what often occurs when there is a problem within a school: simply, it's someone else's fault. The very process of externalizing the source of problems was a way of thinking that Mary had worked hard for the past few years to eliminate.

Blaming someone else for a problem means trouble for sustaining change.

The Power of the Past

The power of what Sarason terms "existing regularities"(which we discussed in Chapter 1) is strong in most organizations, schools included. So often, changes are introduced in a way that adds an additional layer to those existing regularities. As we discussed in Chapter 4, the new ways and the old ways often do battle when change is implemented. But because the old ways have a history, they have a staying power that allows them to shape and reshape the new ways, leading to a process of what Berman and McLaughlin term "mutual adaptation."[1] Too much mutual adaptation can dilute the force of the change effort, leading to situations where existing regularities reappear and threaten sustainability.

Some organizations have ways of minimizing the impact of these existing regularities. Private corporations often do so by eliminating the organizational units that are no longer deemed necessary to the new organizational design. This is the infamous process of "restructuring" or "downsizing" that has received so much attention in the media. Offices that existed on Friday are gone the following Monday, and the employees in those office are politely told not to show up. In the new configuration, new offices are created and new staff are employed to fill those positions. In the current market environment however, most new employees know full well that they could just as easily be tomorrow's casualties, and, as a result, they have diminished loyalty to the newly designed organization.

Although there have been attempts to create similar processes in schools (via restructuring or reconstitution, for example), most schools are not like a private corporation. Accordingly a principal or leadership team can't handle the problem of the omnipresent patterns of the past by unilaterally dissolving the school and bringing in a fresh team. Nor can the leadership team simply mandate an outcome and tell the staff who are reluctant to participate that it's "our way or the highway." Schools, more so than most private corporations, are "negotiated orders," meaning that a substantial ingredient in the way they operate is the very process of bringing members of an organizational culture to a point of common consensus about the nature of an organizational problem and what to do about it.

In schools, change occurs in a negotiated environment.

Sustaining change under these circumstances means that as leaders you have the toughest job of all—recasting the strategies necessary for long-term, continuous improvement. The issue is not necessarily that your staff doesn't want to continue the changes originally envisioned and, accordingly, needs to be threatened to produce results. Rather it's that the staff are under intense and multiple pressures to "step-up" to higher levels of school performance, the antecedents to which are multiple and complex. When those higher levels of performance elude them—when better student performance doesn't happen as rapidly as anticipated—people often look for safety in the past patterns that once seemed so secure (note our reference to the situation in Memphis in the Preface). This, then, is when your leadership capabilities are really put to the test.

The Power of the Past at South Central

Returning to the scenario at South Central School described at the beginning of this chapter, how might you handle the problem? What you know is that the performance of the students at the school had leveled off or, in some areas, declined. What you don't know is why. The team began by following the inquiry process adopted at the beginning of Project Improve and outlined in Chapter 2. This involves the creation of multiple plausible explanations as to the nature of a problem or issue. One hypothesis that was suggested was that this year's eighth grade class was a particularly challenging group, which as a cohort might not be as capable as similar classes the past few years. Another hypothesis was that Project Improve was not being faithfully implemented, and that earlier successes occurred because of a focus on test-taking abilities instead of a firm understanding of reading and mathematics problem-solving skills. A third hypothesis was that, although overall student performance was indeed down (notably in math) some students might have actually done better, but their success was camouflaged by the larger percentage of students who had done worse.

With these ideas in mind, Mary asked for our advice. We suggested that the team first spend some time breaking down the data by classroom and examining the results. Mary asked the district evaluation office to break down the data but was told that this would take three months. Mary called the Superintendent's office and asked if they could exert some pressure to get the data more quickly; it was received within the week. When the Leadership Team examined these data, they were struck by an interesting finding: whereas the aggregate scores in math for the school had decreased, this wasn't true for all classrooms. Indeed, in the class of one eighth grade team, the math scores had increased by 10 percent, and in another team's class by 7 percent. In reading, two other teams' scores had increased by 12 to 14 percent while the school's overall performance remained flat. Why?

The leadership team continued to follow the problem-solving process by proposing hypotheses and testing them to see which ones were plausible. They looked first at how students had been assigned to the teams and concluded that there was nothing to indicate that the

First, problem solving involves testing propositions about "why."

'better" students had been placed in the classrooms evidencing higher scores. Another hypothesis proposed that the teachers in these classes had been better trained to implement Project Improve and that training could account for the differences. Upon close examination however, the team concluded that the teachers in these teams had been

"late adopters" of many elements within Project Improve. The leadership team then focused on the issue of fidelity of implementation—that the core teaching and learning elements of Project Improve were actually being more faithfully implemented in some teams than in others. Could this be true? And if it were, why would it be true?

Could it be that because these teachers were slow to adopt changes in their curriculum or teaching strategies, their classes were less visible and thus not on the normal circuit for visitors who came to witness all of the accomplishments at South Central? Were these teachers among those that normally made visits to other schools to gain the skills that would assist them to improve the performance of their own students?. Could it be that all of the publicity about Project Improve, together with the distractions that this publicity helped to create, was affecting the classroom focus among most of the staff? Were they beginning to listen too much to the rhetoric about school change and paying less attention to that which had made the school successful in the first place? The team raised this as a real possibility.

What a disappointment to realize that what took three years to build could begin slipping away so quickly. However, Mary made the right move to minimize any backsliding that might occur. Calling the Leadership Team together in the summer, although not a popular decision,

Second, problem solving involves examing the data for an answer.

certainly served notice that the data from the student assessments were important and demanded immediate attention (ideally, Mary would have involved the entire staff in this process, but because it was summer, she was fortunate to locate the Leadership Team members on such short notice). Second, rather than speculate as to the causes of

the assessment results, the Leadership Team worked hard to mine the data and search for possible answers. Although they couldn't say with certainty that the school-wide regression on student performance was largely a function of too many distractions and the resultant "watering down" of Project Improve, this seemed to be a plausible conclusion. At Mary's urging, the team decided to further explore, as soon as teachers returned in the fall, the dynamics of teaching and learning in the teams where student performance had increased. Based on the results of these explorations, she would ask the team to work with the school staff to generate a recommendation as to how to get Project Improve back on track. The steps that Mary and the other members of the Leadership Team took are summarized below:

The Use of Data in Problem Solving

- When data that are key to the central mission of the school indicate a problem, involve the staff in the examination of the data.

- Use data to propose plausible hypotheses about the reasons for the problem.

- Don't rush for solutions before exploring all those hypotheses.

- Test the possible solutions to the problem against the data in order to arrive at one or more interventions. Use the data to suggest potential remedies, and discuss them widely prior to implementation.

Leadership and Sustaining Change

We believe that Mary made the right move in doing what she did and it's useful to understand why we consider these to be the right moves.

The role of the principal is important in the evolution of the change process, and nowhere does that importance become more obvious than in the efforts to sustain what has been implemented. Sustaining a change effort is one of the more difficult challenges for school leaders because threats to continued success often appear without warning. It is then that the work that the principal and his or her team have done to facilitate a dynamic and effective leadership approach is put to the test, a point reinforced by Hargreaves.[2]

Allen and Glickman review five qualities of leadership that empower school staffs, making the continuance of the change process much more likely.[3] These qualities are:

Leadership that Empowers a Staff

♦ Encouraging authentic collaboration by establishing goals and processes appropriate to the school's unique characteristics

♦ Supporting teacher innovation and what is learned through innovation.

♦ Modeling the leadership behavior you want others to demonstrate

♦ Supporting shared governance by committing the resources to facilitate it

♦ Creating a culture of appropriate risk-taking

Note that these attributes are not exhibited only at a single point in time (such as when a project first begins). Rather, they are ongoing and integral to the entire change cycle. Mary provided the leadership to help empower her leadership team throughout Project Improve. In the process of thinking through the problem of declining achievement scores, Mary insisted on using the very problem-solving model that the school had adopted (see Chapter 2). Thus, she modeled the strategies that she expected the entire staff to use when confronted with a problem. Once the staff returned in the fall, the Leadership Team in turn worked hard to help the entire staff realize that Project Improve, designed to help all students learn, might need some adjustments based upon the recent student progress data. The team, however, didn't try to force a particular strategy; rather, the team presented the data and used it to engage in a school-wide problem-solving process.

Continuous change is partly a result of building your leadership capacity.

Despite some initial backsliding, the Leadership Team owned up to their responsibilities. But the team's emergence in accepting this responsibility didn't develop overnight. The team was prepared to act in this manner in part because it had been supported throughout Project Improve through regular leadership development directed toward long-term sustainability. The first year of this development training had focused on process skills (Chapter 2) such as visioning and communication, whereas the second year's activities concentrated on content changes, such as leadership for instructional improvement. These topics were addressed during weekly seminars wherein the team could problem-solve ongoing issues, often with the assistance of a facilitator. The team, in turn, was able to work with content-based task groups of teachers who worked to develop many of the curricular and instructional improvements. In this way, leadership to sustain change was diffused throughout the school, permitting the kind of leadership density to which we've referred.

After all, leadership usually is most effective when it strives to look at problems in their complexity rather than striving for quick and easy answers. Looking at the complexity of a situation is a risk, but risk is absolutely necessary in order to sustain the direction of change. It would have been easier for the staff to interpret the declining test scores as the responsibility of someone else—families, TV, the kids themselves, the state for its obsession with multiple-choice tests, etc. Had they done that, Project Improve could have begun a slow death, and the true nature of the problem would not have been confronted. Mary built a culture of trust with her team, and they in turn extended that culture to the entire school community. The risk was that a climate of trust takes time to build, and that the results that emerge from trust are sometimes slow to develop.

Sustaining change involves the risks of accepting complexity.

As Lewis Thomas, the noted biologist has pointed out:

> When you are dealing with a complex social system…you cannot just step in and set about fixing with much hope of helping. This realization is one of the sore discouragements of our century.[4]

Preparing for Project Fade-Out and Staff/Community Turnover

Life in an organization, it is often said, is much like stepping into a river: as it flows by you the river looks the same. However, you never step into the same water twice. So it is in schools. Those who reside in your community come and go each year, changing the dynamics of school involvement and support as well as "who's coming to school" (as we discussed in Chapter 3). In addition, even in the so-called traditional school, where events seem to go on the same year after year, the arrival and departure of staff causes all kinds of subtle and not so subtle changes in school curriculum and teaching strategies. Yet, epecially in a school that is undergoing dramatic changes—one in which school professionals and community members are intentionally attempting to make alterations—the water flows deeper and faster, leading to profound changes in many areas that may have been untouched for years.

Schools change whether intended or not.

If your school is like South Central, well into a change agenda and attempting to sustain changes in the face of possible vision fatigue, it's likely that the players who are part of the change agenda are not the same ones who were there at the inception. Some of the staff who began the journey of change with you are now gone—either through transfers because they didn't support the changes or as the result of retirements. Some of the staff are still with you, but are less enthused about the implementation of change than they were early in the process. Finally, some are new to the school and, in some cases, new to education. Your school

You need to keep up with the changes in your staff.

will find that sustaining change involves sustaining the energy and commitment of school veterans as well as bringing new people into the culture of change. If you fail to understand that your staff is a running river, always changing, you run the risk of discovering very late in the game that you have a very different staff than you had a few years ago.

Fade-Out: Sustaining the Veterans

In any change effort, you hope that everyone participates and contributes to the common vision. Yet, as we discussed earlier, the likelihood of that occurring is small. Instead, you can expect there will be a (hopefully) small percentage of people who are less than enthusiastic about making changes. Sometimes, these are folks who were unenthusiastic from the beginning, but often it's those who were committed in the early stages of initiation and implementation but who have just simply "run out of gas" or are "fading out." Being successful with experienced staff members who may have lost their energy is critical to sustaining change.

Keeping your veteran staff involved is a key to sustaining change.

How do you do this? What strategies can you use? What if, despite your best efforts, you still have a minority of nonsupporters—a vocal minority of nonsupporters!!

During the initiation stage or early periods of implementation, undoubtedly there were some staff members who were uncomfortable with the direction of your change efforts. If this uncomfortableness continued, some of those staff members probably transferred to a different school, and they as well as you are the better for it. Yet, despite transfers and retirements and the like, you still may have a few teachers who aren't as active as you would like—teachers who just don't initiate much in order to accelerate the change process. Given that they are good teachers, albeit ones with a different philosophy, it's important to work hard to incorporate them into the change agenda, despite the fact that they are not as supportive of everything your school hopes to accomplish. In these situations, your strategy must be to find the areas of mutual overlap between their approach and that which your are trying to create throughout the school.

If, for instance, there is a teacher who is more focused on direct instruction than a constructivist approach to teaching, it might be useful to use this individual's skills in areas where direct instruction could be particularly beneficial for students. Certainly in a variety of subject areas (reading and mathematics for example) direct instruction can be a powerful force in helping students to gain some basic skills that will help them to meet the necessary proficiencies. Likewise, teachers who have been in the school for many years can often contribute much to community outreach efforts because they may have ties to the community that newer teachers do not. What we are suggesting is that a major ingredient to sustaining change is to continue to identify where a person's skills can be used to benefit the school meeting its learning goals. As long as you take this approach (building on strengths rather than trying to change people for no reason other than they are "different"), working with a staff with divergent styles and skills can continue to benefit the school.

While recognizing and utilizing the skills of such "veterans" is critical to the sustainability of any change effort, too often we learn this lesson the hard way. Some years ago, Bennis reflected on the lessons learned in a failed attempt to reculture a sleepy state college into an exciting and radically different university, which would set the standard for universities everywhere.[5] Bennis, who was part of the leadership cadre of this new institution (a campus within the State University of New York system), resigned as Chancellor after four years, realizing that a major error that he and others in leadership made was a failure to work with the seasoned faculty, many of whom felt unappreciated and excluded from the change agenda. Bennis commented that organizations don't come into existence just when someone who wants to change them decides that it's time for a new beginning. Rather, any organization has a set of routines and a history into which the change agenda is introduced. If those routines and histories are cast off, then those that lived them are cast off with them. This in turn breeds resentment and resistance, which in turn spawns opposition to the change process.

Eliminating organizational routines must be handled delicately.

But, in case you still need to be reminded, and are looking for concrete ways to sustain the involvement of everyone in your school, regardless of whether they are central or somewhat peripheral to the school's change agenda, we provide a few pointers that meet the guidelines noted below:

Strategies to Link Change to the Past

♦ Don't build the future by tearing down the past.

♦ Create a cadre of supportive alums and former faculty and staff.

♦ Ensure that diverse points of view are represented on committees and councils.

♦ Include everyone in the evolution of change—even the non-believers.

First, look for opportunities to visually recognize the history of your school and the people who have been part of it. This can be done via a school history portfolio, student projects that incorporate the school and community history into the curriculum, and from special recognition opportunities (see the discussion on the "School Journey" in Chapter 4). We know of one school that during the early stages of its change process posted a pictorial history of the school on the wall inside the school entryway. This history noted im-

Celebrate school history: it's the foundation for the future.

portant dates, events, and people and the roles they played since the school was built in 1961. Part of the history included the initiation of the current change initiative, which was appropriately positioned at the end of the pictorial. In this pictorial history, the current change initiative was portrayed as evolutionary—one built on the past rather than as a change that dismissed the past. The fact that this history was displayed early on in the project increased the chances of sustaining the change because it validated prior efforts and their contribution to the school as it had come to be.

Mary did something at South Central that we thought was quite effective. She made it a point to emphasize that what was being attempted in her school was dependent on work that had come before. Wherever possible, she'd remind the staff that a change that they were about to implement (e.g., block scheduling or teaming) either had existed or at least was discussed somewhere in the district sometime in the past. Because Mary had done her homework, in most cases she could even name the people who were involved. In order to better connect the present with the past, she established numerous opportunities to recognize retired teachers who had once taught at the school. This recognition took the form of a luncheon twice a year in the school cafeteria, after which the invited teachers would visit a designated classroom to work with the teaching teams and the students. These retired teachers were so pleased with the program that they formed an organization called "Friends of South Central School." Eventually, this group raised funds that were donated to the school for special purposes. These "friends" came to support the school in such a manner that not to continue the climate of change would have been done at the risk of disappointing the "Friends."

A third way to link a change agenda to a school's culture is to adopt strategies that encourage the continuing support of your veteran staff by ensuring that the membership of committees, councils, and other groups entrusted with the responsibility to provide leadership are inclusive of all members of the staff. It's easy (and in some ways understandable) to want to staff committees with individuals who are likely to make decisions supportive of the changes being implemented. However, failure to include individuals who may have a contrary point of view can both run a risk and prevent an opportunity. The risk is that if differing points of view are not aired publicly (such as within a committee or task force), then they are more likely to be expressed privately—behind closed doors or in other situations where the extent of the dissent is not known to any but the dissenters. It is much easier to deal with opposing points of view when you know what they are.

Involve everyone in a leadership role.

There is still another reason for recognizing the contribution of everyone, even the dissenters. Obviously, as members of the leadership team, you hope that those who have been less supportive of comprehensive school change will be brought along as a result of their regular interaction with the majority who do support the changes. By including varying perspectives in the debates and discussions of the change agenda and how the agenda can move

Opposition to an idea can serve to sharpen the idea.

forward, there are untold opportunities for organizational learning to take place. We don't mean to sound Pollyannaish, but dissenters often do have some valid points, and including those perspectives in the discussions as to how the change can be sustained can improve any steps taken to accomplish that end. Having to make a compelling argument for a change to a person not yet convinced of its value can improve the change agenda by forcing you to ask the question: "if I was against this change, what would I need to change my position?" This is why the literature on change argues for recognition of various points of view through inclusiveness in the decision-making procedures.

Facilitating the Contributions of New Members

We've discussed some of the ways in which your school can be attentive to sustaining change by working with staff who have been participants in the school culture for a considerable length of time. But over time, you'll also bring in new staff members to replace staff who have retired, transferred, or left education for one reason or another. It's important that as you bring new professionals to your staff, they are clear about the school's direction and your expectations for them as members of the school community. This is especially critical when the change process moves from implementation to sustaining change, because eventually it will be the new staff who will define and redefine the change agenda in your school.

How these new teachers are socialized into your school will influence their commitment to sustaining the directions of your school change agenda. The one thing you want to avoid is placing these new staff in an environment where the basic practices necessary for sustaining the change are difficult to learn and develop. Returning again to South Central School, let us examine some of the steps taken to support newcomers to the change process. The four main issues that we will explore are:

Facilitating New Members in the Change Process

♦ Train staff in the change model.

♦ Provide affiliation of new teachers with teaching teams.

♦ Connect new teachers with a qualified mentor.

♦ Link new staff to professional networks.

Training in the Change Model

Whereas you and your staff may have been involved in your change initiative for a considerable time, those staff members that are new to the school probably have not. One of the common errors we see in schools that are trying to sustain their change effort is failing to provide new staff members with the values, beliefs, and training necessary to bring them into the culture that the change model requires.

New staff won't understand your change initiatives the way in which your experienced staff do.

Imagine, if you will, being a new staff member at a school such as South Central, which has been busy in the implementation of Project Improve for the past few years. It would be very difficult to become a member of a teaching team working on differentiated instructional strategies if you had little or no prior experiences working in these conditions. You will need to be trained in the assumptions of Project Improve (the focus on improved student learning, comprehensive change, shared leadership, shared decision making, and reculturing), how Improve has evolved at the school, the various important components at each stage of Improve (from pre-initiation and commitment building through implementation and sustaining change), and the critical role of evaluation and assessment and how this role plays out in the school. In the absence of such training, you are left to pick things up on your own—certainly an inefficient and ineffective strategy if sustaining change is a high priority.

The Important Role of Teaching Teams

Because teachers in the school worked as members of a teaching team for some part of the day, Mary ensured that all new teachers were placed on a team that could help them achieve the skills and perspectives needed for continued development of Project Improve. During their first year at the school, these teachers worked regularly with the members of the team responsible for the 80-some students assigned to them. But, as Mary discovered, teams worked differently, and often each team developed strategies that were more effective than those used by other teams. So that new teachers could be exposed to and learn from these strategies, Mary encouraged the rotation of new staff to the various teams so that they could learn firsthand what was effective practice on different teams. For example, one team had developed some very useful ways that data on student progress could be aggregated and displayed so that the team could keep abreast of student progress on a number of variables. The availability of these data allowed the team to make fine-grained decisions as to what type of instructional strategies might be used for different groups of students. New teachers benefited greatly from seeing how these data were used, and thus were more likely to seek out the same approach in their own work.

Being part of a team helps induct new staff into your school culture.

Mentors and New Staff Members

Another practice that Mary found effective with new faculty was the assignment of a mentor for up to three years of a new teacher's tenure at the school. If the teacher had no prior teaching experience, then the mentorship was almost always for three years, whereas if the teacher had considerable prior experience, the mentor relationship was for one or two years. Mentors usually came from within the team to which the new staff member belonged, and the team made the choice of who the mentor would be. These mentor relationships were made *Long-term mentorship pays off.* with a clear strategy for the future. South Central had as a goal having two National Board of Professional Teaching Standards (NBPTS)) certified teachers (teachers who receive licensure from a national professional board) on its staff within the next two years. Teams worked hard with the staff members who were compiling their portfolio for presentation within the next year. Mary's hope was that the teams would view the mentor-mentee relationships as not only beneficial to the new teachers, but also as a long-term investment in assisting others to become future board-certified teachers. In the process, the idea of teachers working in a community of learners was important in sustaining change.

The Value of Professional Networks

Lieberman and Grolnick recount the importance, as well as the tenuous nature, of educational networks.[6] These educational networks exist for a variety of reasons, the most common of which involve providing a convenient way to connect professionals, thereby providing an arena of shared purpose, collective problem solving, and a feeling of shared identity. We believe that new members of your school staff should be encouraged to participate in a network that supports the overall directions of your school. We saw the advantages that the Association of Project Improve Schools brought to South Central, and are convinced that almost all schools would benefit from such an affiliation. Lieberman and Grolnick outline some of these benefits:

Characteristics of Productive School Networks

- Provide a sense of being an alternative to the existing system.
- Provide a sense of shared purpose.
- Facilitate sharing and psychological support.
- Serve as an effective facilitator.
- Emphasize voluntary participation and equal treatment.

As noted above, membership in these networks is important to the process of sustaining commitment because they serve as a support to the members who are working hard to make changes in their practice. Through the process by which participants build relationships with each other, the fabric of the network is woven and extended. Participants come to see that the issues over which they struggle in their school are usually the same as those with which others struggle. In addition, they learn about the solutions that have been tried by others in the network and the degree of success which others have experienced. As teachers become more secure about what they know, they become more adept at selecting the strategies that others have suggested. Ultimately they move into a zone of learning wherein they extend themselves beyond the narrow boundaries of their classroom or school. This is when true professional development can occur.

Participation in a network helps us to realize that we're not alone.

But, as Lieberman and Grolnick also point out, not all networks achieve these lofty outcomes. Their research concludes that networks that are too directive and tightly organized are quite fragile.[7] Such networks, though they seem capable of staging planned gatherings such as regular meetings, are not as successful at facilitating the informal strategies through which on-going communication could occur among network members. On the other hand, the so called "natural" networks—those that are more informal and less structured, seem to thrive in part because they rise to meet the immediate need of members of the network. As long as that need continues to be met, the network continues to be healthy. When the network no longer fits the need, it withers and another emerges to take its place.

This is an important finding about the process of socializing new members into the school and sustaining their commitment to the change process. One of the worst errors you can make is to direct new staff to participate in a school change network to which the staff does not have any commitment. Such action can run two risks. First, unless teachers are committed to network membership that fits their needs, it is unlikely that they will derive much benefit from participating in that network. Second, because participation in a network is largely contingent upon the teacher's needs being addressed in the network, participation directed by you will probably diminish the teacher's commitment.

A network must fit the need of each member.

With Project Improve, we encouraged the Leadership team to link South Central to the Association of Project Improve Schools—a network of schools involved in the specific assumptions and goals of Project Improve. Furthermore, we proposed that the team invite (but not mandate) teachers to be part of those networks. Over time, most staff members viewed these connections as productive. They served as a forum for the cross-fertilization of ideas through conversations (both direct as well as Web-based), local and regional meetings, and projects on which teachers from various schools cooperated. Most important, the Association gathered educators together and provided them a forum for their values and beliefs, contributing to a movement-like identity. One of the greatest outcomes of a productive network is the development of a moral purpose—one that helps professionals articulate their beliefs about the education of children. That outcome alone helps feed the soul of educators, who are too often empty in this era of narrowly conceived achievement and accountability.

Refocus on Student Learning

As we discussed earlier, a common occurrence in school change is the ever-present pull to move back to the patterns of the past. The more your team is aware of this possibility, the more they can minimize the effect of this pressure. Your school can also decrease the negative consequences of the regression-to-the-mean tendency by being proactive in terms of achieving the intentions of the change—the improvement of student learning. We call this process one of "keeping your eye on the prize."

Keeping Your Eye on the Prize

One of the findings that sheds light on why sustaining change can be so challenging is that there are two types of change: first-order change and second-order change.[8] First-order changes are those that focus on improving the effectiveness of the existing processes but which do not fundamentally alter the existing patterns of teaching and learning. Fullan terms this the "run faster syndrome," that is, doing more of what was done before, only more of it.[9] The remediation of students with learning difficulties is the classic example of first-order change, because most remediation consists simply of extra dosages of what was done (unsuccessfully) before.

First-order change is "run faster" change.

Second-order change, on the other hand, is aimed at a fundamental alteration in the goals, culture, and outcomes of schooling on the assumption that unless this comprehensive restructuring occurs across the school, the impact of change will be minimal. A focus on adapting instructional strategies to the needs of students and reorganizing the teaching culture to meet those needs is an illustration of second-order change. Second-order changes, then, reflect thinking "outside the box" and moving towards transformative change. As Fullan notes:

Second-order change is "deep" change.

> The challenge of the 1990s is to deal with more second-order changes that effect the culture and structure of schools, restructuring roles, and reorganizing responsibilities—including those of students and parents.[10]

When the regression-to-the-mean phenomenon occurs, it's often because the school has (often unknowingly) become satisfied with first-order changes. This was what was beginning to occur at South Central School. Although the avowed goal of the school to focus on improved student learning had not changed, the daily routines of many teachers had become caught up in "showcasing" the accomplishments of the school. This in turn reduced the attention that teachers were placing on ensuring that increased student learning was in fact occurring. Too much first-order change deflected their attention away from examining data that could help steer them back to improved student learning—the overall goal of Project Improve. South Central became a bit too enamored with their successes and had begun to lose momentum because their eye was no longer on "the prize."

Why is this attention on "the prize" so important in sustaining change? How can we develop strategies that help schools to keep their attention on second order changes? A consistent focus on student learning is critical because schools make a difference in student learning. When we lose sight of the potential power of schooling to affect student life, chances are that we are running the risk of exposing students to conditions that can be as damaging to them as the exposure to a toxin such as lead or asbestos. We don't believe this analogy is mere hyperbole.

Focus on student learning is second-order change.

In a review of the research on what accounts for student success, Cuttance argues that 60 percent of the variation in student learning is controlled by classroom or school factors, the other 40 percent being determined by what the student brings to school.[11] Because educators have control over what happens within that 60 percent of the variance, they then have a responsibility to ensure that they provide as much assistance to students as possible so that their chances for success are maximized. To do less—to take our attention away from the importance of what schools can do for students' futures—has negative consequences for students that may last for the remainder of their life. Schools such as South Central then have a responsibility to develop strategies that encourage focus on improved learning for all students. To do less is analogous to exposing them to a toxin—a learning toxin—that might very well be present for the remainder of their lives. We therefore owe it to our students to find ways to keep our focus on the critical second-order changes noted by Fullan and others. We next discuss one of these strategies—the "school review."[12]

The School Review

The school review, a somewhat common process in the British Commonwealth nations, but rarely found in the U.S., is essentially a third-party review by a team of knowledgable critics, based upon reasonable standards of best practice. It is an attempt to provide targeted information to schools so that the prize of increased student learning can be better attained. A school review can be a powerful strategy to sustain student learning because it:

Benefits of a School Review

- ◆ Offers a systematic review and evaluation process.
- ◆ Obtains information about the school's purpose and achievements.
- ◆ Facilitates collegial participation.
- ◆ Provides a process and outcomes shared by the school and review team.
- ◆ Aims at school improvement rather than finding fault.

Because the school review is dedicated to the improvement of student learning, it's important first to note what the school review is *not*. The school review is not meant to "accredit" schools in the traditional sense of the term. Schools that are judged to meet a certain level of proficiency are not placed on an approved list nor are those that do not meet those same proficiencies singled out. Neither is the school review intended as an audit in the sense that most audits examine the fiscal and/or policy and procedure process in order to ensure that the school conforms to certain district, state, or federal requirements.

The school review, however, is a strategy for documenting learning achievements and the related outcomes for students (which can be cognitive, affective, artistic, or others). In the school review, the skills and knowledge of students are assessed *in situ*, that is, in the normal process wherein students acquire/demonstrate these skills. These skills are assessed in reference to their degree of fidelity to what are known to be the best practices in the area. This does not mean that areas that support student learning (e.g., management systems, curriculum, and learning environment) are not examined, but rather that they are seen as means to the ends—student learning—rather than ends in and of themselves.

A school review helps to sustain second-order change.

We suggested to Mary and her team that a school review process be adopted at South Central, and that it follow the guidelines from the Project Improve network (which in turn were adapted from the Accelerated Schools Program).[13] Some of the main dimensions of the school review as outlined by Project Improve include:

Questions to Address in a School Review

♦ Where is the school now? What data have they gathered to accurately answer this question?

♦ Where does the school want to be? How is this reflected in their vision?

♦ What strategies has the school devised to get them to where they want to be?

♦ How do they propose to implement these strategies?

♦ How will they know when they get there?

The school review is different from an accreditation or audit in still another way. The school review is meant to establish a culture of information—one that pervades the school and the community that it serves. Although the process is indeed owned by the school, the review process also benefits from the assumption that continuing improvement occurs from a simultaneous impetus both from the top as well as the bottom. In other words, the school review is also a way in which parents, the community, and the others can obtain useful information related to the core technology of schooling—teaching and learning—and to be able to better assess what the investment in education is producing. The school review can then serve as a forum for dialog about where the school is, where it wants to be, and what it takes to get there.

The school review is predicated on the assumption that change does not happen by mandate or pressure alone. Rather, pressure must be accompanied by an impetus to change found within the grass roots of the organization. Thus, the school review also assumes that the information which comes from the school review is information that the school wants to use in order to sustain its change agenda. The school review can contribute to this process by identifying those areas where the school may need major development while also indicating those arenas in which the school is performing well.

What's important here is not so much that the school review is something that should be adopted by every school. Indeed, the school review, although it does address a set of common issues, is a procedure that can be somewhat variable and designed to meet the situation. What is critical is the utility of the school review to foster student learning, thus the focus on second-order change as discussed by Fullan. The school review, then, is just one example of a strategy that your school can use to keep its eye on "the prize"—something critically important as your school works to sustain change.

Creating a Learning Organization for Continuous Improvement

A school that commits itself to an outside group or agency conducting a school review has established, no doubt, a culture that is different from that found in most schools. It's different because this school doesn't do what so many schools do—hide information that makes it look bad, and, if such information is ever uncovered, then either denies its credibility or claims that the information is being misinterpreted. We believe that the commitment to a school review process symbolizes a healthy organization whose participants are willing to share information and learn from it. For this reason, we were pleased that the South Central staff decided to become involved in the school review process. The school that has committed to such a process is becoming a "learning organization, " which we see as having four related characteristics:

Something akin to a school review is integral to a learning organization.

Characteristics of Schools as Learning Organizations

♦ **Adaptability**—able to make timely changes in curriculum and instructional strategies to meet the needs of students.

♦ **Focus on variation**—not trapped by routine, but rather differentiates teaching and learning practices based on student needs.

♦ **Multiple communication channels**—information flows up, down, and sideways rather than just from the top down.

♦ **Continual review of process and content**—believes in the power of information to improve the end result of the school.

Adaptability

First, a school that is a learning organization will take a hard look at its core technology—that of facilitating student learning. Every student brings to school different experiences and motivations, and a central task of a school is to understand the multiple contexts that influence learning. Furthermore, schools must adapt their pedagogy in ways that best meet the needs of this diversity of student experiences. Does your school focus on adapting its routines to fit the characteristics of the students who enroll, or is it the expectation that all students will adapt to the one way of learning that the school promotes? We believe that schools need to be organized in ways that allow them to adapt to changes in the students whom they serve.

Variation

The presence of variation in students and their abilities does not lend itself well to centralized decision making or standardization of treatment. Yet, when we consider most schools and school districts, the traditional centralized bureaucratic framework dominates. Central office planning moves down to the school level, wherein the school principal encourages school practices in conformity with district policies and practices. School principals are at the apex of the school authority structure, and teachers have the responsibility to instruct students so as to meet district guidelines. Herein, the school works towards maximum predictability and standardization even though the very process of learning defies, for the most part, such standardization.

Variation in student abilities does not lend itself to a standardization of treatment.

To some of you this conclusion may seem a bit of an oversimplification, especially in this era of site-based management and the like. Yet, we believe it is not an oversimplification because, for the most part, administrators are charged with making the major policy implementation decisions and teachers are charged with carrying them out. Of course, this does not mean that teachers don't make decisions with regard to classroom practices or that they don't have a voice in the decisions administrators make. It's simply that, for the most part, teachers and other staff members are not explicitly acknowledged as having a formal and legitimate role in the decision-making structure of the school.

A centralized organizational structure does not facilitate a learning organization because it does not seek out the variability and uncertainties that are inherent in the learning process as input for robust decision making. If, for example, students in a traditional school continue to have difficulty with reading using the district reading materials (which have been selected by the central office curriculum committee), how might the teacher gain access to materials that might better serve those students if these materials are not "approved" by the district curriculum committee? And if her locally adopted practice does achieve desirable results, this teacher has neither the incentive nor the opportunity to share her experiences with her colleagues because to do so would be an admission of noncompliance in the use of the district reading program. The school then, as an organization, learns little if anything from this teacher's experiences. We believe that schools must celebrate variation rather than try to stifle it.

Multiple Communication Channels

A true learning organization encourages a diversity of information to be gathered and shared throughout the organization. This "requisite variety" is purposefully created to permit the organization's mission to be addressed through the best decisions possible.[14] In a learning organization, all organizational members have access to critical information and have an opportunity to use this information to affect how the organization

A learning organization seeks out diverse information.

operates. Teaching teams, then, such as those at South Central School, would share information about their practice, the interventions that have been used, and any assessment of the results. But sharing of information alone is not sufficient in a learning organization. The team uses that information to provide feedback into the decision-making process and thereby raises questions as to how, or if, the results match the values and vision established by the school. In a process known as "double-looped learning" the team might learn not only whether reading levels are improving, but could also raise thorny questions such as whether the gains in reading achievement are consonant with the school's overall values regarding other indicators of learning (such as enthusiasm and motivation). When a school(and its members) engages in this use of information and decision making, then it takes on some of the essential characteristics of a learning organization.

Continuous Review of Content and Process

Establishing the culture of a learning organization is critical to sustaining change. As House and McQuillan argue, successful schools share a number of characteristics, one of which is a culture within which change is the norm. Teachers in successful schools such as Central Park East and others often comment how "everything is always under review," or "we're always looking at what we're doing and how to make it better."[15] Such an environment cannot be created by fiat or be derived from a slogan, but must be carefully constructed

In successful schools, everything is under review.

through a cumulative process involving elements of technical/rational, political, and cultural perspectives.[16] These terms might seem somewhat academic, but actually they convey some important lessons for continuous improvement in your school.

From the *technical/rational* perspective (one that examines organizational structure, or the way in which your school is organized to facilitate student learning), continuous improvement requires the necessary infrastructure to support a normative framework of change. How quickly and efficiently are decisions made, and what information is available to help make those decisions? What are the vehicles for communication, and how accurate and timely is the communication within your building? Once decisions are made, is there a clear process for establishing responsibility and accountability? Answers to these and similar questions begin to tell you something about the structure of your school and the way in which that structure contributes to a continuous improvement process.

If your school has layers of offices that must make a decision on almost every request, if you have trouble getting a straight answer or have trouble knowing the basis on which decisions are made, then the technical aspects of your school organization need to be examined. Also, if communication channels are regularly "blocked" and too much information borders on rumor or being unfounded—and you can't identify where to go to clarify it—then your school organization needs analysis. It's hard to be a learning organization if the structure of the organization inhibits learning.

In considering the role of the *political elements* (who does what, why, and how—and who benefits (or losses) from this process), think about who is involved and who is not, informal as well as formal leadership, and reward structures that support sustaining the change. As we discussed earlier, bringing new teachers and staff into the change effort is critical because those who are instrumental in beginning the change process are not always the same people who will carry it on. And although the role of the principal is key to formal leadership, informal leaders—those who are not in authority but who nevertheless are respected and to whom others listen—are critical to sustaining change. Your team has to identify, cultivate, and support such individuals and recognize that they too may change over time.

Also consider the inducements for sustaining the change. Words alone are not enough, and symbolic rewards, though important, can only go so far. If you want to sustain a learning organization, you need to provide members with the skills they need to continue and move the change to the next level. What do people need to improve their practice, who provides it, and how do they use it? This probably means regular and quality professional development—the type that supports your staff as well as demonstrates to them that they are worth the investment in time and resources.

Finally, a *cultural perspective* on sustaining a learning organization involves addressing the issue of what values matter and how those values are expressed in practice. Are there appropriate rituals in the organization so that significant events are highlighted and recognized? Does your school present the appropriate symbols that signify its vision and purpose? Are the values focused on increasing the performance of all children readily played out in the actions of your school community?

Continuous improvement involves paying attention to articulating the values that are key to sustaining the change agenda, even to the extent that this seems repetitive. For if your school is to sustain a commitment to higher performance of all students, then all members of the school community need to clearly understand what that commitment entails and should feel comfortable asking the key question: how do certain school practices contribute to improved student learning, and how do we know that it does?

A learning organization evolves through a conscious and cumulative effort to build a culture of change. Sustaining change is dependent on this kind of effort. But building such a culture does not happen by itself. It takes a framework for change that has organizational learning built into it. It is for this reason that we believe that a design model (such as Project Improve) and an inquiry process(such as that used at South Central) are so important.

Senge offers some useful questions that can help you know how far your school has traveled on the path to becoming a learning organization:[17]

Determining if Your School Is a Learning Organization

- ♦ Does your school have a clear and honest understanding of its reality?

- ♦ Do you use data that is potentially embarrassing?

- ♦ Does the organization support continued learning?

- ♦ Does your organization have capabilities it didn't have before?

- ♦ Are your energies focused on where you want to go, or are you too busy putting out fires?

Fullan notes that the problems of sustaining change are similar to those of implementation. However, in the process of sustaining change, the roles of those issues become more clearly defined. Certainly, if the dimensions of a learning organization as described above aren't embedded within your school during the implementation process, they will not suddenly appear when you are committed to sustaining your change agenda. Effective schools are in the business of "institutionalizing the long-term capacity for continuous improvement," which means that they are always in the process of reculturing so as to successfully adapt to any change in their environment.[18] That is the fundamental transformation that needs to be made if your school is to be successful at the change game.

> When long-term commitments are made to implementation efforts, a collective experience of shared knowledge about and familiarity with the whole process of innovation and continual improvement is built. Individuals gain expertise and understanding of the system and are better prepared to make needed modifications to constantly improve it.[19]

Chapter Summary

To sum up this chapter, let's review the guidelines you might look for as your change efforts become somewhat routinized. How will you know whether you are well on the road toward a culture of continuous improvement or if you are slowly but inexorably sliding backwards?

First, be aware that there is always a tendency in any change process to drift backwards to the familiar. Don't be surprised or alarmed when this becomes evident, it's almost inevitable. What's most important is to accurately identify the source of the pull toward the past and to minimize its effect. At South Central School, Mary and her team were alerted to a potential problem by examining the student performance data. They hypothesized that one source of the problem was that of a diminished fidelity—that some teaching teams were no longer as attentive to implementing Project Improve in their classrooms. This illustration points to the value of accurate and timely data to track your school's course through the change process. We submit that a school that uses data as the basis for more of its collective discussions will be better able to keep their eye on "the prize" and minimize slipping back.

Second, and related to the issues above, you must continue the active involvement of all members of your school community in the change effort. This is important in the sustaining of change because you will have to contend with the turnover within your staff and school leadership, those leaving and those arriving. Successfully handling such changes is important because any individual who feels marginalized and unimportant in a new culture can do much to sabatoge the activities that you are pursuing and you need to do all you can to get them and keep them committed to the Project. You want to work hard to recognize the contributions of all your staff by demonstrating how present successes can be continued and built on the efforts of the past. In addition, pay attention to conscious and deliberate socialization as new individuals join your staff. Don't assume that they know what you know. Schedule special professional development sessions just for new staff—make them feel "important." Pair each of them up with a knowledgeable experienced mentor who can help guide them through the changes for which you strive.

It's easy to assume that improved student learning remains your primary goal when, in reality, you may be trapped (as was South Central) by the rhetoric about improved student learning. Don't be tricked into this assumption. All of us routinely assume that what we do "is good for kids," or "makes a difference in student learning," but we rarely ask ourselves (or each other) how we will know if it will make a difference. Keep your eyes on the prize (student learning) by forcing your organization to address the hard issue of "how do we know that we know?" If the only way you know is through intuition or feeling, then that's not sufficient to sustain the change process.

Finally, sustaining change means creating a structure and a culture dedicated to continuous improvement. And for continuous improvement to be the norm, your organization must, from the inception of the change effort, be in the process of becoming a learning organization. This means creating a culture of inquiry wherein your school operates like a brain, processing information at one level but also seeking out alternative information and the meaning of that information at another level. Your school then must *learn* from its history and its environment. Fear of failure is inimical to learning in individuals as well as organizations. Commit yourself to seeking out the information you need, not just that which you want.

Reculturing Map

How do know if change is being sustained?

Increase:	*Decrease:*
☐ Viewing change as a journey	☐ Viewing change as a destination
☐ Recognizing slipping back as natural	☐ Becoming discouraged from slipping back
☐ Awareness of what turnover in staff entails	☐ Ignoring the effects of staff turnover
☐ Investing in people	☐ Investing in things
☐ Focus on the "prize" (student learning)	☐ Becoming distracted from the "prize" (student learning)
☐ Recognition of the value of small steps	☐ Getting bogged down with challenges that are too ambitious
☐ Group problem solving	☐ Working in isolation
☐ Comfort with data	☐ Anxiety about data

References

1. Berman, P., & Mclaughlin, M. W. (1979). *An exploratory study of school district adaptation.* Santa Monica, CA: Rand.

2. Hargreaves, A., Earl, L., Moore, S., & Manning, S. (2001). *Learning to change: Teaching beyond subjects and standards.* San Francisco: Jossey–Bass.

3. Allen, L., & Glickman, C. D. (1998). Restructuring and renewal: Capturing the power of democracy. In Hargreaves, A., Lieberman, A., Fullan, M., & Hopkins, D. (Eds.). *The international handbook of educational change.* London: Kluwer Academic Publishers, pp.505–528.

4. Lewis thomas as quoted in Senge, P. M. (1990). *The fifth discipline.* New York: Doubleday, p. 62.

5. Bennis, W. G. (1976). Who sank the yellow submarine? In Bennis, W., Berne, K., Chin, R., & Coney, K. (Eds.). *The planning of change.* New York: Holt, Rinehart, & Winston, pp. 219–227.

6. Lieberman, A., & Grolnick, M. (1998). Educational reform networks: Changes in the reform of reform. In Hargreaves, A., Lieberman, A., Fullan, M., & Hopkins, D. (Eds.). *International handbook of educational change*, op. cit., pp. 710–729.

7. Ibid.

8. Cuttance, P. (1998). Quality assurance reviews as a catalyst for school improvement in Australia. In Hargreaves, A., Lieberman, A., Fullan, M., & Hopkins, D. (Eds.)., *International handbook of educational change*, op. cit., pp. 1135–1162.

9. Fullan, M. G. (1991). *The new meaning of educational change (2nd ed.).* New York: Teachers College Press, p. 29.

10. Ibid., p. 29.

11. Cuttance, P. Quality assurance reviews as a catalyst for school improvement in Australia. In Hargreaves, A., Lieberman, A., Fullan, M., & Hopkins, D. (Eds.). *International handbook of educational change*, op. cit., pp. 1158–1159.

12. Ibid.

13. Rapaport, D. (January 1997). *Mentor toolkit.* Presented at the Accelerated Schools Networking Conference, St. Louis, MO.

14. Morgan, G. (1997). *Images of organizations (2nd ed.).* San Francisco: Jossey-Bass.

15. House, E., & McQuillan, P. (1998). Three perspectives on school reform. In Hargreaves, A., Lieberman, A., Fullan, M., & Hopkins, D. (Eds.). *International handbook of educational change,* op. cit., p. 209.

16. Morgan, G. *Images of organization,* op. cit.

17. Senge, P., Cambron-McCabe, N., Lucas, T., Smith, B., Rutton, J., & Kleiner, A. (2000). *Schools that learn*. New York: Doubleday, p. 552.

18. Ibid., p.90.

19. Cunningham, W. G., & Gresso, D. W. (1993). *Cultural leadership: The culture of excellence in education*. Boston: Allyn and Bacon, p. 233.

HOW DO YOU KNOW WHEN YOU'VE ARRIVED?
Evaluation and Assessment

Chapter Highlights

♦ *Understand the context of standards.* The pressure for all students to meet high educational standards is an important part of life in contemporary schools.

    ☐ Realize that demographic changes in who's coming to school make meeting high standards even more challenging.

    ☐ Help your staff understand where standards fit into everyday classroom practice.

♦ *Value the role of assessment and the school's ability to shape it.* Any healthy organization factors assessment into its regular routine.

    ☐ Teachers need to become more involved in designing and implementing the assessment process that works best in their school.

    ☐ Recognize the difference between standards as guideposts rather than as straightjackets.

♦ *Evaluate the progress of the design model and assess its impact on student learning.* There should be fidelity to the change design as well as positive effects on student learning.

    ☐ Evaluate how well the change model is being followed.

    ☐ Assess the design model's impact on student learning.

♦ *De-emphasize standardized testing through the use of alternative strategies and principles of assessment.*

    ☐ Adopt strategies and principles that can make assessment authentic and "practical" for teachers and students.

    ☐ Use assessment results to influence the decisions that teachers make about what is working as well as what is not—and why.

♦ *Embed assessment into the learning process of the school.* A major problem of many schools is that assessment is "tacked on" and not viewed as key to the school change process.

    ☐ Don't blindly follow past assessment practices; help staff to think outside of the "box."

    ☐ Become a learning organization within the context of standards-based assessment, but don't limit your success to those standards alone.

After reading this chapter, you should be better prepard to assist your staff in creating a viable process for assessment. In reality, a consideration of assessment must address two issues. First is the evaluation of the change process itself: How is it working and how do you know it is working? The second, and admittedly more difficult issue, is that of the assessment of student learning. Herein the question to be addressed is a more complex and important one: Has the learning of students improved and is there any connection of trend lines in student learning to the change impetus? We believe that wrestling with these difficult questions requires a major change in the school culture so that your staff can better use assessment results. And we will introduce you to some specific strategies that can help your school become proactive in creating it's own assessment plan and work to make that plan a "normal" component of the school change process.

Assessment at South Central School

Mary and her leadership team knew that one of the most difficult jobs of Project Improve was in being able to document its progress. Like most educational organizations, neither South Central Middle School nor the district had invested much time or resources for the creation of a supportive culture for assessment. Assessment was viewed as something required by an agency funding a grant or by the state department of education. Assessment criteria were usually externally created and included data on attendance, percentage of students taking statewide tests, and the percentage of students meeting grade-level benchmarks. Whereas these data might be useful to school boards and politicians, they were not particularly salient for most classroom teachers because they told them little about how to improve student learning. Most problematic, however, was the fact that these assessments were annual high-stakes summative experiences rather than ongoing formative activities.

With the situation of either stalled or declining student achievement results, Mary began to see that building a culture for comprehensive and ongoing assessment was something that had not received the needed attention it deserved. Had an ongoing analysis of Project Improve occurred, the leadership team and the staff may have been more aware of the fact that the publicity about the efforts of the project, although welcomed by the staff, had a downside as well—that of distracting too many excellent and well-intentioned teachers from the central purpose of the Project—improving student learning. Mary and her team decided that now was the time to build on past experiences and to effectively weave assessment into the culture of school change at South Central.

Understanding the Context of Standards and their Role in Classroom Practice

Two extremely significant publications greatly influenced the present moment in public education. In 1983, the federal government released the controversial report *A Nation at Risk*[1] in which our educational system was blamed for not doing enough to prepare students for the changing workforce. It was a signal that the nation's global economic competitiveness had been in part diminished by a public educational system that had not adapted to changing political and economic conditions. Education was identified as the problem and the root cause of the country's economic woes.

Then, in 1990, the National Center on Education and the Economy (NCEE) published *America's Choice: High Skills or Low Wages.*[2] This publication, like *A Nation at Risk,* argued that nations such as Germany and Japan were more productive than the U.S. because workers in those countries were better educated. In our own state of Oregon, Portland's current mayor, then a state senator, was an NCEE board member and used *America's Choice* as a blueprint for Oregon's school reform legislation, including such elements as Certificates of Mastery, performance standards, and an expanded school to work program.[3]

In 1989, President Bush (Sr.) and the nation's 50 governors convened an "Education Summit" at the University of Virginia. Here, for the first time, they agreed upon broad national goals for school improvement by the year 2000. Later, the Clinton Administration passed the "Goals 2000: Educate America Act," which encouraged and authorized major content-area groups to articulate standards in their fields for a National Education Standards and Improvement Council. Goals 2000 also urged states and school districts to develop their own standards and means of assessment.

In 1996, American business leaders along with President Clinton and prominent state governors met at IBM's headquarters in Poughkeepsie, New York, for two days of discussion about the creation of educational *standards* and *assessments* for measuring how well the nation's educational system was progressing. President Clinton favored the development of national standards, but business leaders and conservative governors felt that each state should develop its own standards. Thus the process of utilizing national goals to set local standards began. Here, the country would have a top-down vision for the general objectives of standards and a bottom-up process for the states to create and implement the standards. Standards were thought to be the next piece of the educational reform puzzle. Well-conceived and clearly articulated standards, it was argued, would make expectations clear, equitable, and consistent for all students.

Standards were envisioned as making student expectations clear, equitable, and consistent.

National associations such as the National Council of Teachers of Mathematics (NCTM), state departments of education, and school systems began to define and develop educational standards. The Department of Labor put forth a very different set of workplace standards in 1991 known as the Secretary's Commission on Achieving Necessary Skills (SCANS) report.[4] The SCANS report recommended a set of workplace related standards (worker habits and activities, interpersonal relationship skills, information processing skills—oral and written, an awareness of context and a systems perspective, and technological literacy) and a set of foundational standards focusing on intellectual and personal qualities. Thus, in the quest for marketplace competitiveness in a global economy, and within a relatively short 13-year period (1983–96), public education was identified as a key national problem, broad national goals were established, and a standards-based reform movement was initiated.[5]

The consequences of the standards movement are significant. Patricia Graham, in discussing what America has expected of its schools over the past century, points to three fundamental areas of changing expectations: *attendance, access,* and *achievement.*

A central aspiration during the first half of the twentieth century was simply to increase student participation in formal education through greater school *attendance.* There was an assumption that the content of the curriculum was well-established but that too many young people either were not in school or were not there long enough. Of course, the curriculum in place was less of a concern for privileged children than for children who did not have a rich educational environment outside of school. Graham points out:

> We have tended to accept that schooling provided the same experience for everybody, not recognizing that for some schooling was a mere addition of spice to an already wholesome educational recipe, whereas for others it was the entire educational recipe.[6]

Increasing *access* was the hallmark of the second half of the twentieth century. Solving social as well as educational problems became an important function of public education during this period of time. In 1954, the Supreme Court declared that schools could no longer be separate but equal. All children had the right to high quality and resource-rich school programs. No one could be excluded on the basis of race, where he or she happened to live, gender, any handicapping condition, or language. The espoused concern for social justice became paramount.

Finally, in the last decade of the twentieth century, attention focused on the goal of academic *achievement* for all students. With universal attendance through high school and significantly expanded access to educational programs, the nation now expects high academic achievement for all children. It is believed that our very future as a country depends on all of us doing well in school. The new century and the information age demand that all citizens be well educated. Now we must figure out the appropriate curriculum and instructional practices that will facilitate learning for all students. Never before in this country's history have we believed that all children must, and can be, successful.

Yet, the consequences of students and schools not meeting these higher standards are dramatic. They range from increased retention of individual students at grade level (or no "social promotions") to growing numbers of students being placed in special education programs and large numbers being pushed out, or dropping out, of school. Many states are beginning to link teacher and administrator salary to student achievement, and are proclaiming major consequences for educators as well as schools that don't meet these expectations.

A consequence of standards has been more students being "pushed out" of school.

Despite the skepticism that surrounds the standards movement, many teachers report (in a recent national survey conducted by *Education Week*) that as a result of the focus on state standards, the curriculum is more demanding, expectations for students are higher, there is more teacher collaboration, and students are writing and reading more.[7] Thus, it's apparent that many teachers do understand and indeed support the quest of higher expectations for achievement.

Such support for higher expectations, however, has a flip side. As increasingly diverse and needy student populations challenge school systems across the county, there is intense pressure from parents, community activists, business people, and even real estate agents to have all students meet state standards. As a result of these pressures, many teachers feel demoralized and stressed. Teachers view what's happening to them as top-down policy with little or no input from them. Having students meet state standards as measured by standardized multiple choice tests is often viewed as busywork that actually takes away from precious instructional time. Many teachers feel that directives and heightened accountability have actually taken the joy out of teaching. They point out that these standards lead to fewer electives, less enrichment, little in the way of powerful learning, and diminished student enthusiasm. Teachers feel that they need more time, smaller classes, professional development, and greater support from the public. Nonetheless, many teachers believe that standards make sense; it's just how they are measured that is so disturbing to them. They want and need to redefine accountability so that they can enjoy their work again.

A consequence of standards has been the demoralization of teachers.

Valuing the Role of Assessment and the School's Ability to Shape It

South Central's late realization to take assessment more seriously is not unusual. Too often, assessment is viewed as an afterthought and is treated as such. Most schools see themselves as too busy to incorporate assessment into their regular routine because it is not considered to be central to the core technology of schools—teaching students. "How can we take the time to collect and analyze data," is the familiar response, "when we barely have time to cover the content for which we are responsible?" Indeed, even if teachers wanted to be more involved in assessment, many are intimidated by the very concept. What comes to mind are complicated evaluation designs, large investments of time to collect the required information, and the use of esoteric statistics to analyze the data.

Although such can be the case, it need not be. Assessment can become a regular component of the school routine rather than something that arises occasionally, and usually at the most inopportune time. Also, assessment need not be a function fulfilled by a group of specialists armed with long data-collection instruments and sophisticated computer-based analytical procedures. Indeed, it's our premise that unless assessment is "owned" by school practitioners—that is, unless it becomes a process for learning about *Assessment should be a regular component of the school routine.* results as well as using the results to guide teacher discussion about learning—then assessment will continue to receive a low priority in the busy life of most schools.

Let's take a practical example of the value of regular information in the school change process. As a teenager, one of us had a friend who owned a 1929 Model A Ford. This car was the friend's first car (though he was only 14) and it was planned that the car would be rebuilt into a slick roadster. Well, that never happened, but the two of us had a wonderful time running around in the rural community in which we lived. I remember, however, that the dashboard had only one gauge—for oil pressure. Almost every time we cranked the car up (and I mean *crank*, as there was no battery), we had to visually check the fuel tank (by putting a stick in it to measure the level), the radiator (by doing the same), and the crankcase. There was no dial to register electrical current or water temperature, two of the more critical indicators of the effectiveness of an internal combustion engine. Problems were resolved by lifting the hood and physically checking major engine components.

Compare this with present day cars, which not only have a temperature gauge and amp meter, but also a fuel gauge that flashes when there are two gallons remaining, an indicator if there is a major malfunction in the engine, a thermometer that registers outside temperature, a tachometer indicating RPM, and a compass indicating direction. Not only can we better determine how well the car is operating, but we even can determine the general direction we are driving in and what clothing to wear for the temperature outside. Modern automobiles provide a vast range of data as to how well they are running. Sure, there are some pieces of information that aren't absolutely necessary toward that goal (e.g., a compass heading or outside temperature). However, the availability of critical data make the operation of the car not only easier but much more inexpensive. Problems can be identified earlier, resulting in cost savings and possibly increased safety.

The analogy of appropriate data in automobiles carries over to the school change process as well. We need data on how well our children are learning if we are going to make improvements in the experiences we arrange for improved learning. Part of the problem, of course, is that student learning is much more difficult to assess than are the workings of an automobile engine. Because of this complexity, educators are prone to throw up their hands in frustration and conclude that learning is too difficult to accurately assess. But, if we can't account for what changes in learning have occurred and have a reliable indication of why, then it's like driving the 1929 Model A and having to depend upon, at best, crude indications of how well the engine is operating.

We need data on what's working if we are to continue to improve our schools.

Kenneth Wilson and Bennett Daviss make a useful distinction between evaluation and assessment, and this distinction goes to the heart of our discussion.[8] Evaluation is what we do when we want to learn if something is working as it was intended to work. Returning to the automobile analogy, an oil pressure gauge registers whether there is sufficient oil being injected into the cylinders so that the engine will have a steady supply of lubricant. In the case of schools, such as South Central, evaluation would consist of examining Project Improve as a catalyst for shared decision making and cross-grade collaboration—both intended outcomes of the implementation of the Project.

Evaluation focuses on whether a change process is working as it was intended.

Assessment, on the other hand, is a different matter, because assessment centers on the ultimate objective of the change process itself. Again, in the case of an automobile, proper oil pressure is of course necessary to the operation of the car, but tells us nothing about one of its overall purposes—that of delivering people and their possessions from point A to B safely and in a given amount of time at a generalized cost per mile. In the case of South Central, the ultimate purpose of schooling is how well the children have learned as a result of, among other factors, the presence of Project Improve. If children haven't developed a higher level of skills, and if we can't document that Improve has contributed to that process, then we can rightfully ask: "why continue the Project?" As Wilson and Daviss say:

Assessment centers on whether the change is improving student learning.

> By auditing process and result together, educators can gather the data that will allow them to invest consistently in improvements instead of squandering personal and public resources on the merely different.[9]

We invite you to think of the twin role of evaluation and assessment in the story of South Central. In Chapter 5 we describe the situation wherein the state assessment scores for South Central at the end of the year indicated that eighth grade mathematics scores had declined and that reading scores had remained flat. This bit of assessment data might be useful at one level (for example, in school by school comparisons), but the data don't tell us anything about why differences between, or even within, schools might exist. Here, then, it's absolutely necessary to understand the processes occurring at the school level, which is what Mary and the leadership team did as they broke down the data and discovered that the school trends were not borne out in all classrooms, and that there were some unique processes occurring within the school that could explain those cases that did not match up to the rest of the school.

OK, you say, it's important to examine the process (evaluation) as well as the outcome (assessment), but doesn't this place an even higher premium on standardized testing—and is this the real value of assessment? We don't believe so, but first we want to briefly mention a few points about standardized tests in schools.

As noted at the beginning of this chapter, there's a lot that's wrong with standardized tests as an assessment tool. They cover a limited amount of content, and even the content that they do cover (mostly of a factual nature), is not the kind of content that is increasingly demanded in a knowledge society (indeed, the presence of technology increases the availability of "factual" knowledge to an ever wider range of individuals). What's more, the reality that these tests have such "high stakes" for schools (but probably to a lesser extent for students) creates an environment where schools spend large proportions of their time preparing students to take the tests.

Whereas some argue that a focus on norm-referenced tests is a good use of school time (it certainly aligns instructional procedures with desired outcomes), others believe it has become an unwarranted obsession pursued at the cost of student mastery. Yet, assessment through standardized tests that are then norm-referenced will not, we believe, disappear in the near future. Indeed, the federal government under President George W. Bush has proposed more, not less of such testing. We believe that the increase in testing does not, however, tell us much about what students know (though its proponents might think it does), but rather is being used primarily as a tool for increased accountability. Until the public is convinced that its schools are performing well and can document how well they are performing, we think that high-stakes tests will remain the proxy for accountability.

Norm-referenced tests are likely to remain in place for the foreseeable future.

However, the presence of high standards need not necessarily lead to a total reliance on standardized assessment strategies. Darling Hammond calls for "standards, not standardization" and her perspective paves the way for a more enlightened viewpoint on the value of assessment. The perspective put forth by Darling-Hammond is very much the point of view we use in this book and that is described in Project Improve—that student learning is best increased through a problem-solving model for school improvement that is adopted by, and used at, the school-district level. And because the school improvement process can occur in a variety of ways, there can be neither one simple solution to be used at all schools nor one way of assessing how well schools and their students are improving. Darling-Hammond notes that:

It's important to distinguish between standards and standardization.

Standards for student learning can be most useful when they are used as guide-posts, not straightjackets for building curriculum, assessments, and professional development opportunities, and when they are used to focus and mobilize system resources rather than to punish students and schools.[10]

Within this "guideposts" framework, assessment of student learning takes on a somewhat different dimension than is normally considered in the more traditional view of assessment. In this traditional view, student assessment is defined as the aggregate of "scores" reported relative to statewide benchmarks. These assessments are externally driven and data are used externally (e.g., how does South Central compare to another middle school on math?). Teachers have very little involvement in defining the shape of these assessments and know that the purpose of the assessment data is fundamentally for use by a political entity such as the state.

The assessment within the context proposed by Darling-Hammond is, however, dedicated to focusing attention on a wide array of student work. This work can take a variety of forms—projects, papers, presentations, as well as on-demand performances such as those required by standardized tests. This is an important distinction because consistent and meaningful improvement in student work will not occur just because there exists a set of externally-created standards driving school improvement. Improvement will occur only when teachers individually and collectively spend the time to carefully examine the wide range of student work, discuss the criteria by which that work is assessed, and use those assessment data to make the necessary adaptations in the process of teaching and learning.

We believe there is considerable value in an assessment strategy that focuses upon school improvement (i.e., student learning) and not solely on accountability. As we argue in this book, the process of school change is fraught with many challenges, the most formidable of which is the creation of a professional school culture that is truly invested in the improvement of learning for all students. We don't see how that culture can be created under an atmosphere of threat and punishment; indeed, no school has been successful by pointing a gun to its head and threatening to end it all if standards are not met. A productive professional culture can be created *only* when assessment becomes integral to the learning process of not only students but the professionals who teach them as well. The topic of what should be evaluated and assessed is addressed in the next section.

Evaluate the Progress of the Design Model and Assess its Impact on Student Learning

We believe that all schools must address how well they are following the change process and how well their students are learning. Certainly test scores and percentages of students meeting state standards are inadequate and imprecise measures of school change and student achievement. They offer an incomplete picture of how well the school is doing. Rather, what's needed are data on two fronts: (a) the implementation of the change process and (b) its effects on student learning.

Evaluation of the Change Process

As mentioned earlier, Wilson and Daviss describe evaluation as what we do when we want to learn if a change initiative is working as it was intended to work. In the case of South Central, the school community had chosen to follow the Project Improve process of change. It's critical therefore to know how well Project Improve has been followed, because without *fidelity* to the stages and activities in its process, it would be impossible to determine Project Improve's impact on student learning. In fact we could be measuring, as Charters and Jones point out, a "non event."[11] For example, we certainly wouldn't say that the Weight Watchers Diet was a failure if participants who did not lose weight didn't follow guidelines about eating well-balanced meals and regular exercise. The same is true for Project Improve. We wouldn't want to say that Project Improve had failed (or even succeeded) if participants hadn't followed the guidelines outlined in the model's five stages: (a) Pre-Initiation and Initiation, (b) Building Commitment, (c) Implementation, (d) Sustaining Change, and (e) Evaluation and Assessment. If, indeed, you have a design model to guide the content and process of change, then it is critical to have quality data to inform you how well the design model is working.

Fidelity to the change model is necessary but not sufficient for successful change.

The Assessment of Student Learning

Carl Glickman points out that schools typically try on one innovation after another, but rarely determine whether they have penetrated through to classrooms and impacted the core technology of teaching and learning. Glickman notes:

> It is irresponsible for a school to mobilize, initiate, and act without any conscious way of determining whether such expenditures of time and energy are having a desirable effect. This sounds obvious, but most schools move from innovation to innovation, expending great amounts of time developing new curricula, learning new practices, and acquiring new material and equipment. Then, after initial enthusiasm has passed, they have no sense of whether these efforts helped students.[12]

Evaluating how well a school is "using" its innovation or how closely it is following its change process is one side of the equation. Of greatest importance, however, is the assessment of student learning. If we fail to address the impact of changes on student performances, we run the risk of the means of school change becoming the end.

If we fail to address the impact of change on student learning, we run the risk of the means of school change becoming the end.

Beverley Falk argues that a "better way" of assessing student learning is one of powerful learning supported by alternative assessment measures that actually promote learning.[13] She describes powerful learning as the development of critical thinking and "having wonderful ideas" so that students can "inquire, discover, pose, and solve problems that not only make sense of the world but also have an impact on it." Such teaching is a switch from a *teaching as telling/learning as listening* approach that we all too often find in classrooms that are consumed with meeting state standards. She recommends a *teaching as listening/learning as telling* approach. This involves connecting to students' understandings and life experiences and searching for ways to build bridges between existing ideas and new knowledge. The teacher then becomes more of an investigator or detective than a drill sergeant preparing the squad for a precision marching demonstration.

The traditional way of teaching is for the teacher to tell and the student to listen.

An enriched teaching process involves the teacher listening as the student learns by telling.

Falk's ideas are consistent with a constructivist approach to teaching and learning. In fact, many others including Conley[14] and Lambert[15] view constructivism as the overarching instructional concept driving current school reform efforts. The learner actively constructs knowledge. Learners are increasingly responsible for their own learning that is built around their life experiences, interests, and strengths. Learning activities are authentic, relevant, and meaningful. Major national school restructuring initiatives and projects like Accelerated Schools (see Hopfenberg & Levin[16]; Finnan et al.[17]) also view constructivism or powerful learning as being at the core or center of their efforts.

De-emphasize Standardized Testing Through the Use of Alternative Strategies and Principles of Assessment

How can you be true to a constructivist or powerful learning orientation and also demonstrate that students can meet state standards? In this section we address this question by examining alternative assessment strategies and principles and their role in assessing and recognizing the multiple talents of students. We believe that schools must become, as Rick Stiggins says, "assessment literate," but that they can do so only by moving well beyond traditional indices of achievement.

There are numerous ways that schools can become better informed about how well their students are learning. Standardized tests neither provide teachers with a sufficient understanding of what their students actually know nor the information needed to actually teach their students more effectively. These tests, for the most part, are used to compare schools and do not demonstrate relative progress or precise strengths and deficiencies in the learning of individual students. They tell us who is higher or lower than someone else, rather than how well specific students are learning. Some critics believe that tests say more about socioeconomic status and the availability of learning resources. They go on to argue that the most effective way to close the "achievement gap" is to close the resource gap by providing richer opportunities for all children to learn. In the discussion to follow, we hope to move the assessment of student learning beyond its traditional boundaries and to help schools become more critical, assertive, and proactive throughout the assessment process.

We made the following recommendations to the staff at South Central:

> ### Alternative Assessment Strategies and Principles
>
> ♦ Don't become a test prep academy
>
> ♦ Fight for better testing practices
>
> ♦ Build on student strengths
>
> ♦ Make assessment authentic and linked to learning
>
> ♦ Demonstrate learning progress with multiple forms of evidence
>
> ♦ Encourage teachers to adopt a constructivist orientation
>
> ♦ Differentiate instruction to accommodate the needs of an increasingly diverse student population
>
> ♦ Get feedback from outside friendly critics

Don't Become a Test Prep Academy

As a result, in part, of the emphasis on meeting standards, many schools have abandoned what research and professional associations refer to as "best practice." The use of worksheets to prepare for tests often replaces enrichment strategies such as actually reading books, having motivational book talks, creating books, writing reports, conducting independent research, participating in social studies simulations, taking field trips, and performing in school wide plays and concerts. A recent report from the television show, *60 Minutes*, pointed out that in Texas, many schools spend up to a half-day a week on developing students' test taking skills.[18] In our own work in Oregon, we tracked both student achievement and student satisfaction in three low-achieving elementary schools over a five-year period and discovered that whereas "student achievement" in the schools was apparently going up, student satisfaction and the perceived quality of their lives in school was actually declining. Although students may be-

If instruction is designed to build on student strengths, then in the long run students will be able to meet standards.

come better at test taking, more are actually losing their interest in school. Many of these children are at greater risk of dropping out and not becoming curious and risk-taking, life-long learners. How will such a focus on test taking help in the long run, especially in a nation that needs highly skilled and educated information age workers? It's important that you focus on powerful learning and engaging your students rather than concentrating too heavily on test scores. We believe that, in the long run, state standards will be met as long as the student experience is enriching, builds on strengths, and is enjoyable and rewarding.

Fight for Better Testing Practices

We have identified four practices (there are many more) that we consider to be representative of poor testing practice:

We are not against the use of standardized tests, just their inappropriateness in certain situations.

1. the requirement that every student be tested in every assessed content area;

2. the practice of timing tests;

3. the high frequency of tests;

4. using tests as the sole indicator of success for promotion and graduation purposes.

We aren't against the use of standardized tests per se, just their inappropriateness in certain situations.

Many experts, for example, argue that it is not necessary to test every student in every curricular area in order to hold schools and school systems accountable. Alfie Kohn points out that in public opinion polling it is not necessary for pollsters to talk to every voter, and there is no reason to test every student every year if the primary purpose of testing is to ensure accountability.[19] What is recommended is testing a representative cross-section of the student population. One technique is to give selected groups of students a different part of the larger test. By combining the results schools would then have a reasonable assessment of how the student population as a whole performed. This makes sense because accountability requirements could still be met without creating the "test-fatigue" now so prevalent among students and their teachers.

Also, along with many other experts, we also believe that high-stakes tests should not be timed, or at least that the time to complete the work be expanded. There is little correlation between the time to take a test and its relationship to real-world problem-solving activities. We see no value in telling students they didn't meet a standard because of an artificial time limitation.

Furthermore, we see little purpose in testing students every year, as the Bush administration has proposed. *Fair Test*, a Boston based organization that examines testing policy, recommends testing at the 4th, 8th, and 12th grades. In our own state of Oregon, the Department of Education requires testing at the 3rd, 5th, 8th and 10th grade levels. The point is that the amount of testing seems to be rising exponentially, and we see little connection between the proliferation of testing and the value added. We are concerned that scarce resources are being used for test preparation, testing materials, and the administration of the tests, all of which are taking away from resource needs in critical areas such as smaller class size, instructional supplies, and professional development.

> *There is little connection between the proliferation of standardized testing and the value added by such tests.*

Finally, we believe strongly that school success should never hinge on a single test score. Virtually every expert agrees that there must be multiple means of assessment. Relying solely on standardized test scores is universally considered to be poor practice.

Build on Student Strengths

Assessment typically identifies student deficiencies—what they don't know. We believe that assessment should be designed to build on student strengths—what they do know. As earlier mentioned in Chapter 3, we believe that all youngsters are naturally curious and want to learn about their world; they have rich personal life experiences; have expressive and receptive language skills; and have a rich and fascinating cultural identity. Yet, often these types of student interests and strengths are different from those emphasized in school and have little bearing on what is assessed in school. As a consequence, schools have little holding power for many students, and these students too easily become unmotivated, disengaged, and pushed out. What we need to do is design curricula and instructional methods that build on prior learning and complement, rather than contradict, the child's experiences outside of school.[20] Falk points out that schools need to be organized in light of what students can do rather than in light of what they cannot do.[21] Certainly, schools must help students to build their basic skills, but the issue is how best to do that. We believe that it is by emphasizing real or authentic world learning experiences and making connections to students' actual interest and strengths. We believe, then, that assessment too must follow this path.

Make Assessment Authentic and Linked to Learning

Deborah Meier in her recent book, *Will Standards Save Public Education?* points to Chicago as the "home of get tough reform" where test scores have risen by only 3.4 percent over the past three years, an increase that amounts to maybe two or three additional correct answers on the standardized test.[22] In the meantime, school dropout rates continue to be high, raising questions about the overall efficacy of the high-stakes testing program.

A recent report on *60 Minutes* indicates that in Texas only 27 percent of teachers believe rising test scores on the Texas Achievement Test reflect real gains in student learning. Students are reportedly able to pass the test, yet are not able to read or think critically. Indeed, at the same time that the number of students "passing" the tests in Texas has increased, the percentage of students who enter the Texas University system and need remedial work is at an all-time high.[23] Again, tests such as those administered in Texas and most other states provide teachers with little understanding of what students actually know or what can be done to unlock the barriers to learning. Rather, these tests are designed to compare and rank students and schools at a single point in time.

What type of assessments would make more sense? We believe assessments that measure authentic learning experiences (as described in Chapter 3) are the only "tests" that actually promote learning for both the student and teacher. Students can learn from the immediate feedback they receive. Teachers also can learn about what students can do as well as the challenges students face. The only way to obtain this kind of information is through more authentic classroom assessment.

Performance-based assessments can measure student ability to think deeply, to concentrate, and to perform. These assessments examine what students know and can do in ways that reveal what they understand, how they understand it, and the strategies that they use. Such practice can be encouraged through exhibitions of student work in learning portfolios, problem-based learning projects, and actual performances such as speaking, writing and problem solving. Commercially developed norm-referenced tests need to be replaced with assessments that match state standards and measure them in authentic ways. If we are to promote authentic learning rather than rote, then our assessments need to match.

If we are to promote authentic learning, then our assessments need to match.

Finally, good assessments should take into account student growth over time. We need to understand where students start, and then track their growth relative to these starting points. Many students who score low are actually making high relative-growth gains but may still be below an arbitrary point for meeting a standard. When traditionally low-achieving students are assessed, it is to be expected that growth will be measured relative to their starting place. We believe that building on how far a student has progressed should be emphasized rather than dismissed.

Demonstrate Learning Progress with Multiple Forms of Evidence

Experts in assessment all agree that relying on any one measure of student achievement is a poor practice. Yet, in a growing numbers of states, student retention and even graduation are linked to single high-stakes tests. We believe that students should have the opportunity to demonstrate their learning in a variety of formats. We prefer Howard Gardner's proposition, "The question is not how smart you are but how you are smart." Some examples of alternative formats for assessing how students are "smart" include:

The question is not how smart you are; but how you are smart.

Performance-Based Assessments

♦ Portfolios

♦ Problem-based learning projects

♦ Exhibitions or presentations

♦ Science experiments and social studies simulations

♦ Public speaking

♦ Performances

♦ Mathematics problem solving

♦ Written essays

♦ Teacher observation

♦ Videos

♦ Student-led conferences

All of these formats mirror real-world work. They involve students in actually doing what people in the workplace do—writing articles, doing research, performing, giving talks, etc. At Central Park East School, all students must keep a portfolio organized around 14 different areas ranging from literature, history, and ethics to science, math, media, etc. The students then present seven of these areas to a graduation committee (two faculty members, an adult of the student's choice, and another student) for questioning and defense. Our educational administration program at Portland State University utilizes the same approach; students must demonstrate proficiency in 9 of 16 state-developed standards. The examining committee is comprised of the school site administrator/mentor, a university supervisor, and invited guests of the students' choice. The standards are clear, the work is authentic, and the level of concern and commitment to doing well is high. The presentation of the portfolio is an exhibition of student work and a demonstration of their ability to articulate what they did, why they did it, and what they learned.

Teachers do not have to learn a host of new skills in order to assess student learning more holistically; indeed many already do so. We have been impressed by the expanding roles that teachers already play in classroom assessments. In our work, we've already seen teachers giving specific skill tests, keeping a running record of individual student reading fluency, giving unit tests, collecting work samples in portfolios, compiling scores on the learning of math concepts, conducting student interviews, developing tests for independent reading, and breaking down the data provided in the Oregon state tests. We are struck by how skillful and comfortable many teachers have become in assessing their students. Such evidence shows that what many teachers do is a far cry from just "winging it" and claiming that they just intuitively "know" how much their students have learned.

Many teachers already engage in holistic assessment.

We're also encouraged by the growing use of student-led parent conferences wherein students present samples of their work to their parents or guardians. There is time for joint reflection and an expectation for specific family goal setting to support the student in her or his future work. The teacher is available to answer questions, but students are clearly in charge of their own assessment. These conferences provide students with an opportunity to showcase their work as well as to explain how they believe that parents and teachers should assess the quality of their work.

Encourage Teachers to Adopt a Constructivist Orientation

With the rise of high-stakes testing has come an increased tendency to utilize direct instruction, which is primarily a behavioral or skill-based orientation to the curriculum (a teacher in one of our schools refers to this as a "drill and kill" orientation). Worksheets, memorization, and basic-level rote activities tend to predominate. Although some direct instructional practices may be appropriate, a reliance on this approach can supercede enrichment activities such as field trips, science experiments, projects, and simulations. The rise in direct instruction has followed the high premium placed on meeting state standards as measured by statewide assessments. However, given the reality of the standards movement, it is crucial that your leadership team gives teachers the encouragement to adopt a constructivist or powerful learning orientation towards their teaching.

School leadership must encourage powerful learning throughout the school.

As mentioned in Chapter 3, it is important to encourage teachers to think of the characteristics of powerful learning experiences in their own lives as they plan their lessons and learning activities. Teachers should be supported as they facilitate understanding that can only occur when students are actively engaged in creating meaning and new understanding themselves. Teachers will want to establish learning situations that facilitate authentic student experiences, which in turn lead to a clear connection between content and life experiences. As Falk reminds us, we must move away from teaching as telling and toward teaching as listening. We believe that test scores can improve as a by-product of a constructivist orientation and powerful learning experiences.

Differentiate Instruction to Accommodate the Needs of an Increasingly Diverse Student Population

Meeting the needs of an increasingly diverse student population has become a major challenge for schools in the twenty-first century. Most industrialized countries have attempted to handle this problem by adopting strict tracking policies based upon standardized test scores. For example, career choices for students in Japan are pretty much established by the time they complete middle school and enter into a particular type of high school. This process begins in middle school, where students are sorted into one of five levels of high school depending on their test scores and work habits.

A national policy such as this rubs against the grain of espoused basic American beliefs about equity and the opportunity to succeed through public education. Of course, in the U.S. we still have considerable *de facto* tracking based upon residential patterns and we still place students in classes that, in the end, result in tracking. Still, one of our greatest challenges is that of educating increasingly diverse students with differing abilities, interests, and life circumstances.

Our largest challenge is educating diverse students who come to school with differing abilities and interests.

The one-room schoolhouse provides a useful metaphor for how this challenge may be addressed. In this environment, teachers work with a roomful of students of varying ages and stages of learning. In such an environment the teacher usually does little lecturing and typically divides the students into flexible groups based upon the skills to be learned and interest rather than grade level or age. The teacher circulates from group to group, facilitating student learning with individualized assignments and feedback. Oftentimes, the teacher arranges for students to be grouped in a manner that facilitates peer coaching and cooperative learning.

The one-room schoolhouse is really about what some experts refer to as differentiated instruction.[24] A basic assumption of differentiated instruction is that learners need different and multiple approaches to the content, process, products and assessment of learning. It is more than giving some students more or less to do, but involves changing the very nature of instructional strategy. Differentiated instruction is, above all, student-centered and consistent with a constructivist or powerful learning orientation. It is grounded in the belief that learning experiences are most effective when they are engaging, relevant, and interesting. It is a blend of whole-class, small group, and individualized instruction. A variety of instructional groupings are used depending on the desired learning outcomes. Specific content examples include curriculum compacting (as students demonstrate mastery of the curriculum, they are permitted to progress at their own rates) and learning contracts. Process examples include interest centers or groups, interactive journals, and tiered assignments. Products include cooperative group projects, student-initiated projects, and building on diverse learner strengths. Finally, differentiated assessments include peer review, portfolios, and individual conferencing.

Differentiated instruction focuses on multiple approaches to teaching and learning.

Get Feedback from Outside Friendly Critics

One lesson learned from recent school reform work is that schools benefit from regular external assessment or validation of their school change efforts (see discussion of the school review in Chapter 5). The Coalition of Essential Schools uses what they call "critical friends" for dialogue and for providing feedback to their schools. In the Accelerated Schools Project, mentors from the various satellite centers visit the schools periodically to observe classrooms, sit in on task group meetings, and meet with the leadership team and interview participants. A written report is then developed and shared with the school community. Alfie Kohn insists that the best way to judge schools is by visiting them and looking for evidence of learning and interest in learning.[25] He has developed an observation checklist that we recommend (see Tool 6.1, pp. 177–178). The goal of school visits by critical friends is to hold up a mirror to reflect the quality of teaching and learning. Such visits encourage a culture of self-assessment and continuous improvement in the school.

Critical friends can hold a mirror up to current practices and ask: "is this what you want to be doing?"

Embed Assessment into the Learning Process of Your School

In Chapter 2, we introduced the concept of an inquiry process that would be used to help South Central School in the implementation of Project Improve. The inquiry process consists of five phases:

1. Focus on a challenging and meaningful problem
2. Explore solutions
3. Synthesize the solutions and develop an action plan
4. Pilot test the plan
5. Evaluate the results and reassess.

Tool 6.1. What to Look for in a Classroom: A Visitor's Guide

	Good Signs	*Possible Reasons for Worry*
Furniture	Chairs around tables to facilitate interaction. Comfortable areas for learning; multiple "activity centers." Open space for gathering.	Chairs all facing forward or (even worse) desks in rows.
Walls	Covered with students' projects. Evidence of student collaboration. Signs, exhibits, or lists created by students rather than by the teacher. Information about, and personal mementos of, those who spend time together in this classroom.	Bare. Commercial posters. Students' assignments displayed but they are suspiciously flawless, only from "the best" students, or virtually all alike. List of rules created by an adult and/or list of punitive consequences for misbehavior. Sticker (or star) chart or other evidence that students are rewarded or ranked.
Faces	Eager, engaged.	Blank, bored.
Sounds	Frequent hum of activity and ideas being exchanged.	Teacher's voice is the loudest or most often heard. Frequent periods of silence.
Location of teacher	Typically working with students so that it takes a few seconds to find him or her.	Typically front and center.
Teacher's voice	Respectful, genuine, warm.	Controlling and imperious. Condescending and saccharine-sweet.
Students' reaction to visitor	Welcoming; eager to explain or demonstrate what they're doing or use visitor as a resource.	Either unresponsive or hoping to be distracted from what they're doing.

Tool 6.1. Teaching and Learning Observation Checklist (continued)

Class discussion	Students often address one another directly. Emphasis on thoughtful exploration of complicated issues. Students ask questions at least as often as teacher does.	All exchanges involve (or are directed by) the teacher; students wait to be called on. Emphasis on facts and right answers. Students race to be first to answer teacher's "who can tell me?" queries.
Stuff	Room overflowing with good books, art, supplies, animals, and plants, science apparatus; sense of "purposeful clutter."	Textbooks, worksheets, and other packaged instructional materials predominate; sense of enforced orderliness.
Tasks	Different activities take place simultaneously. Activities frequently completed by pairs or groups of students.	All students usually do the same thing. When students aren't listening to the teacher, they're working alone.
Around the school	Appealing atmosphere. Student's projects fill hallway walls. Library well-stocked and comfortable. Bathrooms in good condition. Faculty lounge warm and inviting. Office staff welcoming toward visitors and students. Students helping in lunchroom, library, and with other school functions.	Stark, institutional feel. Award, trophies, and prizes displayed, suggesting emphasis on triumph rather than community.

We believe that an inquiry process such as that used at South Central lies at the heart of a school wherein assessment is integral to the way people think about how to improve student learning. When members of a school community create an inquiry process that requires information (rather than sentiment) to drive decision making, they have taken a bold step. They have begun to move their school or district out of an environment where what is "best for kids" is decided by politics and persuasion to one where decisions stem from the results of reasonable and disciplined inquiry.

Most schools do not have an inquiry process that is integral to their school culture. They tend to make decisions about the direction of change in an *ad hoc* manner, depending, in part, on who is advocating for what and who has power or authority. Oftentimes, what is determined as needed for student improvement is the result of a power struggle between competing interest groups, either within the school or between the school and the central office/community/teacher's association, etc. When these conditions exist—where decisions are made based mostly on which side can overpower the other—then the school or district is caught in an escalating spiral where winning means everything, even if it's at the expense of what is truly "best for kids."

An inquiry process that is dedicated to evaluation as well as assessment issues lies at the heart of a school that is serious about continuous improvement. Senge, *et al.,* talk about a continuous improvement process with a bit of a different twist from that we've proposed.[26] In their model, Senge and his colleagues emphasize that in a continuous improvement process, you never return to the same place from which you began. Rather, you are always moving to a new level—each level being defined from what you've learned from inquiry at the previous level. Like any good research process, then, inquiry is the yeast of further inquiry (see Figure 6.1).

In a continuous improvement process, you never return to the place where you started.

Only by creating an environment for continuous improvement can evaluation and assessment become an activity that permeates your organization. There is, however, a fundamental matter that leadership teams need to address if evaluation and assessment are to become vehicles for such system-wide learning. This issue concerns the key role of leadership teams in facilitating such a shift to system-wide learning and ultimately identifying strategies for successful evaluation and assessment. In the remainder of this section we discuss this issue.

Leadership teams, we believe, must play a key role in facilitating individuals, groups, and organizations in the direction of continuous improvement. These roles, however, must be focused on providing leadership in evaluation and assessment rather than just managing assessment. Stiggins makes a clear distinction between managing assessment and providing leadership in the area of assessment, as summarized below:[27]

It's important to distinguish between managing assessment and leading assessment.

Figure 6.1. Feedback Spiral of Assessment

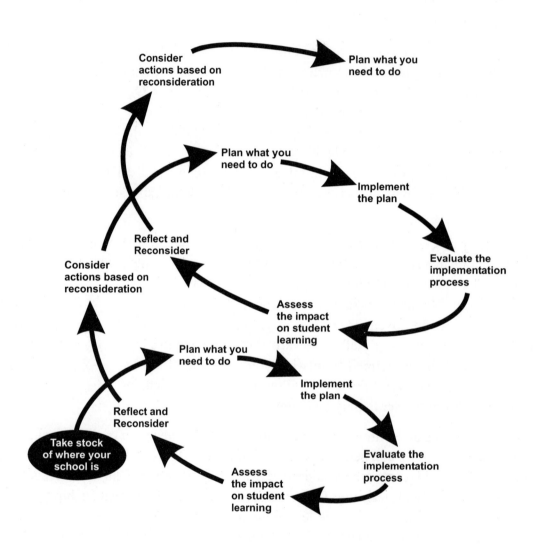

Managing Assessment

♦ Following the existing procedures for assessment

♦ Making sure that teachers do not go outside of current procedures

♦ All policies and procedures are written and followed

♦ Purpose of assessment is raising standardized test scores

Leading Assessment

♦ Developing new procedures to meet new needs

♦ Encouraging teachers to think beyond current procedures

♦ Policies and procedures provide some latitude for implementation

♦ Focus on improving learning; improved outcomes will follow

Note the difference between these two approaches. The management function makes the assumption that you already know what needs to be "measured" and that the school's job is simply to go out and "do it." This places the leadership team in the position of "the enforcer"—making sure that teachers do what is expected of them (usually by some outside authority). This is what we have now in many schools, with principals charged with cracking the whip on teachers in order to raise test scores.

The leadership function, on the other hand, involves an entire staff in a problem-solving approach to assessment. The leadership team encourages system-wide learning by posing the questions and dilemmas of student learning and inviting wide-ranging participation in helping to solve these dilemmas. The team might say, for example, "We know that our students aren't reading as well as they should, and our statewide assessments are one data source that tells us this. How can we create a reading effort that meets the needs of our students—many of whom don't come from an environment where reading occurs?" Although the leadership team sets the context, it invites everyone who will ultimately contribute to the solutions to play a role in designing those solutions and in decisions concerning how they know when the journey is successful.

To accomplish these goals for assessment (as well as many other elements of change) it is important to remember that changing the way in which assessment is viewed and carried out must occur at three levels: *individual, group,* and *organizational.*[28] All of these levels contribute to the culture of organizational learning, which must be pervasive if quality evaluation and assessment strategies are to emerge.

At the *individual* level, it's important for the leadership team to recognize that individuals make changes in the way they evaluate their work when they "confront situations for which old ways are not adequate, which require new ways of thinking and acting."[29] The team's role with individuals is to provide a supportive environment within which individual teachers can

Individuals change when they realize that old practices are not adequate.

grow and change when confronted with information that reveals insufficient student growth. Part of growing and changing involves helping teachers to not only consider giving up some instructional strategies that aren't working but also to consider potentially risky strategies that might work more effectively. And in providing that supportive environment, we mean that the team should first and foremost give individual teachers permission to admit that something at which they worked very hard may have failed, and that in failure are the seeds of future success.

At the *group* level, your team will want to provide opportunities and the needed skills for people to interact and learn from each other. As we know from the literature on effective groups, providing these opportunities for group learning will not work unless you also provide

Groups provide an environment for individual and collective learning.

the support and motivation to work through the complexity of group processes. These typical group processes—termed by Mulford as "formin', stormin', normin' and performin'"—focus on how groups, just like individuals, contribute to organizational learning but in a somewhat different manner.[30] Group learning evolves from the group formation process, working through disagreements, recalibrating the direction of the team, and, finally, setting a new course. Thus, when a group discusses and debates how it is they will "know" when student learning has improved, they are going through a process of collectively discussing not only what the assessment data tell them about student learning, but they are also beginning to consider surrendering some of the practices they once thought were productive. Next, of course, come discussions about replacing these failed practices with new practices, as well as considering the criteria for assessing the impact of these new practices. We believe that schools that work collectively can develop very powerful learning strategies, and it is important for the leadership team to set the parameters for groups to be actively involved in ongoing assessment.

At the *organizational* level, learning about assessment occurs as the school builds into its culture a series of feedback loops that permit and encourage the development of evaluation

Organizations reinforce a culture that encourages individual and collective learning.

and assessment strategies to new and different levels (see Senge model noted earlier in this section). School-wide initiatives designed to have an impact on student learning must be examined within the context of their purpose and the information that addresses that purpose. If the assessment results indicate that those purposes are not being met, then the initiatives need to be rigorously examined. Indeed, the school culture must support eliminating those initiatives or programs that do not meet their goal of improved student learning. Although this might seem a radical step to take (and it would be in some instances), the prospect of such a decision means that, as a school, you've obligated yourselves to specify the criteria for making these decisions. Furthermore, you have established a culture that permits hard decisions to be taken should these criteria not be met.

Organizational learning is important because it commits the organization to make decisions that have system-wide implications. Because schools are, as Sarason has noted, indeed systemic entities, the use of quality information to make these cultural changes must be the primary vehicle for continuous improvement. Only when we use evaluation and assessment results that are discussed and debated by individuals and groups and applied to the organizational level can we truly create a learning organization.

Nonetheless, it is important to understand that organizational learning and continuous improvement in the assessment domain does not necessarily mean that things always get better. All schools are part of a larger environment, and are limited in a number of ways by that environment. The manner in which educational standards are assessed is one of those limitations. Organizational learning means devising ways to be successful within the context of the standards, but not just limiting success to those assessment strategies alone. Said more bluntly, the standards are here for the foreseeable future, and so are the narrow ways in which we measure them. We believe, however, that leadership teams can play a critical role in transforming schools that live within this admittedly less-than-ideal environment and at the same time still work with their teachers and staff to change those very conditions that are so limiting.

Leadership teams can help organizations to learn even when conditions the organization faces are less than ideal.

Chapter Summary

We began our discussion with a brief look at historical trends and contextual issues that have contributed to the current national obsession with raising student achievement and meeting state standards. In discussing these developments, we asked a number of important questions: What are the effects on students and teachers? What are the realities of classrooms in this new accountability environment? How can teachers learn to value evaluation and assessment and view them as part of the school redesign process in which they become proactive change agents?

We concluded by focusing more directly on what it is that must be evaluated and assessed. Evaluation of the actual implementation of change as well as the impact of change on student learning becomes the focus. A variety of alternative assessment strategies that will help schools redefine accountability beyond their reliance on standardized tests were also presented. Finally, we argued that the assessment of student learning needs to become part of the school's standard operating procedures, embedded in a culture of organizational learning and continuous improvement.

In the final chapter, we summarize the points that you'll want to emphasize as you navigate school change in your building.

Reculturing Map

How do you know when you have arrived?

Increase:	*Decrease:*
☐ Problem solving process	☐ Band-aid solutions
☐ Reflective practice	☐ Leaping to solutions
☐ Use of alternative assessment strategies	☐ Reliance on standardized testing
☐ Investment of time and resources for evaluation and assessment	☐ Making excuses that there is not enough time or resources for evaluation and assessment
☐ Internally driven evaluation and assessment	☐ Externally driven evaluation and assessment
☐ Ongoing evaluation and assessment	☐ Episodic evaluation and assessment
☐ All students meeting standards	☐ Only select students meeting standards
☐ Powerful learning	☐ Rote learning
☐ An enrichment approach	☐ Remediation
☐ Identification of student strengths	☐ Identification of student deficiencies
☐ Differentiated instruction	☐ Whole-group instruction
☐ Focus on student learning	☐ Singular focus on raising test scores

References

1. The National Commission on Excellence in Education. (April 1983). *A nation at risk.* Washington, DC: U.S. Government Printing Office.

2. The Commission on Achieving Necessary Skills. (1991). *America's choice: high skills or low wages?* Washington, DC: U.S. Government Printing Office.

3. Cushman, K. (November 1993). How the national standards debate affects the essential school. *Horace, 10*(2). Coalition of Essential Schools.

4. The Commission on Achieving Necessary Skills. *America's choice: high skills or low wages?*, op. cit.

5. Merrow Report. (1997). *In schools we trust.* Washington, DC: Corporation for Public Broadcasting, Annenberg/CPB.

6. Graham, P. (February 1993). What America has expected of its schools over the past century. *American Journal of Education, 101*, 85.

7. Editors (January 11, 2001). Seeking stability for standards-based education: Executive summary, *Education Week, XX*(17), 8–9.

8. Wilson, K. G., & Daviss, B. (1994). *Redesigning education.* New York: Henry Holt.

9. Ibid., p. 138.

10. Darling-Hammond, L. (1997). *The right to learn.* San Francisco: Jossey-Bass, p. 213.

11. Charters, W.W., Jr., & Jones, J. E. (1973). On the risk of appraising non-events in program evaluation. *Educational Researcher, 2*(1), 5–7.

12. Glickman, C. (1993). *Renewing America's schools: a guide for school based action.* San Francisco: Jossey-Bass.

13. Falk, B. (2000). *The heart of the matter: Using standards and assessment to learn.* Portsmouth, NH: Heinemann.

14. Conley, D. (1993). *Roadmap to restructuring.* University of Oregon: ERIC Clearinghouse on Educational Management.

15. Lambert, L. (1995). *The constructivist leader.* New York: Teachers College Press.

16. Hopfenberg, W., & Levin, H. (1993). *The accelerated schools resource guide.* San Francisco: Jossey-Bass.

17. Finnan, C., St. John, E., McCarthy, J., & Slovacek, S. (Eds.). (1996). *Accelerated schools in action: Lessons from the field.* Thousand Oaks CA: Corwin Press.

18. Hartman, R. (Producer). (September 10, 2000). Testing, testing, testing. *60 Minutes.* Columbia Broadcasting System (CBS).

19. Kohn, A. (2000). *The case against standardized testing.* Portsmouth, NH: Heinemann.

20. Means, B., & Knapp, M. (1991). Introduction: Rethinking teaching for disadvantaged students. In B. Means, C. Chelemer, & M. S. Knapp (Eds.), *Teaching advanced skills to at-risk students: Views from the research.* San Francisco: Jossey-Bass, p, 9.

21. Falk. *The heart of the matter,* op. cit., p. 53.

22. Meier, D. (2000). *Will standards save public education?* New York: Teachers College Press.

23. Hartman, R. *Testing, testing, testing,* op. cit.

24. Tomilson, C. (1995). *How to differentiate instruction in mixed-ability classrooms.* Alexandria, VA: The Association for Supervision and Curriculum Development (ASCD).

25. Kohn, A. *The case against standardized testing*, op. cit.

26. Senge, P., Cambron-McCabe, N., Lucas, T., Smith, B., Dutton, J., & Kleiner, A.. (2000). *Schools that learn.* New York: Doubleday.

27. Stiggins, R. J. (2000). The principal's assessment responsibilities. In W. G. Wraga & P. S. Hlebowitsh (Eds.), *Research review for school leaders* (Vol. 3). Mahwah NJ: Lawrence Erlbaum, p. 212.

28. Mulford, B. Organizational learning and educational change. In Hargreaves A., Lieberman, A., Fullan, M., & Hopkins, D. (Eds.). *The international handbook of educational change.* London: Kluwer Academic Publishers, pp. 616-641.

29. Ibid., p. 622.

30. Ibid., p. 625.

CONCLUSIONS—AND (NEW) BEGINNINGS

Chapter Highlights

♦ *Schools must rethink the way they think.* When change is all around, schools must consider making responsible changes in the way they operate. The first step is to change the way they think about what they do.

♦ *Utilize a design model to think through what it is you need to change.* A design model can help to define the problem, provide a problem-solving process, and direct the collection of data on the progress of change.

♦ *Build a culture of change that celebrates learning—in students and in the school organization itself.* A learning culture is the "engine" that drives continuous improvement.

♦ *When all else fails, remember three points:*

☐ A problem well-defined is a problem half-solved.

☐ An inquiry process is key to working through the problem as defined.

☐ Be relentless in the use of quality information to assess the progress you are making on the problem.

Rethink the Way We Think About Schooling

We began this book with a set of five assumptions about the change process. We argued that the change process is highly complex and in many ways occurs within the context of specific local environments. Because the environments within which a school or district exist are indeed so rich and varied, it is almost impossible to import a change effort from the outside and expect it to be successful. The reality is that there is no shortcut to successful change; it needs to be designed, implemented, and sustained from within individual schools.

Yet, we believe that there are factors that are imperative to successful change. These factors are critical regardless of the thrust of the change effort within your school. We've addressed these factors throughout this book, particularly in the chronicling of the change effort at South Central Middle School. Let's briefly review what happened at South Central with regard to these five assumptions.

At South Central, Mary knew the importance of involving the staff in Project Improve. She also believed it was important that a smaller group of teachers work with her in order to design and implement Project Improve. For this reason, one of the first decisions she made in the first few months at the school was to recruit a team of staff and community members to serve on the leadership team. She selected these individuals based upon recommendations of the staff and used some funds from the district office to release team members from some teaching responsibilities during the school year. The responsibilities of the leadership team members were many—advocating, guiding, and helping where needed and, mostly, listening. Listening was especially important, not only because teachers needed to have a place to go where they would be heard, but also because it symbolized the importance which the principal placed upon clear and open communications.

A second (and related) assumption we made about the change process was the importance of it occurring within a democratic environment. Most schools say that they respect democratic principles in the operation of their school, yet unfortunately few successfully practice it. Too often we find change is directed or mandated from a person or persons in authority. Although leaders might say that staff and community members will have "input' into the nature of the change, too often participants discover that their input has little or no substantial effect on the end results.

Bringing about lasting change is too difficult to occur in such a make-believe environment. At South Central School, Mary spent much of her first few months in the school talking to her staff and community members identifying the elements that would make constituents especially proud of their school. She refused to be swayed by the management mythology that there is but a brief "honeymoon" when a new administrator comes to a school, and that big changes need to occur during that honeymoon or they will not occur at all. Instead, she patiently worked (assisted by us as technical advisors) with the staff in a visioning process that resulted in a clearly articulated plan (Project Improve) of where they wished to go. Mary knew full well that there would be many roadblocks in the process of transforming South Central school, and that she'd have to "go to the well' with her staff a number of times. To call upon the support of everyone clearly meant that it was important that everyone have the commitment to overcome obstacles. Such commitment can only come from staff when they know that they play an integral role in the results. Creating commitment means honestly valuing the contributions of everyone, then making the best decisions possible; there are no shortcuts.

Such a broad-based involvement supports broad-based change—comprehensive change. One of the unfortunate and most persistent patterns of change in schools is to adopt discrete change packages (a new reading or math program, a different strategy for student discipline, a different pattern of student grouping) without consideration for how it all fits together. And therein lies the problem—such isolated changes don't reinforce each other and thereby there is too little consideration for the whole. Schools are systems of human ecology, no less interrelated than systems in the natural world—plant and animal systems for example. A central tenet of ecology is that everything is related to everything else, and this is true in human systems as well. We believe strongly that the change effort has to be united by a common and continual effort to address how it all fits together, which is one of the key reasons for our insistence on the place of vision in the school change effort.

All successful change inevitably requires a change in the culture of the school. Seymour Sarason made that point some 30 years ago, and it is even truer today than it was then. Yet, educators are continually surprised and somewhat perplexed by the number of situations wherein change is attempted and ultimately struggles.

A good example is what is happening within the standards movement. The presence of standards and their measurement at various levels of a child's schooling clearly signals the need for teachers to work much more closely together regarding what is taught, when, and by whom. Teaching in a self-contained classroom with little coordination between teachers is not the type of school structure that will optimize the meeting of educational standards. Furthermore, superimposing a new structure without considering the values, practices, and rewards that accompany a new structure is bound to be a force field that acts against successful change. This was recognized by the leadership team at South Central, which is why they eventually restructured the school into teaching teams of two to four people who remained with the same group of students for their entire three years at the school. It's also why Mary didn't stop at the creation of teams, but began the process of reculturing so that new values and norms could support the teaming effort. Different goals, then, often require different educational arrangements, and we must be willing to seek out the arrangements that best meet the objectives of the change initiative.

And what about all of this is related to student learning? How easily we often forget that any effort at school change had better make a difference in student learning or it probably isn't worth the effort. This is even more important in an era wherein the expectations for student learning are so high, in part because the consequences of large sectors of our society not being well prepared are also so great. Although we believe strongly that a focus on student learning can produce positive results, we don't support the current system wherein student achievement on norm-referenced tests is equated with student learning. Achievement scores are only a small element of learning, and we are committed to change that supports a broad-based view of student learning rather than just drilling students to do well on standardized tests.

To paraphrase Einstein, when everything changes around us, we need to change our way of thinking about what is around us.

Utilize a Design Model to Guide the Change Process

As we introduced in Chapter 2, South Central School realized early in the change game that they could not tackle comprehensive change without the aid of a design model for thinking through change. They needed to be aware of the critical issues that might be raised at different points in time and to have helpful clues as to how to solve these problems when they arose. The school selected Project Improve because they saw it as a design model that would aid them in these steps. Project Improve was helpful, because as the amorphous and oftentimes chaotic process of change swept over the school and created in the school staff a felling of helplessness, the guidelines of the Project provided useful touch points of how to think about change and how to problem-solve. Project Improve was by no means the only change design model that the South Central staff could have utilized and, in some instances, it may not have been the best model. But it worked for them, and that's what was important.

Wilson and Daviss argue that the absence of a design process is ultimately what kills the change process in schools. They believe, and rightly so, that almost every time we consider major change in our schools, we start from scratch. Educators fail to take advantage of what's been learned in the past and go about the process in an almost random manner, trying a little of this and a little of that, hoping that eventually something will "work" and create the desired effect. If aircraft were designed on the premise that we had learned little or nothing about aircraft design since Kitty Hawk, then we'd still be flying with a few people in each plane for very short distances at extremely low altitudes. It's no wonder, then, that change in our schools seems to be so fraught with dead ends, partial successes, and, ultimately, failures.

We increase our chances of successful change when we have a design for thinking about change. Although design models may differ, a useful design will help a school leadership team in a number of important ways. First, it should assist the team in thinking through the identification of a high-stakes problem and the rationale for selecting that problem. Remember, this problem is going to be the hallmark of your change effort—the "brand" that indicates what your change effort is attempting to achieve, and why. When the going gets especially tough and you ask each other why you're still persisting in the face of so much difficulty, it is this crucial problem identified earlier to which you will return over and over.

Second, the design model should be of assistance as you develop a routine for problem solving. At the end of Chapter 2 we present an inquiry model that is based on Deweyian principles that has been used successfully in the Accelerated Schools Project. This inquiry model is useful because it helps remind us that there is a deliberate manner by which we can encounter problems and come up with possible solutions. Use of such an inquiry model helps slow down the rush to solutions that is so typical in school change. So often, we create solutions that are based on virtually everything except a considered process of examining the reasons why the problem exists and then identifying alternatives and choosing from among them. In the absence of an inquiry model, solutions arise out of power and influence of the people who propose them rather than a deliberate process of identification and testing.

The third essential value of a design model is the critical role of accurate assessment and evaluation data. Inasmuch as possible, decisions about what to adopt, modify, or eliminate should be made on the basis of reliable data that sheds light on the focus of the change effort. Now, we don't for a moment believe that one can ever find enough data that will point the way with such precision that there will never be questions and doubts. However, we do believe that the availability of good assessment and evaluation data helps to frame the questions pertaining to important decisions in the change process. As Wilson and Daviss point out, the evolution of commercial aircraft depended upon reliable information from prior trials and experiments, which, in turn, led to design modifications and subsequent tests of those modifications. Although children's learning is probably much more complex and unpredictable than even the flight of an airplane, change can become more substantive when it follows a similar trajectory of using good information to inform the change process.

Build a Culture of Change that Celebrates Organizational Learning

Having a way of thinking about change is more than just a tool to direct action, though that in and of itself is a definite improvement over what exists in most schools. As a way of thinking becomes embedded in the very fabric of your school, it then starts to become a way of doing things—your way of doing things. A design model such as that described in this book became, for South Central, the South Central model for school improvement. Over time, what began as a design for thinking "morphed" into a way of organizing people, a way of decision making, a way of relating to outside groups, and a way of distributing resources, both real as well as symbolic. A well thought out design for change emerges into the threads that bind together the tapestry that reflects the nature of the school. Because these threads are not randomly arranged but arranged with a purpose, they contribute to a tapestry with an identity. It's what can be called a "system."

Systems are elements that are interrelated to produce a greater whole. Understanding the elements means awareness of how they work together to create that whole. But systems are not static; rather, they continually change. How they change is the key issue for schools. The system can change in the absence of intentionality on the part of the members, and that change might be either beneficial or harmful to the overall purpose of the whole. On the other hand, systems that are understood and then designed and redesigned have a better chance of producing beneficial results than those that change without such design. When a school has a design model that involves staff in constructing a culture of change and learning from the results of trying things out, then we say that the school is becoming a learning organization. That is exactly the direction South Central was traveling.

Peter Senge is notable in his attention to the importance of learning organizations in the change process. He talks about three essential components of learning systems. First, every organization is a product of how its members think and interact. This follows what we reviewed above—that the way of thinking in a school directly influences how the school will operate. Too often in schools, we focus on changing the operations of the organization without addressing the way in which members think about the organization. This is what Sarason meant when he noted that, in school change, the more things change the more they remain the same. We can't just overlay existing perspectives, values, and ideologies with a new structure or program and expect it to work. A learning organization understands the need to examine how the organization thinks and therefore what needs to be addressed first is the thinking process. This takes time, but in the long run is more powerful than jumping to solutions.

Second, Senge argues that a learning organization realizes that learning is connections. When students enter a school, they have little conception about knowledge being segmented into things we call "subjects" and (later) "disciplines." Students have questions, interests, and curiosities, which often involve more than a single subject or way of thinking about that subject. In turn, students will be more motivated to learn when the connections that they bring to a question remain intact (one of the compelling reasons for project learning or problem-based learning). Accordingly, a learning organization understands the importance of the connections between elements—that problems cannot just be isolated into reading problems or computational problems or motivational problems. Rather, these are learning problems that must be addressed. The design process is a vehicle for doing just that.

Finally, and this will not be surprising, learning is driven by vision. A learning organization can better utilize the many elements of a system because its members have a vision of what the overall tapestry should look like. They are unwilling to settle for random patterns that may or (most likely) may not lead to an intended outcome. Schools as learning organizations have a powerful vision around which they organize their thinking and their action. It's no wonder that schools with a working vision are most likely to produce an ongoing series of artful tapestries; that's what they intended to do.

Remember the "Keys" to the Future of Change in Your School

We end this book with an observation from Michael Fullan, one that we believe summarizes the essence of our message:

> The shame of educational change is the squandering of good intentions and the waste of resources in light of personal and societal needs of great human consequence. The capacity to bring about change and the capacity to bring about improvement are two different things. Change is everywhere, improvement is not. The more things change the more they remain the same, if we do not learn our lessons then a different mind-and action-set is required.[1]

Improvement is, as Fullan notes, the real meaning of educational change. The literature on the process of educational change is replete with study after study of things that didn't work; conversely, there is a paucity of literature on what did work. The purpose of this book has been to give you guidance so that you can increase the odds of school change leading to school improvement.

We know that there is a lot of material to digest in this book. But the most important element of the change process is not as much what facts, knowledge or tricks you've accumulated as it is how you think about the change process. As a leadership team, one of your main responsibilities is to play a key role in managing the change process, and this means helping all the people in your school community sift through all the "stuff" and be able to focus on what's important more than on what's urgent. And without a template to aid you in the management of the change process, it's too easy to become distracted, lose focus, or be involved in change, not improvement.

In the Preface to the book we mentioned a school district (Memphis) that had just decided to terminate its five-year experiment with comprehensive change as advocated in this book.* Although we are too far removed from the Memphis situation to fully understand the district's decision, we wonder: what was learned from this experiment? Was the fact that standardized test scores hadn't increased the only reason for the decision? Did the district consider the impact of the decision on the hundreds and thousands of people who had put so much energy into

---

* Indeed, in November 2001, *Education Week* published an article in which recent research from RAND on comprehensive school reform was summarized. While the article reported that a comprehensive reform has yet to make a definitive difference in student performance, it also points out that it is too early to say whether or not such initiatives "really work." We believe that, properly implemented, they will. See Viadero, D. (November 7, 2001). Whole-school projects show mixed results. *Education Week, 21*(10), 1, 24–25.

these changes over the past five years? We wonder also about the advertised return to the enhancement of fundamental skills and why that is believed to be a solution? Most importantly, does the district have a design model guiding its decision on these matters?

Because it seems that most good advice comes in threes, let us leave you with three "must remembers."

**Three "Must Remembers" for
More Successful Change**

♦ Know what it is that needs to be changed

♦ Have a design process that leads you through the change process

♦ Have an evaluation/assessment plan that tells you how you are doing

---

First, remember Dewey's recognition that a problem well-defined is a problem half-solved. Think carefully and regularly about the problems you need to tackle and the improvements you need to make in your school. As much as possible, begin with information that helps define the nature of the problem, then think through the destination you wish to reach. We believe that student learning should lie at the heart of a school's journey, and that a comprehensive vision is critical to the improvement of student learning. As the journey moves along, keep in mind the destination you wish to reach.

Second, develop or use a process for thinking through how you'll plot the course toward the desired destination. We've argued throughout this book (through the Project Improve analogy) that you must have a process in mind for thinking about change as well as managing change. By thinking about pre-initiation, building commitment, implementation, sustaining change, and evaluating/assessing change, you can concentrate your energies on certain activities that need attention at certain developmental stages of the change process. By having an approach to problem solving, you develop a process that guides decision making and helps to build a culture of continuous improvement. This is critical because we need to get away from beginning each change effort as if we have no history on which to build. Your goal must be to arrange the building blocks of a significantly different school culture.

Finally, remember the importance of evaluation and assessment. Too often neither of these occurs. We believe that if the change does not lead to improved student learning, then it's unlikely that school improvement is occurring. Your team must manage change so that evaluation and assessment become part of the school culture, and that your community continually seeks out these sources of information as they manage change.

Mary will be the first to tell you that successful school change is challenging. She'll also be the first to tell you that she and her team made mistakes along the way, and learned from those mistakes. We can also tell you that, five years after Mary took over at South Central Middle School, it is an improved school. The staff has a clearer idea of what they need to be doing, they are better equipped to do it, and student learning has increased. When Mary finally retires in a few years, she'll leave a wonderful legacy—a school community so committed to continuous improvement that they will demand that the new principal be well equipped to take over where Mary left off. And Superintendent Jennifer, knowing the value of a principal who can empower and enable the change process, will make sure that the school board insists on the appointment of such an individual. And so it will go on —through a culture of continuous school improvement. Yet, Mary has no need to be seen as a savior. Her reward is a quiet comfort knowing that the process will build on what came before. For as Lao-Tzu notes, it was said of the successful leader, "we did it ourselves."

Reference

1.   Fullan, M. (1991). *The real meaning of educational change (2nd ed.)*. New York: Teachers College Press, p. 345.

DOESN'T SOMEBODY OUT THERE HAVE A CHART? Lessons Learned about Change

Chapter Highlights

♦ *Initiation.* How do you begin the change effort? The first phase of the change process is commonly called initiation. Here the school community engages in a discussion of the need for change and begins to search for a means of changing their school.

♦ *Building commitment.* What are the keys to gaining support for school change? Building early and foundational staff enthusiasm is critical so that staff will make a significant and long-term commitment to change.

♦ *Implementation.* How do you put your ideas into practice? During implementation, the school community begins to fulfill or accomplish its school change goals. Schools typically adapt the change to fit their own needs and existing cultural regularities.

♦ *Sustaining change.* What can you do to maintain your direction? Few changes in education are sustained long enough to make a long-lasting difference. Long-term participation, a focus on teaching and learning, and a culture of continuous improvement are needed to sustain change.

♦ *Evaluation and assessment.* Are you making a difference? Both the process and outcomes of change must be assessed. The school community must evaluate the means used to change their school and assess its effects on student learning and dispositions toward learning.

Note: Reading this chapter may be done in its entirety or it may be read selectively. Each main heading corresponds to the book's preceding chapters (Chapters 2–6). So, if you have been working on change for a while and are most concerned with sustaining change, you could concurrently read the section in this chapter on sustaining change and Chapter 5. Also, we begin each section of this chapter with a "lessons learned" box, so if you are a busy practitioner and simply want the basic ideas, you can begin there. Some of you may prefer to get conceptually grounded in this chapter before you move into Chapters 2 through 6 whereas some of you may want to leap into the "how to" chapters right away. How you read the book is entirely up to you.

After reading this chapter, you'll gain a better perspective about how the research has addressed many of the questions that leaders like Mary invariably wrestle with as they engage in the process of change. Some of these are:

♦ What do you need to do to actively initiate comprehensive school change?

♦ How do successful schools build a commitment to change?

♦ What are the key elements to moving from vision to implementation?

♦ How do you keep a change agenda fresh and interesting?

♦ How can you tell if the change efforts have been successful?

As you will see as your read this chapter, we have discovered that there is a host of research and advice out there. Nevertheless, in our opinion, as we point out in Chapter 1, the leadership of school change boils down to vigilantly addressing seven key elements:

♦ **Use a design model to guide the change effort**. Once defined, the purpose of change should be carried out through a well-developed design model, informed by previous work, best practice, and research. Such a model provides a template for decision making and helps connect the pieces of change into a coherent whole, thereby minimizing the tendency to tinker anew each time a change is proposed. (Chapter 2).

♦ **Build staff capacity for change.** It is critical to build the capacity of your staff in the content of school change (what needs to be done and why) as well as the process of change (how to do it). Change can be sustained only through the shared leadership that grows out of enhanced staff capacity. Failure to invest in this capacity-building process almost always guarantees subsequent failure (Chapter 2).

♦ **Create meaning and purpose**. The purpose of any change effort should be to enhance teaching and learning. This purpose must be clearly defined through a visioning process involving all relevant stakeholders. Change happens best when a problem is well defined, owned, and personalized by those who will carry out the change (Chapter 3).

♦ **Work toward changing the culture of the school.** Understanding the present culture of a school (how people think and act) is fundamental to successful change. Even more important is to understand the elements of that culture that are in need of change. Making these changes is called the reculturing process, and is the critical link between the words of change and the actions of change (Chapter 4).

♦ **Create a culture supportive of continuous improvement**. Change must be viewed as integral to everyday life in schools, rather than as an "add-on" with a finite life cycle. This continuous improvement must become a focus of the reculturing effort in schools (Chapter 5).

♦ **Focus school change on improved student learning**. Change must facilitate all students to meet high standards. However, it's important to understand the role of state/national standards to benefit all students while also going beyond these standards to create a more powerful learning environment (Chapter 6).

♦ **Develop a means by which to measure progress.** Schools must evaluate their fidelity to the change process and assess its impact on student learning. The evaluation and assessment of change are key to continuous improvement, and must be built into your design model from the earliest stages (Chapter 6).

How Do We Launch More Schools like South Central?

Superintendent Jennifer Craig was so pleased with the South Central story that she asked us to summarize for her and the school board key lessons we had learned along the way. The district wished to launch other schools and thought that it would be helpful to draw from our knowledge and experiential base. Jennifer wanted her other schools to become as mindful and thoughtful about the change process as possible.

We responded to her request by drawing from some of the best literature about school change/improvement and of course from our most recent work with South Central School. We emphasized to Jennifer that the literature tells us that there is no theory of change that is so well supported that one can act with certainty upon it. Rather, there are numerous processes that connect the "usually messy, unpredictable, and quite often convoluted dynamics of changing."[1] As Fullan says, "it is not possible to solve the change problem, but we can learn to live with it more proactively and more productively."[2] Fullan also tells us "there are no hard and fast rules rather a set of suggestions or implications given the contingencies specific to a local situation."[3]

However, there are some models, frameworks, and strategies that have been designed and developed over time. Each model, framework, or strategy has value for giving us greater understanding about change. Therefore, we must learn to use them thoughtfully and selectively; to move between models, frameworks and strategies, having the knowledge to match them to different contexts, situations, and challenges.

Moreover, we decided to review the research related to topics about which there are questions that leadership teams like South Central's usually ask about the change process. (These topics/questions also served as titles and organizers for the preceding chapters in this book.) We cautioned Jennifer, however, that our review would not be exhaustive, but representative of what we have learned from compendiums of educational change and school leadership, from books and monographs we consider to be "classics" in the field, and from our own work with Mary and the South Central School Leadership Team. Thus, our recommendations and advice are intended for other emerging leadership teams that wish to launch their schools in the future.

Pre-Initiation and Initiation: Launching the Ship—How Do We Prepare This Thing to Float? (Chapter 2)

Lessons Learned

♦ **Capacity building**. How do you enhance the capacity of your school for change? A focus on a firm understanding of the content and process of change is a good start.

♦ **Defining the problem**. What is your change initiative about? Be clear about the challenge you are trying to address and its relationship to student achievement.

♦ **Building a foundation of support**. How do you help people "get on board?" Create a foundation of understanding, meaning, and commitment to change during the initiation process.

♦ **Collaboration**. How do you organize people for change? Create collaborative work groups in which leadership is shared. These groups have the best chance of being successful throughout the change process.

♦ **Inside out and outside in**. Where does the impetus for change begin? Change is more readily initiated if the impetus comes from both inside and outside of the school.

♦ **Initiation is easier than implementation**. Does initiation of change always lead to successful implementation? Be prepared for the "hard work." Many schools are seduced at initiation and abandoned at implementation.

The first phase of the change process is commonly called initiation. Others talk of adoption and/or mobilization. In our own work, we refer to this phase as the "courtship" or "buy-in" period.[4] Within this phase, the early initiators of school change engage the school staff in a discussion of the need for change and explore models for change, attempting to garner the initial commitment and support needed to embark upon comprehensive school change. In the case of South Central School, Mary and her leadership initiated the change, and we served as university mentors and technical support persons. The goal of courtship is to begin building a shared meaning and commitment to a change model and to achieve a critical mass of staff support so that efforts to change the school can begin.

There is no one process of school change.

Courtship is intended to build shared meaning and commitment.

Compelled by powerful ideas and pressed to make school change happen quickly, school leaders frequently ignore or underestimate the importance of building commitment and creating shared meaning during the initiation stage. We stress the importance of building a strong foundation so that change can move ahead and be long-lasting.

 Fullan in his influential work, *The New Meaning of Educational Change* describes initiation as "the process that leads up to and includes a decision to adopt or proceed with a change."[5] Fullan[6] and others such as Giacquinta[7] tell us that there are relatively few solid studies of initiation. So, turning to the literature for advice on initiation does not provide us with a lot of guidance. Furthermore, researchers typically study this phase of the change process after the fact, i.e., they get involved after a decision to change is already a done deal. Accordingly, this is largely virgin territory and we must rely a lot on our own experience and good sense. Yet, we are also able to infer what happened during the initiation phase by examining the many failed attempts to implement change.

What do you need to consider at the initiation stage? As" meaning-makers" and initiators of change at your school, you will need to become informed and critical consumers of the educational change possibilities before you. Together, you will face a complex, confusing, and competing set of choices or possibilities. You will need to build your understanding of the content and process of change. You will need to learn about a wide range of possibilities and tools ranging from comprehensive redesign models and curricular innovations to change resources and tools, external technical support, and new financing and grant opportunities. Furthermore, be aware that many change possibilities are overly abstract and not that connected to practice or are just too simplistic. Moreover, most schools are chronically underfunded and their teachers suffer from role overload and face greater pressures for increased student achievement than ever before. As a consequence, most changes too often represent quick fixes or piecemeal change rather than comprehensive or cultural change. These quick fixes or "bricks" as Slavin[8] calls them might take the form of prepackaged curricular or instructional packages that some might call "teacherproof." Although useful in some instances, "bricks" have definite limitations as well. The South Central staff eventually chose to work with Project Improve because of its fit with the school's culture, its research-based design process, and its ability to provide systematic technical support and mentoring.

Too often, change ends up being piecemeal and a "quick fix."

We also must ask ourselves the question, "why change in the first place?" What challenge or problem are we trying to address, and how do we know if what we choose to do is a good fit for the contingencies we face as a school community? Typically, changes in community demographics such as increasing student diversity, growing poverty rates, and declining test scores are the impetus for many school change efforts. Recently, the standards-based movement and high-stakes testing have also precipitated vast changes. So, especially in the current environment, the questions you ask must focus on changes that will increase student engagement, promote powerful learning, improve student achievement and meet state standards. In the case of South Central, the release of the state's first report card was a critical incident that served as a catalyst for school change.

Levin points out, "most theory, advice and cheerleading on educational change come from those who have not themselves engaged in sustained efforts to work with schools collaboratively to obtain deep changes."[9] Outside experts will happily give you their advice, but not take the risks themselves. When the change fails, it becomes the school's fault. Often, these experts fail to see the connection between theory and practice. Their advice only represents hypotheses for change because the proposals haven't actually been tested.

Experts may give good advice, but in the end the school takes the risks.

To further complicate things, many people get into change for the wrong reasons. It's imposed rather than voluntary. Your school may initiate change because of an opportunity for increased funding or a "money grab" rather than as a way to build staff capacity to solve their own problems and challenges.[10] So, you need to determine whether your team's motivation is symbolic or substantive. Do you really want to improve teaching and leaning practices, or are you playing politics by responding to community pressure, wanting to appear innovative to gain resources and favor? A main lesson learned about initiation is that frequently change is not implemented because a foundation of understanding, meaning, and commitment was not laid during the initiation process.

Gaining a foundation of meaning and commitment is critical.

Another important lesson learned from the literature is that *collaborative work groups in which leadership is shared have the best chance of being successful throughout the change process.* Together, they help to develop a shared meaning and provide needed psychological support as a school moves through the change process, as noted by Lieberman and Grolnick[11] and Giacquita.[12] It is also important to hire new teachers who "embrace social change as part of the job."[13] In our own work with schools, new teachers have often provided the enthusiasm and idealism needed to initiate change and keep it going. Change also appears to be more readily initiated if it comes from both the "inside-out" and the "outside-in."[14] Fullan also recommends "*top-down*" and "*bottom-up*" *change, which occurs simultaneously,* as a strong motivator in the initiation of change.

Think of change as outside/inside and top down/bottom up.

Not only will your leadership team need to pay attention to the change itself, you will also need to pay attention to the people it affects and help them make the needed transitions from the work they once did to a different way of doing business.[15] In facilitating these transitions, it is important to understand that most change is what some call first-order and involves add-ons, tinkering, and superficial change rather than second-order change, which focuses on changes in teaching practices and culture[16] (see also Fullan[17] and

Second order change is more important than first order change.

Pincus[18]). Knowing this will help you to assist your colleagues to look and dig deeper for solutions to your problems and challenges.

Giacquinta speaks of schools being seduced at initiation and abandoned at implementation.[19] He points out (as do others) that initiation, as difficult as it may be, is much easier to achieve than adequate implementation. He also states that receptivity to innovation during the initiation process is determined by three factors: (a) the innovation is specific, (b) it is advocated or championed by high-status people, and (c) the cost-benefit factors are clear. In a similar vein, Fullan stresses the need for strong advocates of the change approach, a clear model for carrying out the change, and active initiation of change so that lapses which can kill initial enthusiasm and motivation don't occur.[20]

Building Commitment: Is Everybody on Board? (Chapter 3)

Lessons Learned

- **Involvement.** Who needs to be part of the change process? Involve all stakeholders from the community to play a role in charting a course for themselves and your school.

- **Understanding.** Is the research on school change important? The process of change needs to be fully understood and participants should regularly consult relevant research and best practice as they proceed.

- **Vision.** How useful is a vision for change? Create a vision and regularly review it. Successful schools have learner-centered visions and focus on improving student learning.

- **Reculturing.** How do you change a culture so that it supports change? Align your actions with your beliefs. From the beginning, schools need to reculture themselves for deep and long lasting change.

What does the literature on change have to say about how your leadership team can help facilitate significant and long-term commitment to change within your school? How can meaning, purpose, and the "fire" needed to make a difference be ignited? Answers to these questions are rather apparent, but they are frequently overlooked.

Key elements of building commitment.

The first lesson from the change literature is that *all of your teachers and stakeholders must be involved from the beginning,* not after the fact when something has been adopted or mandated from above. They must feel ownership and support (from both you and the school district), and must choose to make the change themselves. Introducing teachers to the innovation after it has been adopted can only lead to a lack of involvement and commitment, increased resistance, and possibly even sabotage. In many of the newer comprehensive school redesigns, the staff actually vote on whether to accept or reject the proposed change. The literature talks about a "substantial majority" or as high as 80 to 90 percent acceptance required. Thus, informed consent is critical. At South Central, 93 percent of the staff eventually voted to work with Project Improve.

Many change redesign models even require contracts and agreements that specify length of commitment, steps to be followed, allocation of resources, outside technical support, and a clear commitment from the district superintendent and school board. District commitment is critical and is cited by many researchers as important. Some districts go so far as to encourage uncommitted teachers who can't support a change process to transfer to other schools. Yet, although districts should provide direction and support, the actual change process needs to become the responsibility of the individual school. Whatever changes are adopted should become a school-selected priority and ideally be a good fit with the direction the school is currently heading. Thus, teacher involvement will be stronger when there is a shared perception that fellow colleagues and district leadership are truly committed to change over the long haul.

Real change is the school's responsibility.

Many schools report that they gain added involvement, commitment and legitimacy by associating with reputable reform efforts sponsored by major universities or professional associations. Being part of a change network such as Accelerated Schools, Coalition of Essential Schools, or Expeditionary Learning can enhance teacher involvement and commitment because of the strength of being part of a national movement. But, along with this legitimacy can also come an inherent uncertainty and ambiguity about what may be lost and what new requirements may be imposed. Evans discusses how people are "characteristically ambivalent" at the beginning of any major change.[21] Schools are frequently hurried or pressed to make change happen, and, coupled with ambiguity of the change process or redesign models, it creates a great deal of stress. Even when good choices are made, a school staff will still require significant support and counseling as they move through the change process. These issues are discussed in depth by Zemelman[22], Olson[23], Evans[24], Fink[25], Bodilly[26], Allen[27], and Giaquinta.[28]

In a complex and ambiguous school reform environment, your leadership team will need to be actively involved, model the process, and send strong signals of being knowledgeable, confident, and possessing a "can do" attitude. Joyce, Hersh, and

The less explicit the change, the more confusion there is.

Mckibbin, in reviewing the research on implementation of innovations, state, "The less explicit the characteristics and rational of the innovation, the more likely there will be user confusion and frustration and a low degree of implementation."[29] They further add, "Results seem to boil down to the common sense proposition that the more thoroughly one understands something, the more likely one is to master it and be committed to using it." Thus, your leadership team's primary responsibility in building staff involvement and commitment will be to strive toward building an understanding and internalization of the proposed change. Teachers need considerable information, opportunities for critical dialog, visits to other school sites, and a process for sharing their concerns and findings with one another.

Second, your team will need to pay careful attention to the process of change. In the press to make school reform happen quickly, too many schools shortcut the early foundational phases of meaning making and laying the groundwork for changing

Focus on the process is as important as the content of change.

their school's culture. Traditionally, there has been excessive emphasis placed on the rationality of the change itself whereas insufficient attention is paid to the process of change, i.e., how staff members actually deal with it. Such awareness and sensitivity is especially critical for your leadership team at the early and foundational stages of the change process. It's one thing to develop what appears to be an exciting innovation and another to have staff make it meaningful, internalize what the change will require of them, and, finally, commit to using it. Furthermore, the designers of change often do not understand that staff resistance to change is a predictable and naturally occurring event. You will need to work with your staff as they make the transition from an initial sense of loss of the past to making a commitment to the proposed changes of the future. It's often good to consider that in the early stages of the change process, your team should focus equally between the change to be implemented and the transitions from what those changes may replace. Further elaboration is provided by Evans[30], Bridges[31], Miles[32], and Chenoweth and Kushman.[33]

Our third lesson about pre-initiation is that your school must develop a shared and learner-centered vision of its future. Successful schools have a vision that guides and inspires their work. Fink points out that schools need to possess a "shared sense that staff members know where they are going."[34] Allen adds that schools need to know "what are we working towards?"[35] He argues that only a shared vision will make new governance structures and action research meaningful so the school can make appreciable school-wide progress in teaching and learning. On the other hand, schools without a clear vision often fail because they are not able to mobilize staff around a common focus. Stringfield describes these schools as "hitchhikers."[36] They are desperate and want to move on, but are aimless as to their destination. These schools, he claims, "stick out their thumbs" and travel without having carefully chartered their course.

House points out that many comprehensive school redesign models come with built-in visions that focus upon a deep respect for students and a common belief that they all can succeed.[37] One of the most promising ways of developing a learner-centered vision is by examining the latest research and best practices related to teaching and learning. Here we find new conceptions of knowledge that enable learners to construct knowledge in depth and apply it to real situations as noted by Bereiter and Scardamalia[38], and Zemmelman.[39] Your team should also realize that currently greater attention is being paid to "constructivist"-inspired forms of teaching and learning that builds on student strengths and "multiple intelligences," as discussed by Levin[40] and Gardner.[41] Means, Chelmer, and Knapp note the growing recognition and value placed on prior student knowledge, life experiences and culture.[42] All in all, there is a movement away from viewing learning problems from a deficit approach (e.g., the student doesn't have the skills to learn) and toward an enrichment perspective of teaching and learning (e.g., it's the job of the school to enhance learning opportunities). Thus it's not what students cannot do but rather what they are able to do that serves as the basis for establishing the instructional culture of the school. According to Miles, we may be moving into a well-defined and more stable approach to authentic pedagogy.[43] We have learned from Lortie that what is most motivating to teachers is connecting with their students and watching them learn.[44] Thus, grounding your school vision in teaching and learning will help to engender teacher commitment and hope for the future. It's why your teachers became teachers in the first place: to make a difference in the lives of the children they *teach*. Making a difference is really about making a commitment and has a moral and uplifting quality about it. The South Central staff became significantly more committed to school change as they moved towards building on student strengths and following an enrichment approach in their teaching and learning activities.

A school vision should be learner-centered.

Finally, our fourth lesson is that *building staff commitment is about "reculturing" your school*. Reculturing means developing new values, beliefs, and norms that are focused on teaching, learning, and your professionalism. Improving schools requires building a greater sense of collegiality, creating norms of continuous improvement, valuing risk-taking, and providing mutual support.[45] Furthermore, in a recultured school, leadership is defined as the quality of interactions and the extent to which work is collaborative.[46] Such leadership then becomes pervasive and actively shared. Such a culture will be challenging to achieve, but incredibly rewarding when experienced. Schools that reculture develop educational meaning and a shared sense that "staff members know where they are going, and it is present throughout the school."[47]

Reculturing means establishing new values and beliefs.

Implementation: Did You Say to Turn Port or Starboard? (Chapter 4)

Lessons Learned

- ◆ **Adaptation.** Does a change look different from school to school? Know that once initiated, schools adapt the change to meet the conditions of the their school culture.

- ◆ **Policy.** How useful are policies in the change process? Even the best policy can't mandate what matters. Focus on the meaning of change as it emerges within your school.

- ◆ **Culture.** How important is your local school culture? The implementation of change often has a low success rate because program developers fail to consider specific cultural elements of the school(s) in which changes are embedded.

- ◆ **Behavioral patterns.** How does the past affect the future of change? Any effort at change will run into, and be affected by, an already existing pattern of thinking or acting within the school.

- ◆ **Contingency theory.** Can the implementation of change be a rational process? We must identify conditions that increase the probability of change rather than search for immutable and universal laws.

At one time, the term "implementation" was commonly used to describe a phase of the educational change process. Reading programs were "implemented," as were new ways of organizing classrooms (remember open-space schools?) Moreover, classroom management strategies were also implemented (remember assertive discipline?). Effecting change in schools was viewed as comparable to the process used in any other organization. After all, new technologies are routinely implemented in industry, new strains of seed are implemented in agriculture, and different surgical procedures are implemented in medicine. Why should change in schools be any different?

Implementation is the "doing-it" phase of change.

Taken literally, implementation means to carry into effect, fulfill, or accomplish. The term has a sense of completion attached to it—signifying something done toward the latter stages of a process—toward the end or near the end. So if a change is implemented in a school, the connotation is that much of the development of the change occurred prior to the actual implementation process. And like the development of a new technology or a new strain of hybrid corn, we can safely assume that the change was developed (for the most part) outside the organism (the school) into which it is to be implemented. This was one of the fundamental problems identified by some who studied the change process.

Jeffrey Pressman and Aaron Wildavsky were among the earliest to note that the implementation of federal programs hardly occurred in the linear fashion that their developers thought they would.[48] Indeed, implementers often didn't do what was "expected" of them, nor did they always act to maximize program objectives. Programs that were implemented, then, often fell short of their intended objectives because they were not implemented as planned. In the early 1970s, we learned that much the same process occurred in schools. Charters and Pellegrin concluded that *schools don't so much implement change as much as they adapt changes.*[49] They begin a change (e.g., curriculum, technology, or an organizational configuration that might have been developed outside the school) but once initiated, schools adapt the change to meet the conditions of their environment. Unlike a hybrid corn seed used on the farm or a new machine brought in by a factory, most educational changes are not just "used" in their natural state, but rather are shaped to suit the perceived needs of the school. As a result of the variability of what comes out of the implementation process, implementation can become, as Charters and Jones noted, a "nonevent."[50]

Change is not a linear process.

Schools don't implement—they adapt changes.

A series of studies conducted by the Rand Corporation in the mid to late 1970s further documented these patterns. Known as the Rand Change Agent Studies, these studies examined the attempts by the federal government to stimulate change in local schools. The assumptions of these efforts were that an outside agency such as the federal government, through program development (good ideas) or external funding (augmented resources)—or both—could jump-start the change effort at the local level. A variety of curriculum efforts (especially in mathematics and the sciences) as well as teacher training efforts (e.g., Teacher Corps), fit this model.

The Rand studies revealed that, in schools as in other organizations, change usually doesn't occur in such a straightforward manner. Although most of the initiatives sponsored by the federal government were successfully "adopted"—meaning that the local school was committed to implement the change as developed, a lot happened after that. In the end, the Rand studies concluded that only a few of the programs adopted were successfully implemented, and even fewer continued after the financial or technical support from the government disappeared.

McLaughlin recounts three additional conclusions from the Rand studies.[51] First, the action *is* at the local level. Regardless of the sophistication of the program design or the presence of outside funding, policy means little until it is put into practice at the local school or district. Second, *even the best policy can't mandate what matters.* Schools are embedded in a local economic, social, and political context, and those who work in schools are part of this context.

No matter how much educators might be committed to the value and integrity of a program that they are attempting to implement, the context in which educators work is the overall driving force affecting implementation. Finally (and we have noted this before), when all is said and done, *implementation is really a process of local adaptation.* Sometimes, such adaptation means the complete breakdown of the policy and program intended to be implemented; more often, however, local adaptation means that some things will be faithfully implemented as designed, whereas others will be altered to meet the local conditions.

Change is local, context-dependent, and adaptive.

The Rand studies established a watershed of sorts because they documented how complex it is to put policy into practice and that change is hardly the predictable pattern that policymakers would like to believe it is. But if implementation of change efforts in schools is so complex, your team needs to understand why. To better understand some of the reasons, it's useful to examine the key points raised in a contemporary classic on implementing change in education, *The Culture of the School and the Problem of Change* by Seymour Sarason.[52]

Sarason's book was published during the externally-directed change efforts such as those referred to in the Rand studies. Sarason is a psychologist interested in education, but from a social/cultural (rather than individual) perspective. In his years of working with schools, he learned, through observing and participating in numerous attempts to change school practices, that the "more things change, the more they remain the same."[53] As Sarason reflected on this observation, he realized that the implementation of change has such a low success rate because program *developers often fail to consider the specific cultural elements of the school(s) in which changes are embedded.* That is, changes are often developed in the abstract—based upon a mixture of ideals, intentions, and estimations of what should happen. Such estimations, however, usually are not grounded in a thorough understanding of the research about school culture. As a result, political ideology and personal values play a major role in the design of educational change, notwithstanding their practicality to be implemented. One of the key reasons South Central chose Project Improve is that it isn't a "cookie-cutter" reform program in that it values staff autonomy and depends on the professional judgment of staff members to identify and solve their own problems.

Sarason makes an important point about making change happen: *that any effort at change will run into, and be affected by, an already existing pattern of thinking or acting within the school.* Thus, change efforts conceived outside the culture of the school invariably are changed by the already existing patterns of behavior within the school. How teachers think about the best ways to learn, how they teach in order to maximize such learning, and how they "know" when learning has occurred—are elements of a culture of schooling through which change efforts must pass. Failure to recognize and understand the existence of this culture then, is a primary contributor to the mutual adaptation process described by the Rand studies.

Fullan who, like Sarason, has at times been perplexed by the change process reinforces the importance of understanding and eventually using the school culture as the locus of school change. Like many of us, Fullan experienced the period of the 1960s and 1970s wherein it was believed that we could engineer school change to produce desired results. If these desired results were not forthcoming, then it was back to the drawing board in order to reengineer the process so as to solve the problem. "Doing change" was a problem of designing and building a foolproof process, and there was much optimism that this was a worthy goal.

Fullan now notes how we have to break out of this way of thinking if we're going to seriously understand the change process. Critical to this is his notion that the implementation of change does not require the engineering of the perfect process/technology in a laboratory whereupon it will be introduced into the classroom. Instead, Fullan says that "change mirrors life itself,"[54] and is a process and state where events *Change mirrors life.* are neither in perfect harmony nor in perpetual chaos, where people both overperform as well as underperform, and where there is neither complete certainty nor rampant uncertainty. We know that schools and universities fit this characterization, and that there is no final solution to the "change problem," no prototype from an engineering laboratory that we can drop into a school, plug it in, and make it happen.

In the end, then, *change is contingent on a multitude of interacting factors*, and the messiness of the change problem is one with which we must live. First, if change mirrors life itself then, like life, change is bound to be contradictory, uncertain, complex, and unpredictable—usually all at the same time. If change mirrors life, then like life itself change is better understood as a process and not a product. Second, once we accept the messiness of the change process, we can begin to ask questions about how we would encourage school change in such a complex environment. Indeed this reorients our perspective to change, for we do not have to hold to rational ideals about change which, for the most part, are false. As Firestone and Corbett noted some 15 years ago, "there are no universal rules for changing organizations."[55] Yet, if there are no rules, then how are we to productively use the research that has been done on implementing change?

We can begin by reaffirming that the implementation of change is very context-dependent. What Principal A does in his school to cause significant improvement in student learning may not be what Principal B finds is successful in her school. Thus, it's important to understand that contingencies play an important role in affecting the change process. *Change processes aren't easily transferable.*

Indeed, in the organizational literature there is something called contingency theory, based on the belief that "there is some middle ground between the existence of universal principles of management that fit all organizational types, and that…each organization is unique and therefore must be studied as unique."[56] In accepting contingencies, we try to identify the conditions that increase the probability of a desired outcome rather than searching for an immutable and universal law. In many ways, an examination of the contingencies that affect successful implementation is not unlike an examination of contingencies affecting the weather. We know too well that prediction of the weather does not guarantee anything. Certainly, predictions for a 24-hour period are more accurate than those for 5 days in the future, but even a 24-hour prediction can be wrong if the "right" conditions come into play. The best that a forecast can do is to examine the contingencies, assess their interaction, and then produce a scenario based upon probabilities.

Examining the factors that can increase the success of implementation then is very useful. As an example, Corbett, Dawson, and Firestone examined curriculum change in 14 schools and discovered *8 factors that influenced the success of the project.* Not that these factors guaranteed success, but like a weather forecast, the probabilities certainly were increased.[57]

The first factor is a *close match between the objectives of the project and district priorities.* This may seem like common sense, but it's amazing how frequently there can be a disconnect between school initiatives and district priorities. In fact, not only should there be-tween a close match between the school's objectives and district priorities, but the authors went so far as to note that if the school's change efforts fell below the district's top two priorities, the likelihood of successful change diminished significantly.

The second factor focuses on the *cohesion among the faculty.* Faculties that are divided and have competing interests regarding teaching and learning are difficult to bring together. The authors found that those schools where the faculty had a common purpose in terms of how education should occur were again more likely to successfully implement change.

The amount of *faculty and administrative turnover* is the third factor contributing to successful implementation. Obviously, some amount of turnover is the norm—and is healthy for the organization. However, excessive turnover means that the change effort is forever beginning anew as people familiar with the intent of the change leave the school and new members must continually be socialized into the expectations of the change initiative. Although turnover at all levels can diminish the inertia of a change agenda, it is often catastrophic at the administrative level because there is a tendency to slow, or even stop, the pace of change until new leadership is established.

A fourth area affecting the implementation process is that of the *connection between new initiatives and current practice.* On the one hand, a change initiative will always represent a departure from current practice, and signify the desire to improve practice by moving beyond the present. Yet, any change initiative that proposes to obliterate all current practices and introduce new ones in one cataclysmic move is not likely to achieve its objectives. The authors concluded those changes that showed respect for current effective practices, and built upon them as a basis for change, were more likely to be successful.

The fact that, quite often, *change begets change,* is a fifth lesson to come from these studies. Schools with a history of successful implementation have a better chance of knowing the ropes and building on past successes, whereas schools new to the change process often experience a steep learning curve. Oftentimes, some form of technical assistance (especially in the early stages) to schools new to change helps to buffer the struggles which inexperience can bring.

The *linkages between building and district operations* also seem to affect successful implementation. Schools are "loosely-coupled" organizations, meaning that units within schools and districts have a fair amount of autonomy and normally are not tightly controlled or constrained by other units. As an example, one of the common complaints of many teachers is that the grade level from which a student came didn't teach students what the current teacher thinks should have been taught. Such loose articulation has its advantages because teachers can often make changes in their classroom without having to coordinate with other teachers. Yet, such a system doesn't work very well when attempting to coordinate change throughout a building. A successful change effort is promoted when the effort to change is fostered at the smallest level of the organization at the same time it is supported and enhanced at the higher levels.

The *rewards for being involved in change* are the seventh area identified by Corbett, Dawson, and Firestone. Why should educators change their practices if there are few, if any, rewards for doing so? Although the rewards that come from students being successful are important to teachers, these are not always sufficient to generate commitment to change. Other incentives must be present, and often those that enhance the feeling of professional competency (such as support for new training) are important.

Related to rewards is the last condition—that of *resource availability*. Successful change requires an adequate allocation of resources to support the change effort, and those resources need not always be directly tied to dollars. If asked what they need the most to implement change, teachers invariably will respond with one word: "time." Making change without allocating sufficient time to address the issues related to the change is a surefire recipe for frustration and disappointment. Although admittedly difficult, the successful implementation of change requires attention to the resources needed to support the change effort.

These eight factors speak to implementation as a process and not a standard to be rigidly followed. They illustrate the necessity of understanding schools as organizational systems and cultures in which change is developed and shaped by a variety of interacting contingencies. Returning to Sarason: "any attempt to introduce change into the school involves some existing regularity, behavioral or programmatic."[58] The implementation of change efforts routinely fails because of the inattention given to this almost axiomatic conclusion. We believe that productive change can occur in schools, but only if embraced by all within the school community, and only if the community is willing to examine the existing regularities that stand in the way of successful implementation.

Sustaining Change: Was This Rock on the Chart? (Chapter 5)

Lessons Learned

- **Supporting participation.** The ability to sustain change is dependent on the genuine and long-term participation of all stakeholders. How do you enhance that participation? Your leadership team must create a broad-based culture of participation from the earliest stages of the change process through its continuation.

- **Enhancing teaching and learning.** What are the keys to sustaining a focus on student learning? For school reform to succeed in the long run, your leadership team will need to focus on meaningful student learning, what it requires, and how it can be supported.

- **Continuous improvement.** How do we make change the norm and not the exception? If comprehensive school change is to be sustained, it must be viewed as integral to everyday life in schools rather than as an "add-on" with a finite life cycle. Only if we are willing to "reculture"—create a new system of values and norms to which we can all subscribe—do we have any chance of creating a culture of continuous improvement.

Tyack and Cuban remind us that for over a century and a half, "Americans have sought to perfect the future by debating how to improve the young through education."[59] Despite these sometimes-utopian intentions, most changes in education have been of an incrementalist nature, and have fallen short of the visions for education held by many. Indeed, recent overviews about what we've been able to sustain through over a century of "reform," and most particularly the reforms of the past three or so decades, are uniformly pessimistic. In the recent *International Handbook of Educational Change*, Fink and Stoll echo Tyack and Cuban's conclusions and note that with all the reform activity of the past few decades, there is little evidence that these efforts have substantially altered life in most classrooms. Most changes have a short half-life, they argue, and few are sustained long enough to make a mark on the landscape of schooling.[60]

Change has a short half-life.

Sustaining change, then, is a formidable challenge. Darling-Hammond summarizes nicely the challenges of trying to sustain change in our schools: "it's one thing to engender enthusiasm, good intentions, and even action around school restructuring; it's another to actually build new structures that allow those good intentions to take root and flourish over the long haul."[61] The key to sustaining change centers on the attempt to maintain and build upon those cultural regularities that must be in place to support the change effort. Darling-Hammond mentions two such regularities—supporting participation in a change effort and creating an environment that enhances teaching and inquiry. In this section we add a third—developing a structure of continuous improvement.

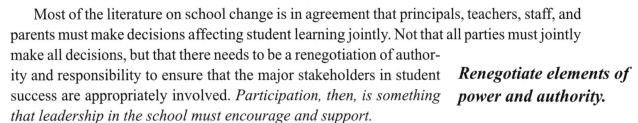

Most of the literature on school change is in agreement that principals, teachers, staff, and parents must make decisions affecting student learning jointly. Not that all parties must jointly make all decisions, but that there needs to be a renegotiation of author- ity and responsibility to ensure that the major stakeholders in student success are appropriately involved. *Participation, then, is something that leadership in the school must encourage and support.*

Renegotiate elements of power and authority.

Working out this delicate balance is, as you well know, no easy task. If you work in a school district of any significant size, you are well aware of the difficulty in establishing the proper balance in decision making between Boards of Education, central office, building ad- ministration, teachers and staff, students, and parents. At each of these levels, there is some set of policies and procedures governing what can be done by whom and the procedures for initi- ating such action. In such a system, pinpointing accountability and responsibility is exceed- ingly difficult to do. When any change designed to enhance student learning doesn't have the desired effect, each level of the bureaucracy looks to the other level for the source of the prob- lem, all the while the change effort withers on the vine.

Investing stakeholders in the change process involves a fundamental alteration in the con- nection between responsibility and accountability, and is an important component of sustain- ing the change agenda. Examining the Accelerated Schools Project (ASP) and the School De- velopment Program (SDP, but better known as Comer Schools)—two of the most prominent large-scale change efforts—provides a glimpse of how the base of participation can be sus- tained.

The basic outlines of ASP were first outlined by Levin in *Educational Leadership*.[62] In a retrospective piece, Levin reflected with candor how it was that the Accelerated Schools Pro- ject (ASP) was launched over a five-year period of time. During those five years, many of the components of ASP were developed and tested in a number of pilot schools. The project was then expanded into some new schools that "implemented" the ASP model.

Early problems, however, were evident. Levin reported that only about a third of the new schools seemed able to sustain the change initiative that they had begun. An additional one-third of the schools struggled to make the changes, while another third did not make any changes at all despite what seemed to be a carefully orchestrated training program with the staff of the new schools. As Levin notes: "to put it mildly, we were very disappointed."[63]

The problems were manyfold. In some cases, schools that were thought to be implementing the ASP model were doing so in name only, and primarily as a result of the principal announcing to the staff that the decision had already been made. The staff in those schools was understandably hesitant to proceed with training under those conditions. In other schools, a schism existed between the school team (perceived by some as "insiders"), which had received ASP training in preparation for implementation, and the rest of the faculty (many of whom felt like "outsiders"). In other situations, staff development time, which had been scheduled was not provided, and once the school year began, it was difficult to fit such training into an already full agenda.

Levin and his colleagues began rethinking the processes needed to continue and sustain the change efforts. They realized that part of the problem was that the ASP had not followed the model developed by the project with the pilot schools. In this model, each school had been assigned a "coach" whose responsibility it was to work with the school on a regular basis in order to assist the school team with implementation and continuity issues. The coach's level of involvement varied from school to school, but a key ingredient was to provide training and support to the entire school community. Full-scale participation was the key, but participation in and of itself was not sufficient. Rather, participation had to be of the nature that it could engage the entire community in such a way that the "values, ideas, and practices are fully embedded in activities undertaken by trainees."[64]

Levin and his colleagues learned that the ability to sustain change is dependent on a genuine participation that allows the school community to wrestle with the articulation of values and beliefs, which in turn drives the change process. Such participation is deliberate and cumulative, building a firm foundation on which specific teaching and learning activities can subsequently be built. Participation at this level cannot be mandated, nor will it occur quickly. Rather, it must be nourished and expanded, and deeply embedded, so as to sustain change. ASP seeks to accomplish this end through a model that relies heavily on the role of a coach (who normally is not a staff member of the school). Other projects take different approaches.

Participation in the change effort must be expanded.

The School Development Program (SDP), better know as Comer Schools—is another large-scale change effort with sufficient longevity that we can learn important lessons about sustaining change. The specifics of SDP are outlined by Comer.[65] Although similar to ASP in that the change effort is school-based and thus focuses on developing participation of stakeholders in the change process, SDP differs in that it prescribes an organizational restructuring to facilitate that process.

SDP specifies the creation of three different teams that are assigned the responsibility of managing the comprehensive school plan, the monitoring and assessment of the goals of the plan, and the staff development organized around the plan. The first team (called the School Planning and Management Team) is the major decision-making body of the school and draws its membership from staff and parents. The second team is the Student and Staff Support Services Team, and its responsibility centers on coordinating and assessing the variety of school- and nonschool-based services for individual students. This team also assists individual teachers in their work with students who are in need of these additional services. The third team (called the Parent Team), focuses specifically on building a strong bridge between school and home. Because parents from this team are represented on the School Planning and Management Team, parents are directly connected to the creation and management of the comprehensive plan.

The structure as outlined above is clearly intended to create a broad base of participation from the earliest stages of the change process through its continuation. Like the ASP, the SDP does not stipulate a particular curriculum or program for the school to develop. Instead, it leaves those decisions to the various committees whose collective responsibility is to target initiatives that support teaching and learning. By creating a culture of participation, the SDP hopes to be better able to sustain change than have many other change efforts.

Build a culture of participation.

Unfortunately, most change efforts are not directly centered on student learning. Although those individuals who advocate many changes believe that their efforts indeed will improve student learning, this is usually an assumption rather than a concerted effort directed at changes in student learning. *A specific focus on improved student learning however mobilizes the school community* to examine how students learn in school and the role of the adult community in facilitating such learning. We believe it is a necessary ingredient in sustaining change. As Darling-Hammond notes, "For school reform to succeed in the long run, policymakers and educators need to act on a shared understanding of what meaningful learning is, what it requires, and how it can be supported."[66]

What drives successful change is student learning.

What do the comprehensive change efforts previously discussed tell us about a strong commitment to student learning? ASP focuses on what is termed "powerful learning." Powerful learning is neither a single technique nor a strategy for improving a specialized skill such as reading comprehension or computational abilities. Rather, powerful learning is a way of coordinating the school's structure (such as class schedules, organization of grades or levels, etc.) with curricular material tied to instructional strategies. Powerful learning is predicated on the ASP guiding principle of "building on strengths," which means that enhanced student learning is based first on assets—what the student does well—rather than focusing on deficits—what the student does not do well.

Bringing about powerful learning is difficult because the culture of most schools is established on a deficit model that assumes that students who are not learning well have some negative characteristics or experiences that prevent them from being successful. Sometimes, those attributes are difficult to change and stem from factors outside the school (e.g., poverty, unstable family environ-

Powerful learning is key.

ment, etc.), and other times, they are difficult to change and stem from factors within the school (e.g., inadequate preparation in prior grades, large class size, etc.) Regardless of the source, students with learning difficulties are usually "remediated," which means that they are usually given more of what didn't work in the first place (more reading instruction, more drill on math computations, etc.). Powerful learning, on the other hand, makes the assumption that children have some attribute that defines them in a positive way, even though that way may not speak directly to a skill that the teacher is trying to teach. Concentrating on that positive dimension (such as an interest in sports or an ability to read in one's first language) then becomes a launch point for developing academic skills in each child.

Like ASP, the SDP schools do not use a specific curriculum to address the improvement of student learning. Rather, these schools make it clear that it is the responsibility of the three teams, (but especially the School Planning and Management Team) to choose the curricular and instructional strategies most appropriate for their school. In addition, the team must monitor these activities in order to ensure that there is a clear alignment between curriculum, instruction, and assessment.

One of the major "ah-has" which Comer himself noted bears reviewing. Often, teachers and staff can become embroiled in debates as to which curriculum is "best" in what area. These debates, although ostensibly focusing on what is best for the students, more frequently center on the curriculum or instructional strategies that teachers prefer. Yet, rarely is there definitive evidence addressing the impact of the program on student learning. Comer realized early in the development of SDP that such was the case, and this is one reason why the SDP does not push any particular learning approach. Instead, the Comer program advocates a clear specification of instructional objectives, regular assessment to check progress towards those objectives, alignment of curriculum to meet the objectives, and regular feedback to the students and their families. What matters is not so much which program is chosen, but "the process utilized, the degree of staff involvement, and the level of gut commitment."[67] Too often, educators don't understand the process described by Comer and others (or don't want to understand it), and thus change initiatives flounder because of petty squabbles over efficacy in the absence of any reliable data to inform the discussion.

The choice of which program to use isn't always the most important decision.

In many organizations (schools included), the prospect of change evokes sighs and groans from most participants. "I can't wait for this to be over," or "doing it the way we always did it was much easier" are thoughts typically heard during the change process. Clearly, most of us see change as something that has a clear beginning and, usually, a definable end—and we can't wait for it to end.

No wonder change is often viewed as an aberration to our regular routine. Our position in this book, however, is clearly different. If comprehensive change is to be sustained, *change must be viewed as integral to everyday life in schools* rather than as an "add-on" with a finite life cycle. To repeat a commonly heard phrase,   ***Change is learning.*** change is the constant, stability the aberration. When we all adopt a viewpoint that change is part of the learning process, then the schools which we lead will begin a journey toward being truly dynamic organizations.

This stance involves fostering a learning community, one wherein learning is not just the acquisition of defined skill sets but also as a culture where learning and relearning are integral. Schools should foster such elements as learning through multiple pathways, utilizing diversity rather than trying to standardize everything, opening themselves to the larger community, and stressing the importance of how to learn rather than just what to learn. It is then that they will have adopted an open-systems model predicated on the need for regular feedback as a key ingredient of continuous improvement.[68]

This is one of the reasons why Cuban urges us to embrace the dilemmas of our practice. By dilemmas he means "conflict-filled situations that require choices because competing, highly valued choices cannot be fully satisfied."[69] Said differently, our practices are filled with multiple choices, which require our best reasoning   ***Embrace the dilemmas of*** power as well as moral frameworks. How do we allocate scarce re-   ***practice.*** sources in our school? How can we voluntarily become more accountable to families, even though we then open ourselves to increased criticism? How do we analyze data about what it is we are doing in a way that leads to honesty rather than self-serving postures? These are some of the difficult questions that we must be willing to confront if we are indeed serious about continuous improvement.

We don't for a moment pretend this is an easy process. The call by Darling-Hammond for greater networking and community building among educators is one strategy designed to develop an infrastructure for professional conversations about improved instruction.[70] Cuban himself believes that the serious examination of "uncertainties, ambiguities, and moral dilemmas of teaching students at different levels of formal schooling is precisely one basis for assembling intellectual communities among educators."[71] Some have argued that even the prospect of educational standards, now so widespread and yet seriously flawed, provides one of the most opportune moments we have to engage in serious discussion about the nature of teaching and learning and to create an environment of continuous improvement.[72] South Central slipped a bit during its third year, but because staff were able follow a systematic problem-solving process and refocus on teaching and learning, the school was able to get back on course. The school was able to face its setback because a reculturing process had taken hold, and setbacks and problems were now viewed as a normal part of the change process—something to be dealt with rather than avoided.

We subscribe to all the positions above. Sustaining change is indeed difficult yet still necessary work. Only if we are willing to "reculture"—create a new system of values and norms to which we all can subscribe—do we have any chance of creating a culture of continuous improvement. The absence of continuous improvement is sure to doom change efforts to a process of "waiting it out" until we can return to the comfortable teaching practices that no longer serve students very well.

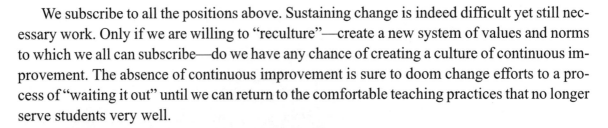

Assessment: How Do You Know When You Have Arrived? (Chapter 6)

Lessons Learned

♦ **Effects of change**. Are the effects of change well-known? The change process in schools has evolved over the past 40 years with little attention given to assessing the ongoing or formative effects of change. School change leaders have been much more compelled to initiate change than to implement, sustain, and assess its effects on students.

♦ **Evaluating and assessing change.** What's the difference between evaluation and assessment? We need to understand both the process and outcomes of change, i.e., the means used to change schools and the effects on student learning and student dispositions toward that learning.

♦ **Standards.** Are standards the only game in town? Meeting state standards has become the primary policy issue of the 1990s and early twenty-first century. Your school should develop a strategy to assess more than what is reflected on standardized tests. How you do this will determine your ability to move "beyond" standards.

♦ **Redefining accountability.** How can schools demonstrate that they are accountable? Schools must explore and search for alternatives to standardized testing based on multiple-choice questions. School-specific questionnaires, benchmarks, validations visits, and alternative assessments will need to be encouraged and developed.

There is little written in the change literature dealing with the formative or ongoing assessment or evaluation of change efforts. This is troubling, given the current standards-based accountability movement sweeping across the states. Most of the change discussion focuses simply on the many failed attempts at implementation and sustaining change. Louis and Miles' review of school improvement literature *Assessment is too often an* points out how they "were struck by the absence of evaluation as a *afterthought.* vehicle for change."[73] What seems to be clear is that for many, *assessment as a tool for school change appears to have been either a nonissue or an after-the-fact concern.* Even in our own work with the Accelerated Schools Project, an internal school assessment tool kit was developed and implemented some 10 years after the project was initiated. For a variety of reasons, possibly a blinding passion for their own ideas, school change leaders have been much more compelled to initiate change than to assess its effects on students.

In a relatively short amount of time, wave after wave of school change has crashed onto the school improvement scene. Fullan identifies four phases in the study of educational change: (a) *adoption* (1960s); (b) *implementation failure* (1970-1977); (c) *implementation success* (1978-1982); and (d) *intensification versus restructuring* (1983 to the present).[74] Each of these four phases of reform appeared abruptly with little if any thought or means of assessing their impact. At best, assessment was an afterthought.

Standards have become the primary policy issue of the 90s and the twenty-first century. The assessment of standards is to be based on student performance criteria rather than the assignment of grades. Likewise, graduation is meant to be based upon what students know and can do rather than the seat time they spend in class. Nevertheless, school practitioners are still scrambling to determine what the standards are (content standards), how they will be assessed (performance standards), and the consequences for not meeting them. Moreover, districts and states are struggling to develop curriculum frameworks that will guide teachers in the process of helping students meet these new learning standards. In some ways, schools are caught in a crossfire trying to change themselves while responding to the externally imposed standards that typically emanate from state or national sources.

An essential problem is that *the attainment of standards is usually measured by multiple-choice standardized tests, which focus on very limited dimensions of analytic thinking.* Sternberg posits that most of these tests do not measure any components of creative or practical intelligence.[75] Some experts like Sacks see no connection between testing and student chances of success in the classroom or in the "real" *Standardized tests have* world. He feels that these tests simply serve to trivialize student learn- *limited value.* ing and that the only winners are career politicians and large testing companies.[76] Regardless of the validity of these norm-referenced tests, the consequences for low-achieving schools range from school districts being placed in "receivership" or taken over by their states, to schools being "reconstituted" or closed down by their school districts.

For students who fail to perform well on these tests, the consequences range from increased retention at grade level to growing numbers of students being placed in special education programs.

The recent spread of a national standards-based movement means that increased attention is being paid to using content- and performance-based standards and their assessment as a means of initiating, implementing, and sustaining change. Linn points out that today, policy makers find testing a very appealing lever for school reform.[77] Testing initiatives are relatively inexpensive, can be externally mandated, can be rapidly implemented, and can offer visible results.

Tests are largely being used to drive a school agenda.

Linn reports that testing and assessment initiatives also present many challenges. Standardized achievement tests all suffer from what one critic has termed the "Lake Wobegon effect" where numerous school districts and states report that their students are all above average.[78] Aggregated data fail to provide the specificity needed to understand relative student strengths and weaknesses. Moreover, newly developed state content and performance standards vary a great deal in specificity and emphasis. In numerous states, student gains on National Assessment of Educational Progress (NAEP) were significantly less than gains on state-developed assessments, leading to speculation that different assessments and standards vary widely and measure different constructs depending on the specificity, thoughtfulness and comprehensiveness of the standards at hand.

Another problem with standards is the dual goals of high expectations and the inclusion of all children. Absolute goals set at high (or world-class) levels are expected to apply to all students. Yet, Linn points out that it is quite possible to have high standards without the standards being the same for all students. Furthermore, it is one thing to strive for high standards and another to uphold them. Standards, as they are established at both the national and state levels, are currently resulting in the failure of many students. Grade-level retention will apparently lead to a sense of failure for extremely large numbers of children around the country. There is also concern that these students will not receive the necessary help and services they will need. Linn leaves us with his sobering finding that "the problem of setting standards remains as much a fundamental, unsolved problem as it was 20 years ago."[79]

Can we have uniformly high standards for all students?

Many school reform experts like Levin and Darling-Hammond advocate for advisory (rather than mandatory) standards in which content frameworks serve as guidelines to be considered and adopted by schools.[80] Darling-Hammond believes that standards should not be prescriptions, but should be shared professional norms and knowledge. They should be tools for inquiry and serve as guideposts, not straightjackets. She further recommends curriculum frameworks structured around content and performance stan-

We should use standards as guidelines, not straightjackets.

dards. She argues for standards developed by professional associations like NCTM. They offer a compass, not a blueprint for change. *The standards are clear enough to help teachers develop curricula, but not so extensive and prescriptive as to require superficial content coverage or to limit teachers' inventiveness in bringing ideas to life for their students.*

As a result, it is critical to strive for a curriculum of understanding rather than one of exposure. Here, greater depth, rather than breadth, is strived for and reflects what Ted Sizer describes as "less being more." Critical and deep learning will only occur when fewer important topics are learned well and in-depth. On the other hand, racing through the curriculum and trying to cover it all leads to shallow and superficial learning experiences. Curriculum frameworks, then, should provide a basic structure of ideas and serve not as curriculum straightjackets, but as a bridge between standards, at the one end, and what happens in the classroom, at the other.

Deep learning is more important than broad learning.

Some educators call for "diversifying assessment" by using a wider variety of evaluation strategies and not relying simply on standardized tests as the sole criterion of students' abilities and achievement. They feel that standardized testing will only perpetuate inequities in educational opportunities of various groups. Darling-Hammond also calls for multiple performance-based opportunities ranging from essay and oral exams, reviews of class work, and research papers, to student interviews and portfolios of their work. Students should have some choice and be able to defend their work before jurors. Darling-Hammond recommends that we find a middle ground between standards that are largely symbolic and those that are laundry lists of facts and skills with no unifying conception for developing understanding. There needs to be a balance between over-prescription of standards, on the one hand, and excessive school autonomy to develop those standards on the other.

Above all it's important that assessment be embedded in the teaching and learning process, rather than delivered out of context during discrete testing moments. We, too, believe, along with Darling-Hammond, that the process of change is "inherently constructivist" and that each school must struggle with assessment issues for itself if it is to develop deep understanding and commitment needed for major changes in practice.[81] Unfortunately, too few of the standards-based programs and ideas currently rest on teachers' and administrators' opportunities to learn, experiment, and adapt ideas to their local context.

Constructivism is at the heart of powerful learning.

School leaders are under an intense pressure to produce, though they have very little control over the standards or assessments on which their schools are to be judged. In an attempt to assist schools in the change effort, Congress initiated the Comprehensive School Reform Demonstration (CSRD) Program in 1997 as a means of jump-starting comprehensive school change. Congress actually specified nine criteria for applicants to consider and named 17 research-based school designs as possible vehicles for school change. Over 1600 schools are currently receiving CSRD grants ranging from $50,000 to $75,000 per year for three years to comprehensively redesign ways in which they operate. Programs such as CSRD (as well as programs like Title I) are required by law to be much more concerned about formative feedback and assessment of their outcomes. With so much money targeted to low-achieving students in at-risk schools, there is a greater expectation for school improvement and a heightened sense of accountability.

Still, with so much change happening at once, and the expectation for results being so high, determining the type of assessment that makes the most sense is difficult. In fact, Slavin states "schools must be seen as differently ready for different kinds of solutions,"[82] while *Assessment is critical to the growth of your school.* Stringfield says that we often make the mistake of applying the "wrong strategies to the wrong settings."[83] Thus, it becomes clear that the assessment effort needs to occur at the earliest stages of the change process so that schools can know if they are ready for change and are making the right choice for the right situation and the right reasons. A major purpose of evaluation and assessment, then, is to help school communities make informed decisions about how they will go about changing their school. We need to help build the local capacity of teachers to make these informed decisions about change. There is still lively debate about what reforms are best for what types of schools. We also know from the literature that there should be more attempts to "scale-up" from what we have learned about the different approaches to change.[84] Understanding these approaches to change can enable us to tackle the problems of school improvement more effectively.

In closing, schools will need to focus on whole-school, rather than piecemeal, change. Assessment will need to focus on a balance of process and outcome variables depending upon which change model or process they choose to follow. Improvements in teaching and learning will need to be fundamental. But there also must be attention paid to the implementation of the change itself. If change is not implemented with some degree of fidelity to the original intentions, then schools are likely to be assessing nonevents. School questionnaires, benchmarks, validation visits, and alternative assessments will need to be explored and developed. Furthermore, the school culture will need to be monitored and assessed, especially the area of its beliefs about how students learn. Finally, standardized achievement test scores and their relationship to state-developed content and performance standards will need to be continuously examined and monitored. After three years, the South Central staff learned to simultaneously evaluate their fidelity to the Project Improve process and to assess its impact on student learning and their dispositions towards that learning.

Chapter Summary

As we note at the beginning of this chapter, the literature on change provides some useful directions but does not point to a definitive model of change that will work in all places at all times. Perhaps this isn't so surprising when we consider that school change is an immensely complex process that involves a myriad of stakeholders, all of whom may have somewhat different perspectives on the ultimate goals of change. Yet, this doesn't mean that there is no value in examining the research on change. Indeed, we believe that a change effort is enhanced to the degree that this literature is used as a base from which the change effort proceeds.

We note, too, at the beginning of the chapter that one of the central tenets that this literature suggests is that schools must utilize a *design model*—that is, a logic to guide their change effort—that incorporates some of the central findings of research and past experience. To not develop or utilize such a model runs the risk taken too often—of beginning each change initiative from scratch, as if there wasn't any other educator who had the same issues that you have. This is why we organized our recommendations for South Central School around one such design model—Project Improve.

Project Improve offered South Central a systematic and tested process for creating shared *meaning and purpose* primarily centered on the improvement of teaching and learning. During the school's "buy-in" period, a high-stakes student achievement problem portrayed in the school's state report card, was identified and eventually owned and personalized by the school staff. The Project Improve design model also provided a systematic process for *building the capacity* of staff around the content (the what) and process of change (the how) so that staff could better identify and solve their own context specific challenges and problems. Throughout the literature on school change, we also found a heightened awareness of the significance of changing *school culture* (how people think and act) so that new practices embedded in the change process can be aligned and reconciled with new and emerging ways in which the staff thought about student ability and potential for learning. Over a three-year period, South Central School went through a reculturing process in which the school changed from a culture of resignation and complacency to one of *continuous improvement*. School change and improvement at South Central became a normal part of the school's everyday life rather than another add-on with a finite life cycle. Finally, in order to determine whether progress was being made, the South Central leadership team plotted their voyage by regularly *evaluating* their fidelity to the Project Improve process and by frequently *assessing* its impact on student achievement as well as student dispositions about their learning experiences.

Superintendent Jennifer Craig thanked us for sharing these lessons learned from both the change literature and from our experiences facilitating South Central School's change voyage. We hoped that launching new schools in the future would become a reality for the Bridgeport School District and that our knowledge and experience would inform the process.

References

1. Larson, R. L. (1993). Making sense of change: What we know from research and practice. In J. R. Hoyle & D. M. Estes (Eds.), *The first yearbook of the national council of professors of educational administration*. Lancaster, PA: Technomic Publishing Co., p. 278.

2. Fullan, M. G. (1994). *Change forces*. London: Falmer Press, p. vii.

3. Fullan, M. G. (1991). *The new meaning of educational change (2nd ed.)*. New York: Teachers College Press, p. 47.

4. Chenoweth, T. G., & Kushman, J. (1996). Building initial commitment to accelerate. In Finnan, C., St. John, E., McCarthy, J., & Slovacek, S. (Eds.), *Accelerated schools in action: lessons from the field*. Thousand Oaks, CA: Corwin Press, pp. 145–168.

5. Fullan. *The new meaning of educational change*, op. cit., p.47.

6. Ibid.

7. Giacquinta, J. (1998). Seduced and abandoned: Some lasting conclusions about planned change from the Cambiere school study. In Hargreaves, A., Lieberman, A., Fullan, M., & Hopkins, D. (Eds.), *International handbook of educational change*. London: Kluwer Academic Publishers, pp. 163–180.

8. Slavin, R. (1998). Sand, bricks, and seeds: School change strategies and readiness for reform. In Hargreaves, et al. (Eds.), *International handbook of educational change*, op. cit., pp. 1299–1313.

9. Levin, H. (1998). Accelerated schools: A decade of evolution. In Hargreaves, et al. (Eds*.), International handbook of educational change*, op. cit., pp. 807–830.

10. Berman, P., & McLaughlin, M. (1979). *An exploratory study of school district adaptation*. Santa Monica, CA: Rand.

11. Lieberman, A., & Grolnick, M. (1998). Educational reform networks: Changes in the reform of reform. In Hargreaves, et al. (Eds.), *International handbook of educational change,* op. cit., pp. 710–729.

12. Giacquinta. Seduced and abandoned. In Hargreaves, et al. (Eds.), *International handbook of educational change,* op. cit.

13. Cochran-Smith, M. (1998). Teaching for social change: Towards a theory of teacher education. In Hargreaves, et al. (Eds.), *International handbook of educational change*, op. cit., pp. 916–951.

14. Joyce, B., & Calhoun, E. (1998). Conduct of inquiry on teaching: The search for models more effective than the recitation. In Hargreaves, et al. (Eds.), *International handbook of educational change*, op. cit., pp. 1216–1241.

15. Bridges, W. (1991). *Managing transitions: Making the most of change*. Reading, MA: Addison–Wesley Publishing Co.

16. Tyack, D., & Cuban, L. (1995). *Tinkering toward utopia: A century of public school reform.* Cambridge: Harvard University Press.

17. Fullan. *The new meaning of educational change,* op. cit.

18. Pincus, J. (1974). Incentives for innovation in public schools. *Review of Educational Research, 44*(2), 113–144.

19. Giaquinta. Seduced and abandoned. In Hargreaves, et al. (Eds.), *International handbook of educational change,* op. cit.

20. Fullan. *The new meaning of educational change,* op. cit.

21. Evans, R. (1996). *The human side of school change: Reform, resistance, and the real–life problems of innovation.* San Francisco: Jossey-Bass.

22. Zemelman S., Daniels, H., & Hyde, A. (1998). *Best practices: New standards for teaching and learning in American schools (2nd ed.).* Portsmouth, NH: Heinemann.

23. Olson, L. (November 2, 1994). Learning their lessons. *Education Week,* 43–46.

24. Evans. *The human side of school change: Reform, resistance, and the real–life problems of innovation,* op. cit.

25. Fink, D., & Stoll, L. Educational change: Easier said than done. In Hargreaves, et al. (Eds). *International handbook of educational change,* op. cit., pp. 297–321.

26. Bodilly, S. (1996). *Lessons learned from the new American schools development corporations development phase.* Santa Monica, CA: Rand.

27. Allen, L., Rogers, D., Hensley, F., Glanton, M., & Livingston, M. (1999). *A guide to renewing your school: Lessons from the league of professional schools.* San Francisco: Jossey-Bass.

28. Giaquinta. Seduced and abandoned. In Hargreaves, et al. (Eds.), *International handbook of educational change,* op. cit.

29. Joyce, B. R., Hersh, R. H., & McKibbin, M. (1983). *The structure of school improvement.* New York: Longman, p. 71.

30. Evans. *The human side of school change: Reform, resistance, and the real-life problems of innovation,* op. cit.

31. Bridges. *Managing transitions,* op. cit.

32. Miles, M. (1998). Finding keys to school change: A forty year odyssey. In Hargreaves, et al. (Eds.), *International handbook of educational change,* op. cit., pp. 37–69.

33. Chenoweth & Kushman. Building initial commitment to accelerate, op. cit.

34. Fink & Stoll. Educational change: Easier said than done. In Hargreaves, et al. (Eds.), *International handbook of educational change,* op. cit.

35. Allen, L., et al. *A guide to renewing your school.* op. cit.

36. S. Stringfield as quoted in Olson, L. (April 14, 1999). Following the plan. *Education Week, 18*(31), 29.

37. House, E., & McQuillan, P. (1998). Three perspectives on school reform. In Hargreaves, et al. (Eds.), *International handbook of educational change*, op. cit., pp. 198–213.

38. Bereiter, C., & Scardamalia, M. (1998). Beyond Bloom's taxonomy: Rethinking knowledge for the knowledge age. In Hargreaves, et al. (Eds.), *International handbook on educational change.*, op. cit., pp. 675–692.

39. Zemmelman, S., Daniels, H., & Hyde, A. *Best practice: New standards for teaching and learning in American schools*, op. cit.

40. Levin, H. (1996). Accelerated schools: The background. In Finnan, C., St. John, E., McCarthy, J., & Slovacek, S. (Eds.), *Accelerated schools in action: Lessons from the field.* Thousand Oaks, CA: Corwin Press, pp. 3–23.

41. Gardner, H.C. (1983). *Frames of mind: The theory of multiple intelligences.* New York: Basic Books.

42. Means, B., Chelemer, C., & Knapp, M. (1991). *Teaching advanced skills to at-risk students*. San Francisco: Jossey-Bass.

43. Miles, M. Finding keys to school change. In Hargreaves, et al. (Eds.), *International handbook of educational change,* op. cit., pp. 37–69.

44. Lortie, D. C. (1975). *Schoolteacher*. Chicago: University of Chicago Press.

45. House, E., & McQillian, P. Three perspectives on school reform. In Hargreaves, et al. (Eds.), *International handbook of educational change*, op. cit., pp. 198–213; McLaughlin, M. W. (1998). Listening and learning from the field: Tales of policy implementation and situated practice. In Hargreaves, et al. (Eds.), *International handbook of educational change*, op. cit., pp. 70–84.

46. West, M. (1998). Quality in schools: Developing a model for school improvement. In Hargreaves, et al. (Eds.), *International handbook of educational change,* op. cit., pp. 768–789.

47. Fink, D., & Stoll, L. Educational change: Easier said than done. In Hargreaves, et al. *International handbook of educational change,* op. cit.

48. Pressman, J., & Wildavsky, A. (1979). *Implementation*. Berkeley: University of California Press.

49. Charters, W. W., & Pellegrin, R. (1972). Barriers to the innovation process: Four case studies of differentiated staffing. *Educational Administration Quarterly, 9*(1), 3–14.

50. Charters, W. W., Jr., & Jones, J. E. (1973). On the risk of appraising nonevents in program evaluation. *Educational Researcher, 2*(11), 5–7.

51. McLaughlin, M.W. Listening and learning from the field: Tales of policy implementation and situated practice. In Hargreaves, et al. (Eds.), *International handbook of educational change,* op. cit.

52. Sarason, S. (1971). *The culture of the school and the problem of change.* Boston: Allyn and Bacon.

53. Ibid., p. 2.

54. Fullan. *Change forces*, op. cit., p. ix.

55. Firestone, W. A., & Corbett, H. D. (1998). Planned organizational change. In N. J. Boyan (Ed.), *Handbook of research in educational administration..* New York: Longman, p 333.

56. Hanson, E. M. (quoted in Firestone & Corbett). Ibid., p. 333.

57. Corbett, H. D., Dawson, J. A., & Firestone, W. A. (1984). *School context and school change: Implications for effective planning.* New York Teachers College Press.

58. Sarason. *The culture of the school and the problem of change,* op. cit., p. 3.

59. Tyack & Cuban. *Tinkering towards utopia,* op. cit., p. 1.

60. Fink & Stoll. Educational change: Easier said than done. In Hargreaves, et al. (Eds.), *International handbook of educational change,* op. cit.

61. Darling-Hammond, L. (1995). Policy for restructuring. In A. Lieberman (Ed.), *The work of restructuring schools: Building from the ground up.* New York: Teachers College Press, p. 169.

62. Levin, H. M. (1987). Accelerated schools for the disadvantaged. *Educational Leadership. 44*(6), 19–21.

63. Levin, H. (1998). Accelerated schools: A decade of evolution. In Hargreaves, et al. (Eds.), *International handbook of educational change,* op. cit., p. 819.

64. Ibid., p. 820.

65. Comer, J. P. (1980). *School power.* New York: Macmillan.

66. Darling-Hammond, L. (1997). *The right to learn.* San Francisco: Jossey-Bass, p. 105.

67. Comer. *School power,* op. cit., p. 165.

68. Keating, D. (1998). A framework for educational change: Human development in the learning society. In Hargreaves, et al (Eds.), *International handbook of educational change,* op. cit., pp. 693–709.

69. Cuban, L. (1992). Managing dilemmas while building professional communities. *Educational Researcher, 21*(1), 6.

70. Darling-Hammond, L. Policy for restructuring. In Leiberman (Ed.), *The work of restructuring schools from the ground up,* op. cit.

71. Cuban. Managing dilemmas while building professional communities, op. cit., p. 9.

72. Ingvarson, L. (1998). Teaching standards: Foundations for professional development reform. In Hargreaves, et al. (Eds.), *International handbook of educational change,* op. cit., pp. 1006–1031.

73. Louis, K. S., & Miles, M. (1990). *Improving the urban high school: What works and what doesn't.* New York: Teachers College Press.

74. Fullan, M. G. *The new meaning of educational change,* op. cit.

75. Miele, F. (1995). Interview with Robert Sternberg on the bell curve. *Sceptic Magazine, 3*(3), 72–80.

76. Sacks, P. (1999). Standardized minds: *The high price of America's testing culture and what we can do to change it.* Cambridge, MA: Perseus.

77. Linn, R. L. (2000). Assessments and accountability. *Educational Researcher, 29*(2), 4–16.

78. Koretz, D. (1988). Arriving at Lake Wobegone: Are standardized tests exaggerating achievement and distorting instruction? *American Educator, 12*(2), 8–15.

79. Linn, R. L. Assessment and accountability, op. cit., p. 11.

80. Levin, H. Accelerated schools: A decade of evolution. In Hargreaves, et al. (Eds.), *International handbook of educational change.* op. cit.; Darling-Hammond, L. *The right to learn,* op. cit.

81. Darling-Hammond, L. *The right to learn,* op. cit., p. 227.

82. Slavin, R. Sand, bricks, and seeds: School change strategies and readiness for reform. In Hargreaves, et al. (Eds*.), International handbook of educational change*, op. cit., p. 1302.

83. Stringfield, S., Millsap, M. A., & Herman, R. (1998). Using promising programs to improve educational processes and change. In Hargreaves, et al. (Eds.), *International handbook of educational change*, op. cit., p.1314.

84. Calhoun, E., & Joyce, B. (1998). "Inside-out" and "outside-in": Learning from past and present school improvement paradigms. In Hargreaves, et al. (Eds.), *International Handbook of educational change*, op. cit., pp. 1286–1298.

PORTS OF CALL IN YOUR FUTURE NAVIGATIONS: Resources for Change

In this section, we provide you with an inventory of "ports" in which to anchor so that you can learn even more about comprehensive school change.

This inventory is by no means exhaustive. There are literally thousands of sources available that can be of use to you as you plot your course. However, the sources listed below do provide valuable information that for the most part support the assumptions of this book (that change must focus on student learning, be comprehensive, occur through a democratic process, involve leadership across the school and community, and create a new culture to support these changes). What's more, these sources are either mentioned in this book or extend your thinking by introducing you to new information and people/organizations.

Like Mary and her leadership team, all of you are busy and are not full-time change agents. Thus, we don't expect that you have the time to sift through reams of books and web sites to find out where to begin. As we did for South Central School, we have arranged some of what we consider helpful sources into seven major categories:

- ◆ **Organizations** with resources that can help you with the change process in general.

- ◆ **Educational laboratories and research centers** that have specific missions on comprehensive change and who regularly consult with schools.

- ◆ Specific **comprehensive school-reform "models"** (most of which are mentioned in this book) the developers of which provide technical assistance to schools.

- ◆ **Organizations and associations whose work is content- or subject-based** and who can assist you with curricular issues in the areas normally assessed in schools (math, reading/writing, science).

- ◆ **Printed resources** such as books, periodicals, and research sites that you can access in a library, bookstore, or on-line.

- ◆ **Tools** such as reports, videos, and general catalogues/web sites.

- ◆ **Assessments** of comprehensive change.

In each of these sections we provide you with a small number of sources that you can use to augment your resource base. These sources were chosen in part because our experience tells us that they are key to your journey and/or because they link you to other sources that can augment your search. To repeat, this is not an exhaustive list; however, it is one that gives you a good place to start. As captains of your own vessel, we're sure that in your search you'll find other gems that are of particular value to you.

Organizations

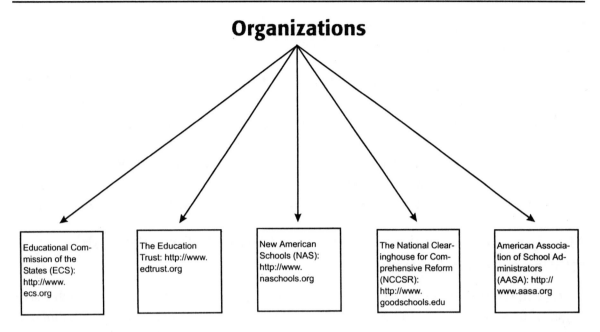

Educational Commission of the States (ECS): http://www.ecs.org

The Education Trust: http://www.edtrust.org

New American Schools (NAS): http://www.naschools.org

The National Clearinghouse for Comprehensive Reform (NCCSR): http://www.goodschools.edu

American Association of School Administrators (AASA): http://www.aasa.org

Educational Commission of the States (ECS): http://www.ecs.org

ECS is an interstate compact of 49 states and the District of Columbia that is dedicated to improving education through an exchange of perspectives between educational leaders and policymakers. ECS focuses on major ideas and policies affecting education rather than on specific "how-to" issues. They are quite committed to school change/reform in general and work primarily in the area of providing technical assistance to states, recommending legislative testimony on a variety of issues, and conducting policy audits. Their web page has a link to a number of educational organizations as well as comprehensive school reform sites.

The Education Trust: http://www.edtrust.org

The Education Trust is a nonprofit organization that has as its goal making K–12 schools and postsecondary institutions work for all students. They are particularly interested in the connections and articulation between public schools and colleges/universities. The Trust has published a number of excellent reports on a number of critical issues, one of which is the changing nature of the student population (see the discussion in Chapter 3 of this book). Their web site has useful linkages to sites on comprehensive school reform and the standards movement.

New American Schools (NAS):
http://www.naschools.org

NAS is a nonpartisan, nonprofit organization that is helping more than 3,500 schools across the county to improve student performance. After 10 years of working in schools, New American Schools has become a leading authority on comprehensive school reform approaches. Since 1991, New American Schools has done extensive research and development to determine what works and what does not work in schools through its support of 10 comprehensive school reform approaches, known as Design Teams. These approaches are built around proven research and are producing positive results for students and schools today.

The National Clearinghouse for Comprehensive Reform (NCCSR):
http://www.goodschools.gwu.edu

NCCSR collects, analyzes, synthesizes, and disseminates information on comprehensive school reform in K–12 institutions. The clearinghouse is operated by George Washington University in partnership with the Council for Basic Education and the Institute for Educational Leadership, under a grant by the U.S. Department of Education. This site is clearly geared towards practitioners and offers a singular focus on comprehensive school change.

American Association of School Administrators (AASA):
http://www.aasa.org

AASA, founded in 1865, is the professional organization for more than 14,000 educational leaders across America and in many other countries. AASA has four major focus areas: (a) improving the condition of children and youth; (b) preparing schools and school systems for the 21st century; (c) connecting schools and communities; and (d) enhancing the quality and effectiveness of leaders. This site offers many useful resources and links to important school reform information.

Educational Laboratories and Research Centers

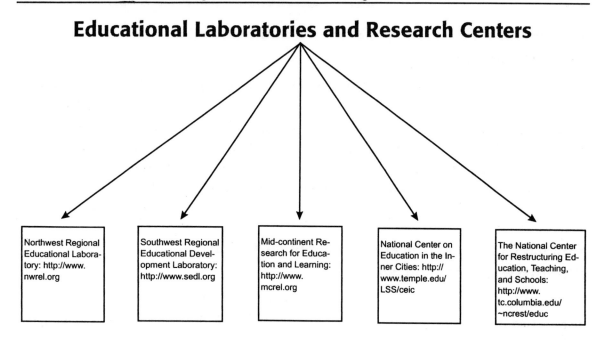

Northwest Regional Educational Laboratory: http://www.nwrel.org

Southwest Regional Educational Development Laboratory: http://www.sedl.org

Mid-continent Research for Education and Learning: http://www.mcrel.org

National Center on Education in the Inner Cities: http://www.temple.edu/LSS/ceic

The National Center for Restructuring Education, Teaching, and Schools: http://www.tc.columbia.edu/~ncrest/educ

Northwest Regional Educational Laboratory: http://www.nwrel.org

NWREL is located in Portland, Oregon, and is one of the original federally supported regional educational labs. While NWREL is involved in educational assistance nationwide, its primary clients are in the Pacific Northwest and Alaska. NWREL's current activities include assessment and evaluation, comprehensive assistance to schools and districts, school improvement, and strengthening the relationship between schools, children, and families. The NWREL web site has links to comprehensive school reform and development (CSRD), which includes (a) information on CSRD the Northwest, (b) a catalog of comprehensive school reform models, (c) contacts for assistance and resources, and (d) a listing of CSRD schools.

Southwest Regional Educational Development Laboratory: http://www.sedl.org

SEDL is located in Austin, Texas, and is also one of the original federally supported regional educational laboratories. It serves the Southwest and has linkages to school districts throughout the region. Current programs include a focus on improving student achievement in low performing schools, improving the involvement of families and communities in local schools, and assistance to non-English speakers in schools. SEDL is a partner with the Southeast Comprehensive Technical Assistance Center, which specializes in assistance to schools involved in comprehensive school reform.

Mid-continent Research for Education and Learning: http://www.mcrel.org

Located in the Denver area, MCREL is deeply involved in comprehensive school reform. Current programs include a comprehensive school-reform center, a computer-based early-literacy program for schools, and a major initiative on science and mathematics. MCREL's web site has useful links to various school reform models, sites where those models are being implemented, and contact information for those sites. Like the other laboratories, MCREL also provides technical assistance to schools nationwide, but especially to those in the mid-continent region.

National Center on Education in the Inner Cities: http://www.temple.edu/LSS/ceic

This Center focuses on research and development around the question, "What conditions are necessary to improve the learning of children and youth in the inner cities?" Although the Center is located in Philadelphia, it is a consortium of three institutions: Temple University, University of Houston, and University of Illinois–Chicago. Among the Center's current programs are (a) identifying the characteristics of exemplary schools in fostering resiliency in students, (b) examining the conditions of effective Title I programs, and (c) establishing productive school-community connections. The web site has useful connections to other sites on comprehensive school reform. You might also review the web-site of the Mid-Atlantic Educational Laboratory for Student Success (LSS) at Temple www.temple.edu/lss

The National Center for Restructuring Education, Teaching, and Schools: http://www.tc.columbia.edu/~ncrest/educ

Better known as NCREST, this Center has been at Columbia University since 1990 and was the home of scholars such as Linda Darling-Hammond and Ann Lieberman, both of whom are quoted widely in our book. NCREST's primary mission is to improve school organization, pedagogy, and school governance. The essential means for reaching these goals is through the restructuring of teacher learning and professional development. In this way, NCREST is probably more teacher-centered than most other labs and centers, although its main activities are more research oriented than application oriented.

Comprehensive School Reform Models

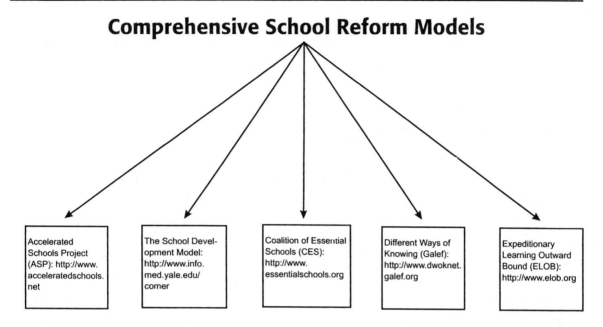

| Accelerated Schools Project (ASP): http://www.acceleratedschools.net | The School Development Model: http://www.info.med.yale.edu/comer | Coalition of Essential Schools (CES): http://www.essentialschools.org | Different Ways of Knowing (Galef): http://www.dwoknet.galef.org | Expeditionary Learning Outward Bound (ELOB): http://www.elob.org |

Accelerated Schools Project (ASP): http://www.acceleratedschools.net

The model has been primarily used at the elementary and middle school levels, but some high schools are beginning to use the model as well. Powerful learning approaches used to educate talented and gifted students are used with all students. Instruction is active, "hands-on," well paced, collaborative, and designed to meet the needs and interests of students so that they are genuinely motivated to learn. The model provides a systematic design process for collecting baseline information on the state of the school, developing a vision, setting priorities, creating site-based governance structures, and initiating inquiry to address school challenges. Three guiding principles direct all decisions related to the school curriculum, instruction, and organization: Unity of Purpose; Empowerment coupled with Responsibility; and Building on Strengths. The national center for the project is located at the University of Connecticut. Satellite centers located around the country provide school leadership teams with training, technical support, and assistance.

The School Development Model: http://www.info.med.yale.edu/comer

The primary goal is to build shared purpose and meaning between the home and school in order to attend to unfulfilled child development and relationship needs which typically impede academic progress in schools. A school planning and management team (SPMT) develops and monitors a comprehensive school improvement plan, while a student and staff support team (SSST) helps to improve the social climate of the school. A parent team promotes parental involvement in all aspects of the school program. "Comer" schools are supported by the national center at Yale University, regional professional development centers, and partnerships with urban school districts and universities around the country.

Coalition of Essential Schools (CES): http://www.essentialschools.org

Originally focusing on high schools, CES' scope now includes K–8 schools. The schools share a set of ideas known as the common principles of which there are 10. Highlights include helping students learn to use their minds well and a belief in having students learn fewer things in depth, portrayed by the aphorism "less is more." Also there is a strong belief that no teacher in the middle or high school should have responsibility for more than 80 students, and in the elementary school, no more than 20 students. The student rather than the teacher is viewed as the "worker" and the teacher is more of a facilitator who helps students learn how to learn. Moreover teachers must be "generalists first and specialists second" in which multiple obligations as teacher–counselor–manager are expected along with a greater sense of commitment to the entire school. Assessment is based on real tasks in which students must "exhibit" their expertise. There is an assumption that no two schools look the same and what the school becomes depends on how it interprets the common principles. Coalition of Essential Schools' work is supported by a national office in Oakland, California, and regional centers around the country.

Different Ways of Knowing (Galef): http://www.dwoknet.galef.org

The model offers a program of professional development known as Different Ways of Knowing, which offers a three-year course of study for teachers blended with powerful curriculum tools. The curriculum integrates the study of history and social studies with literature and writing; math and science; and the performing, visual, and media arts. The arts focus of Different Ways of Knowing is an important pathway to children's understanding and expression of deep knowledge in all disciplines. The model assumes that students learn best what matters to them and that they must construct meaning for themselves. The model also views the "world as its laboratory," values students working in collaboration rather than isolation, and espouses that learners never stop learning and that the measure of true learning is not recall of material, but the generation of new questions that address new possibilities. The model is supported by national offices in Los Angeles and Kentucky and by teams of coaches who periodically provide training and visit the schools.

Expeditionary Learning Outward Bound (ELOB): http://www.elob.org

Student work is organized around interdisciplinary "learning expeditions," long-term, in-depth investigations of themes or topics that engage students in the classroom and the outside world through authentic projects, fieldwork, and service. Students stay with the same teacher or groups of teachers for more than one year and teachers participate in a series of professional development activities. Design principles include strong values for "self-discovery," collaboration with peers, respect for the natural world and ecological sustainability, solitude and reflection, and community service. The main offices are in Cambridge, Massachusetts, and Garrison, New York, and 11 Outward Bound schools and centers serve as regional offices and training centers.

Content- or Subject-Based Reforms and Associations

First Steps: http://www.firststeps.com	Reading Recovery: http://www.readingrecovery.org	National Writing Project: http://www.writingproject.org	Connected Mathematics Project (CMP) 6–8: http://www.mth.msu.edu/cmp
National Council of Teachers of Mathematics (NCTM): http://www.nctm.org	National Council of Teachers of English (NCTE): http://www.ncte.org	Eisenhower National Clearinghouse (ENC): http://www.enc.org	National Council for the Social Studies (NCSS): http://www.socialstudies.org

First Steps:
http://www.first-steps.com

First Steps is a K–10 reading language arts model developed in 1989 by the state Education Department of Western Australia. It has been available in the U.S. since 1995 under the management of Heinemann Publishers, USA. More than 600 schools in Australia, New Zealand, Canada, and the United Kingdom currently use First Steps. It is also currently being used in 191 school districts throughout the United States. First Steps concentrates on reading, writing, spelling, and oral language development. Training and curricular materials focus on a developmental continuum that is a diagnostic framework for mapping out individual student stages of language and literary development. Resource books are also provided to help teachers with the creation of appropriate classroom activities. First Steps serves teachers and school systems well by creating a common learning and assessment language and by providing a very practical resource tool for monitoring and assessing student learning in the language arts. Professional development is customized to meet the needs of schools and school systems. The national headquarters is located in Portsmouth, New Hampshire, and consultants are located across the states and in Australia.

Reading Recovery:
http://www.readingrecovery.org

New Zealand educator and psychologist Marie M. Clay is the creator of the Reading Recovery design model. The program first came to the United States through Ohio State University in 1984. It has spread to more than 10,000 schools in the U.S. In *Redesigning Education*, Kenneth Wilson refers to Reading Recovery as probably the closest thing to a process of research, development, design, and marketing that U.S. education reform has seen yet. In all types of school systems, the program consistently helps more than four of every five failing first grade readers reach average levels of classroom performance in reading in just 12 to 20 weeks of daily half-hour lessons with a specially trained teacher. Teacher training is rigorous and occurs at only approved sites throughout the country. There are currently 23 university Reading Recovery training centers and some 429 teacher training sites across the country. Frankly, we are surprised that given Reading Recovery's track record that it hasn't spread to all of the nations schools. Costs and politics associated with using specially trained teachers in one-on-one tutorials at only the first-grade level have certainly limited Reading Recovery's proliferation.

National Writing Project:
http://www.writingproject.org

The National Writing Project (NWP) is a nationwide professional development model begun in 1974 at the University of California, Berkeley where its founder, James Gray, established a program for K–16 teachers called the Bay Area Writers Project. The primary goal of the project is to improve student writing by improving the teaching of writing in the nation's schools. The writing process itself and writing across the curriculum are typically stressed. Additional areas of focus include emergent literacy, assessment, English-language learners, the writing and reading connection, and academic standards. Through federal funding, the project is able to serve more than 130,000 teachers every year. Writing project sites are typically housed in universities. Currently, there are 167 sites in 49 states. The model is based on the belief that the key to education reform is a network of exemplary teachers of writing who work with schools and school districts around their particular professional development needs. Summer institutes invite teachers to demonstrate and examine their approaches to teaching writing and then bring back new ideas to their schools and school systems. Each local site supports its own cadre of teacher leaders who provide professional development tailored to the needs of its particular community. The National Writing Project hosts yearly meetings, conferences, and retreats for teacher leaders. The national center also conducts annual reviews of all local sites.

Connected Mathematics Project (CMP) 6–8: http://www.mth.msu.edu/cmp

The Connected Math Project was first developed in 1991 and has spread to over 3,200 U.S. schools. The national center is housed in the Department of Mathematics at Michigan State University. CMP is a mathematics curriculum for middle schools that helps students develop an understanding of important concepts, skills, procedures, and ways of thinking and reasoning in number, geometry, measurement, algebra, probability, and statistics. Features include being problem-centered, encouraging skills-based practice, being research based, and demonstrating positive effects on student learning. The Show Me Center at the University of Missouri and Scott-Foresman/Addison-Wesley also support the CMP through the dissemination of information and the development of curricular materials. CMP trainers are recommended to school districts by the national center at the University of Michigan.

National Council of Teachers of Mathematics (NCTM): http://www.nctm.org

NCTM is the world's largest mathematics organization with more than 120,000 members in the U.S. and Canada. It has developed a widely used and cited set of content, instructional, and assessment based standards for mathematics. These standards have inspired the development of numerous curriculum programs and have also been incorporated into most of the recently published textbooks. NCTM also publishes several journals, maintains a web site, and sponsors annual meetings and professional development institutes.

National Council of Teachers of English (NCTE): http://www.ncte.org

The NCTE is comprised of 77,000 members and is devoted to improving the teaching and learning of English and the language arts at all levels of education. NCTE and the International Reading Association (IRA) have developed a set of standards that have become the definitive national description of good teaching and learning of literacy. They also developed a set of books that illustrate the standards in classroom practice. NCTE publishes a newspaper, at least 12 journals, numerous books, and an annual catalog. NCTE also sponsors annual regional conventions, conferences, assemblies, and special interest groups. NCTE advocates for teachers' academic freedom and sponsors research projects.

Eisenhower National Clearinghouse (ENC): http://www.enc.org

This organization identifies, collects, and provides the best selection of math and science education resources (K-12) on the Internet. It also offers a free subscription to *ENC Focus: A Magazine for Classroom Innovators.*

National Council for the Social Studies (NCSS): http://www.socialstudies.org

NCSS is the largest association in the country devoted solely to social studies education. Globally, there are some 26,000 members ranging from K–12 to higher education. NCSS has developed a set of standards that provides for an articulated K–12 social studies program and serves as a framework for the integration of other national standards from history, civics, geography, global education, and economics. These standards ensure an integrated social science, behavioral science, and humanities approach in the development of curriculum and the teaching of social studies. NCSS maintain a web site that will help you find many resources, professional development opportunities, and Internet links.

Printed Resources

We divide printed resources into three categories: books (foundational and specific), periodicals, and research services. The resources listed below have been very useful for us as we wrote this book, but we recognize that other sources might be useful for other approaches to change.

Foundational Books

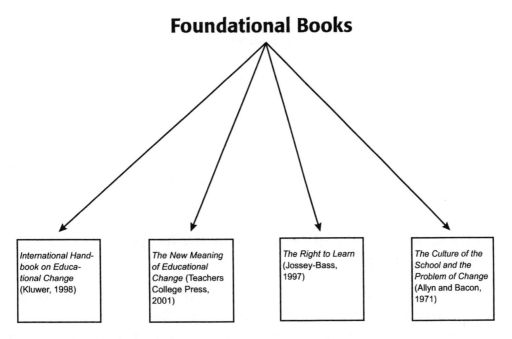

International Handbook on Educational Change (Kluwer, 1998)

The New Meaning of Educational Change (Teachers College Press, 2001)

The Right to Learn (Jossey-Bass, 1997)

The Culture of the School and the Problem of Change (Allyn and Bacon, 1971)

We believe that four books are foundational in understanding the change process. These books are somewhat more "academic," but are essential to understanding the principles of comprehensive change as discussed in our book.

International Handbook on Educational Change (Kluwer, 1998)

This is an excellent up-to-date compendium on many of the most critical concepts on educational change. The two-volume set (edited by Hargreaves, Lieberman, Fullan, and Hopkins) is divided into four sections with more than 60 chapters on a variety of topics. Individuals who have spent their entire career studying school change author many of the chapters. For those who want to understand the roots of many of the issues discussed in our book, this book is a "must read."

The New Meaning of Educational Change (Teachers College Press, 2001)

Now in its third edition, this book by Michael Fullan has become a contemporary classic in the change literature. Fullan artfully combines findings from the research on change with useful directions that educators can follow in order to be more successful in their change endeavors. Chapters that address change and its implications for various school roles (e.g., teachers, principals, district administrators, students, and parents) help the reader to apply the general literature on school change to the roles which they occupy.

The Right to Learn
(Jossey-Bass, 1997)

Published five years ago, this book has already been widely acclaimed and used as a model for school change. Linda Darling-Hammond's premise is that all students have a right to learn and that schools have a duty to teach them to learn. While an advocate of school standards, Darling-Hammond is not a supporter of standardized tests as the only way to assess learning. Instead, she advocates for more professional judgment on the part of teachers who, she argues, must be taught how to flexibly and creatively work with the standards and their assessment. The author is a firm believer in the intersection between top-down and bottom-up changes if educational professionals are involved in their creation and play the main role in their implementation.

The Culture of the School and the Problem of Change
(Allyn and Bacon, 1971)

One of the classics on educational change, Seymour Sarason raises a fundamental question: "Why is it in school reform that the more things change, the more they remain the same?" He addresses this question by arguing that those who advocate changes rarely address the underlying cultural patterns of schools; instead, they overlay changes on top of the patterns. Because these patterns (such as those reinforcing autonomy and the isolation of teachers from one another) often contradict the very changes being implemented, it is no wonder that change rarely seems to take hold. This is a foundational book, and one that leadership teams should read and discuss before they rush to solutions that might not work.

Books with Specific Approaches to Change

The books below are less foundational and more focused in their approach. Each advocates a particular approach to school change, and offers detailed strategies as to how to approach the change process. These are books we recommend because they are consistent with the assumptions in our book.

Implementing Change: Patterns, Principles, and Potholes (Allyn and Bacon, 2001)

This is the second edition of a popular book that centers on what Gene Hall and Shirley Hord term the Concerns-Based Adoption Model (CBAM). This model focuses on three elements: individuals who implement change, facilitators who provide assistance, and the resource system that supports change. This book is particularly useful for leadership teams because it provides helpful research-based suggestions for facilitation and intervention.

Lessons from the New American Schools Scale-Up Phase (RAND Corporation, 1998)

Susan Bodilly's book describes the result of the New American Schools attempt to bring about widespread comprehensive reform in a variety of schools across the nation. RAND was asked to evaluate this effort and the book is a summary of that evaluation. Yet the book goes beyond just reporting results, and draws a number of conclusions about the implementation process that correspond to what we discuss in *Navigating Comprehensive School Change: A Guide for the Perplexed.*

Teaching Advanced Skills to At-Risk Students
(Jossey-Bass, 1991)

This book, written by Barbara Means, Carol Chelmer, and Michael Knapp, is intended especially for educators who work with children who attend high-risk schools. It presents six instructional models that have been successful in teaching advanced skills (mostly in mathematics and literacy) to students who typically do not do well in traditional school environments. As advocated in our book, the authors avoid a deficit model of learning and instead focus on strategies that build on student strengths.

Best Practice: New Standards for Teaching and Learning
in America's Schools (Heinemann, 1998)

This is an excellent overview of what Steven Zemelman, Harvey Daniels, and Arthur Hyde call "best practices" and their application in a number of content areas. Best practices are characterized as follows: student centered, holistic, authentic, reflective, collaborative, democratic, and constructivist. The authors take these practices and show how they can be applied to writing, reading, math, science, social studies, and the arts. They also discuss how these practices can fit into many of the issues of concern to policymakers and others—issues such as school standards, ability grouping, parental issues, special education, and the training of teachers.

Redesigning Education
(Teachers College Press, 1994)

Kenneth Wilson and Bennett Daviss offer a fresh perspective on the frustration of educators (and the public) about the frequent lack of success of so many approaches to school change. The authors argue that education lacks a "design model" approach to change—that is, a systematic approach for building on what has been learned in the past. Because of this, we reinvent change over and over again, and never build a body of knowledge about the change process. In our book, we offer Project Improve as one such design model and argue that this or other design models must be utilized if we are ever to create a culture of continuous improvement in education.

The Human Side of School Change
(Jossey-Bass, 1996)

As the title suggests, Robert Evans' book centers on how we understand change and what we do with this understanding. The book talks about people issues—fear, resistance, resources, leadership—and the role these factors play in the implementation process. William Bridges also discusses some of these issues in his book, *Managing Transitions.* Evans is an organizational psychologist with experience as a high school teacher who knows schools and the people in them. As a result, he is able to offer thoughtful strategies for school leadership teams as they deal with the day-to-day problems of leading and managing the change process.

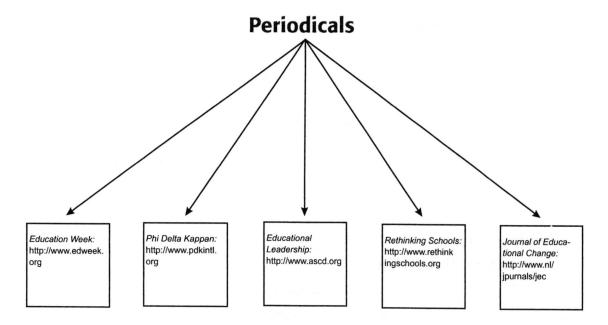

Education Week: http://www.edweek.org

If you want to keep up with news about educational change, you need to follow *Education Week.* In addition to up-to-date information about issues at the federal, state, and local levels, *Education Week* is known for its high quality and accessible features. Recent "special reports" have covered issues such as the quality movement in education, the changing nature of high schools, and leadership (the data that Mary presented to her fcaulty in identifying a "high stakes" problem, as discussed in Chapter 3, came from *Education Week*). Also appearing from time to time are "hot issue" reports, and recent issues have included charter schools, bilingual education, school assessment, and professional development. This web site also has useful links to other sites.

Phi Delta Kappan: http://www.pdkintl.org

For decades, the *Kappan* (as it is known) has featured interesting and well-written articles on topics of interest to professional educators and policymakers. In the past decade, this journal has carried articles on a number of topics discussed in this book: school leadership, educational standards, assessment, professional development, and school restructuring. The Center for Evaluation, Development, and Research (which is part of Phi Delta Kappan) conducts inquiry into important topics such as the use of technology, student retention, and school choice. You can log on to the web site and conduct topic searches of all the Kappan publications.

Educational Leadership:
http://www.ascd.org

This well-known journal, published by the Association for Supervision and Curriculum Development, always has relevant and timely articles about the content and process of school change. Some educators mistakenly believe that *Educational Leadership* is only for school administrators. In reality, the journal is very well suited for school leadership teams as advocated in this book. *Educational Leadership* often runs theme issues on topics related to school change. Recent themes include educational standards, school assessment, class size, and school reform.

Rethinking Schools:
http://www.rethinkingschools.org

Fifteen years ago, a group of teachers in Milwaukee gathered to discuss the absence of quality materials for teachers who work with students of color and/or from poor neighborhoods. Rethinking Schools was born and it has grown into a national organization with a number of quality publications. The organization publishes a quarterly newspaper containing interesting articles on a variety of interesting topics. Rethinking Schools also has produced specialized books and monographs on topics such as testing, school finance, and teaching for equity.

Journal of Educational Change:
http://www.nl/jpurnals/jec

This is a relatively new journal and is currently edited by Andy Hargreaves, one of the editors of the *International Handbook on Educational Change*. Although early articles seem more appropriate for an academic audience, there are articles that would be of interest to school practitioners. Authors whose work appears in recent issues include Michael Fullan, Nel Noddings, Tom Sergiovanni, and Linda Darling-Hammond, all people whom you've encountered in this book.

Research Sites

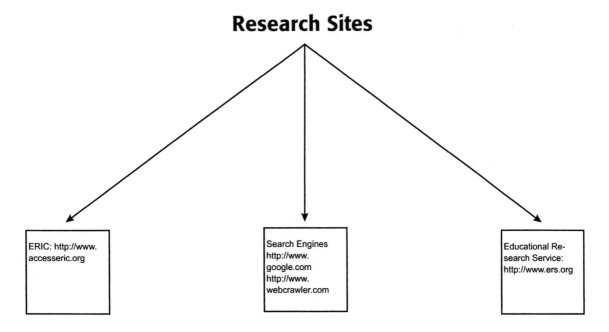

ERIC:
http://www.accesseric.org

The Educational Resources Information Center (ERIC) is the most comprehensive single source for conducting background research on virtually any educational topic. Through a series of descriptors, searches can be conducted by topic, author, publication dates, etc. Almost every educational periodical is listed in the ERIC system, as are books, monographs, technical reports, papers, and dissertations. Most college and university libraries subscribe to ERIC, as do a number of school districts.

Search Engines
http://www.google.com
http://www.webcrawler.com

The Internet allows for access to a multitude of research and information on educational change. However, one needs to be careful; just because something is accessible on the Internet doesn't mean that it is of high quality. Look for sources produced by reputable organizations and which have been reviewed by an independent source. While virtually any search engine can lead you to research information, we have found Google and Webcrawler to be particularly useful.

Educational Research Service:
http://www.ers.org

The ERS was begun by a number of educational organizations that saw the need for a central source for research information needed by many agencies. Thus, organizations such as the American Association of School Administrators, Council of Chief State School Officers, and National Association of Secondary School Principals are linked to the ERS home page. The ERS, through its print and electronic resources, can provide research data on a wide range of educational topics. For school districts that subscribe to the ERS, customized searches on virtually any topic can be provided to meet the needs of the individual district. This is a valuable source for schools and districts engaged in continuous school improvement.

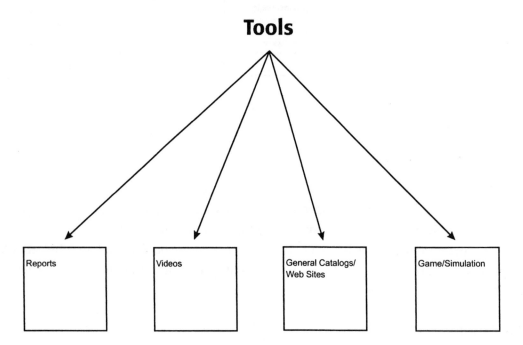

Reports

Comprehensive School Reform–Making Good Choices:
A Guide for Schools and Districts, North Central Regional
Educational Laboratory (NCREL): http://www.ncrel.org

This excellent resource provides an overview of comprehensive school reform, a school self-evaluation tool, and a profiling tool which will help a school chose a comprehensive school reform model that best fits its particular needs.

Comprehensive School Reform–Making Good Choices: Districts Take the Lead, North Central Regional Educational Laboratory (NCREL): http://www.ncrel.org

This is also an excellent resource and offers set of tools focused on school district capacity building and decision making for comprehensive school reform. Seven concrete action steps and eighteen tools for district use are offered.

Comprehensive School Reform, Northwest Regional Education Laboratory (NWREL) http://www.nwrel.org

NWREL offers a variety of excellent tools for comprehensive school reform. We list only a few:

- ◆ Evaluating Whole-School Reform Efforts: A Guide for District and Staff
- ◆ Catalog of School Reform Models: User's Guide
- ◆ Assessment of School Readiness
- ◆ District Leaders' Guide to Reallocating Resources
- ◆ Challenges of Comprehensive School Reform
- ◆ School CSR Self-Assessment Tool

Videos

Enterprise Media: http://www.enterprisemedia.com

Enterprise Media offers training videos and CD-ROMs for organizations going though changes. We particularly recommend the work of Joel Barker (*The Power of Vision* and *The Business of Paradigms*) and Jennifer James (*Windows of Change, Survival Skills for the Future,* and *A Workout for the Mind*).

Teachstream: http://www.teachstream.com

Teachstream offers the very helpful *Video Journal of Education* series. There is a particularly good "change collection" of videos featuring Michael Fullan (*Managing Change*), Michael Fullan and Ann Hargreaves (*What's Worth Fighting for in Education*) and Albert Mamary (*The Spirit of Change*). Other related collections focus on school reform and standards.

Annenberg/CPB Video Catalog:
http://www.learner.org

This catalog offers a variety of videos ranging from the Merrow Report to New American Schools focusing on school change and reform.

General Catalogs/Web Sites

American Society for Training & Development (ASTD):
http://www.astd.org

ASTD provides many excellent organizational development, team building, and training resources and tools.

Association for Supervision and Curriculum Development (ASCD):
http://www.ascd.org

ASCD offers great curricular, instructional, and assessment resources directly applicable to K–12 schools.

Human Resource Development Press (HRD Press):
http://www.hrdpress.com

HRD Press has some excellent change management guides and tools.

Jossey-Bass Pfeiffer:
http://www.pfeiffer.com

This publisher provides many excellent organizational development, change management, team building, and training resources and tools.

NTL Institute for Applied Behavioral Science:
http://www.ntl.org

NTL offers training and publications focusing on change management and related topics. NTL was a pioneer of the T Group and still values the use of small group learning at the heart of its work.

Quality and Productivity Improvement Bookstore: http://www.qualitycoach.net

This site offers many tools and resources to support team and organizational improvement. Features the *Memory Jogger* and related tools for continuous improvement and effective planning of change initiatives.

University Associates Inc: http://www.universityassociates.com

University Associates is dedicated to improving organizational effectiveness through consulting, training and resources. It offers numerous books, videos, tools kits, training modules, and activities specifically focused on change management.

Game/Simulation

Making Change for School Improvement, The Network Inc. Andover, MA 01810. An excellent tool for simulating change in education settings. Players have fun while they learn to manage change in schools.

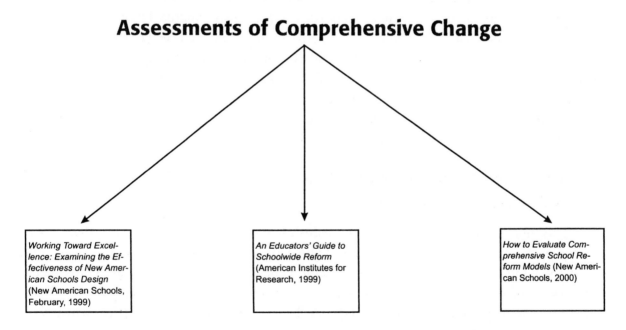

Now emerging are some useful guidelines for the assessment of comprehensive change. These guidelines indicate the questions that need be asked when evaluating how well comprehensive change is working. Three such guidelines are summarized below.

Working Toward Excellence: Examining the Effectiveness of New American Schools Design (New American Schools, February, 1999)

This publication is designed to assist educators in making "informed decisions about NAS designs by sharing lessons learned from the past five years in the field." Evidence of the potential of eight different design models (e.g., Little Red Schoolhouse, Expeditionary Learning) are discussed, along with the potential for comprehensive change across four large urban school districts. The assessment sought answers to such questions as: "What is the research behind each design? What is the evidence that the design can help school improvement? Is there evidence that the design has helped students succeed in areas other than test scores? What are the circumstances in which schools have failed to achieve the desired results?" This document is particularly useful in providing sensitizing concepts and questions that all schools undergoing comprehensive change will want to address.

An Educators' Guide to Schoolwide Reform (American Institutes for Research, 1999)

This guide, prepared for five different educational organizations including the NEA and AFT, is an attempt to "rate" 24 whole-school or comprehensive approaches to school reform. The guide provides data over a number of criteria, among them the extent of evidence of positive effects on student achievement, the extent of support provided by the design developers, and the costs for the first year of the design. Each of the 24 designs is reviewed and discussed in some detail. Some of the criteria adopted, as well as the way in which the data were interpreted, are subject to debate. However, the guide does provide educators with important questions to be posed when making decisions about the efficacy of comprehensive reform models.

How to Evaluate Comprehensive School Reform Models (New American Schools, 2000)

This monograph is one of eight in the series titled *Getting Better by Design,* all of which focus on strategies to enhance the success of all-school design models. This one on evaluation is designed to help school leaders promote comprehensive school reform and to provide the necessary guidelines to evaluate the implementation and assess the outcomes of such efforts. The monograph presents, in clear language, the basic steps in a useful evaluation plan as well as some very useful cautionary notes for the interpretation of the data collected. As an example, the author points to the importance of focusing on "value-added" data (how far the school has come relative to where it began) rather than concentrating on data that report the percentage of students that met a particular standard at one point in time.

Index